Teach Ye Diligently

Teach Ye Diligently

Revised Edition

Boyd K. Packer

Illustrated by the Author

Deseret Book Company
Salt Lake City, Utah

Visit us at deseretbook.com

First printing in hardbound 1975
First printing in paperbound, revised edition 1991
First printing in hardbound, revised edition 2005

Library of Congress Catalog Card No. 75-22704

ISBN 0-87747-558-X (hardbound)
ISBN 0-87579-476-9 (paperbound, revised edition)
ISBN 1-59038-425-3 (hardbound, revised edition)

Printed in the United States of America   18961
R. R. Donnelley and Sons, Crawfordsville, IN

20 19 18 17 16 15 14 13 12

Contents

CONTENTS

Foreword

To fully appreciate this book, there are some things you should know about Elder Boyd K. Packer.

Elder Packer was born September 10, 1924, in Brigham City, Utah, the tenth in a family of eleven. The fact that there were many brothers and sisters to welcome Boyd Kenneth to the family of Ira and Emma Jensen Packer made a significant difference in his life. Those who know the Packer family attest that few families are so united.

From his father he inherited his ready wit and keen sense of humor. From his little Danish mother he inherited a deep spirituality. She taught him some simple lessons: that if you are living righteously and are prayerful, you have the right to live by the Spirit. Those close to him know he learned this lesson well.

He learned early to love nature—and he still does. He loves animals and especially birds. Outside a large window he provides a feeder for quail and pheasants during the winter, and hangs a feeder for hummingbirds during the summer. He knows the names and habits of all the birds of this area and many of the exotic ones. He can describe or draw them. He will point out a hawk in the sky and say, "That is a goss hawk. You can tell by its swift, graceful wings, and its long tail feathers."

vii

At their home his children have all of the usual kinds of pets—dogs, rabbits, horses, chickens, ducks—but at the present time no cats. Cats and birds do not mix—properly. And he likes birds better than cats.

Elder Packer is an artist. I wish all of you could see his home. His handiwork, evident in every room, bespeaks his love of the beautiful, the good, and the appropriate. He is a carver of wood. He paints and draws. He molds and sculpts. He mounts various birds. He painted the portraits on the cover and did all of the illustrations in this book.

He has tremendous powers of concentration and capacity for work. He finishes quickly whatever he starts. He has an unusually keen mind. No one yet has plumbed the depths of this man.

One of the reasons his mind ranges on so many different interests and covers so wide a scope is because this was encouraged in his childhood home. His hands are always busy. He thinks better when he is creating something. I have heard him say, "I'm going to work on a carving tonight. I think better when I do that."

His children have inherited this artistic talent. Their home abounds with homemade objects of both beauty and utility, made by each of the children.

Elder Packer's hobbies and interests are all home-centered. His total life is centered in his home and family. Part of this comes from the example in his father's home. He measures the value of all other activities by the effect they will have on his family. Nothing takes precedence over his commitment to his home and family. Nothing! He understands that as a gospel commitment.

He understands the gospel well. His serious gospel study began during World War II when he was a pilot in the Army Air Corps. He took with him his servicemen's copy of the Book of Mormon. It was read numerous times and marked thoroughly. This book has had a profound influence upon the life of Elder Packer.

There is one source of inspiration available to Elder Packer that is not available to anyone else. That is Donna. She has been his strength in a quiet and sustaining way. She won his heart when she was Box Elder County Peach Days Queen. In all the years I have known him, I have seldom heard him refer to Donna in any other way than "my bride." She is the one who has borne their ten children—and borne much of the responsibility of rearing them, due to his call as "special witness." She it is who is his sweetheart, his friend, and his quiet support. Because of her he can say, with complete honesty, "I know there are families where parents can live together in love without a single argument for thirty years and more."

The ten children born to this couple have provided some of the greatest learning experiences in his life. He has said, "All that I have ever learned that has been most worthwhile, I have learned from my children."

Elder Packer has been successful in his chosen field of education. He received an associate of science degree from Weber College and the bachelor of science and master of science degrees in education from Utah State University. He holds a doctor of education degree from Brigham Young University.

He taught seminary for six years. His teaching abilities were recognized and he was appointed as supervisor of seminaries and institutes of religion. He also served on the administrative council of Brigham Young University.

Of all the fields in which he excels, it is as a teacher that he is a master among men. I know of no man who is his superior in teaching a gospel concept. He is blessed with unusual gifts. He has the capacity to translate an ethereal verbal concept to an understandable activity in everyday life. He understands the principles of teaching and their practical application as the Savior taught.

We are fortunate that he has now made available these principles of successful teaching. This book is written to parents as well as to all other teachers. This is important since parents are the most influential of all teachers. In this book all can learn principles that will qualify them to carry out the injunction of the Savior, " . . . teach one another the doctrine of the kingdom. Teach ye diligently and my grace shall attend you. . . . " (D&C 88:77–78.)

Elder Packer's words are simple, common words. Most of us know and understand them. He could have used the jargon of the educator, but as usual, he deliberately kept the words as simple as possible. That is why it is so readable. You will soon discover that what is explained so clearly and obviously was neither clear nor obvious before he explained it. This is the contribution of this book. It becomes a resource, a library to which we can return again and again to get ideas and help for both teaching and living.

This is a unique book on the art of teaching. No one has done before what he has done. Elder Packer has tackled not only the most difficult of all subjects—the art of teaching—but has added another dimension of difficulty in the process, how to teach moral and spiritual values. He has succeeded because he has unfolded, clearly and well, how the Master did the same thing.

ELDER A. THEODORE TUTTLE
First Council of the Seventy

CHAPTER ONE

You Have Some Teaching to Do

Early in World War II a company that specialized in the manufacture of lenses for optical equipment received a large order from the government for special lenses to be used in bombsights. The relatively few lenses they ordinarily produced were hand-polished by one master craftsman who had learned his art in Europe as a youth. It would be manifestly impossible for him to polish even a fraction of the lenses that were already on order.

In order to resolve the problem, he needed some help. Because the company was an essential defense industry, it was given special priority on workers. A large group of men was tested to find those who would likely make good lens grinders, and those who emerged from this screening process were put into a class with the master craftsman as the teacher. He was simply told to teach them to polish lenses.

Though the old teacher was a competent craftsman, somehow he was not able to teach the students how to polish lenses. He demonstrated repeatedly, and day after day they worked, but they were unable to produce a perfect lens. The situation was becoming critical.

Finally one enterprising young student became con-

1

vinced there must be an answer to this serious problem, so he watched more carefully than he had before. Then, at the close of the day, he took home some of the castings of lenses and some grinding compound.

The next morning he presented his teacher with a perfect lens, the only one produced after all the instruction. The students, who were all surprised at what he had been able to do, were startled when he said, "I can show you all how to do it." And so he could, and so he did.

"I noticed," he said, "that we have been holding the glass casting against the polishing wheel gripped in our hands as we have been shown to do. However, there is this difference: The master craftsman holds his wrist very rigid and turns his arm only at the elbow. Our wrists have been left loose, and for some reason we have been unable to get the same control. If we keep our wrists rigid as we hold the lens to the grinding wheel, we'll be able to polish perfect lenses too."

A Trick to the Trade

There was a trick to the trade, and he had observed it—a simple thing that any of them could do once they were shown.

So it is with teaching. Among the myriads of things that can be successfully taught is the art of teaching. There are certain principles that apply to the teaching, or the learning, of almost any subject. In teaching we find what might be called tricks to the trade. Some of these techniques are little things that anyone can do; others need to be studied and practiced. But with many of these techniques, it is enough for us just to have them pointed out. We need to be alerted to those things that successful teachers do, for they may well mean the difference between success and failure. Certainly they will make us much better teachers.

Everyone Is a Teacher

Much of what we do is teaching. Showing a youngster how to tie his shoe, showing a boy how to run the lawn-mower, teaching a young person how to drive a car, helping a daughter with a new recipe, giving a talk in church, bearing testimony, conducting a leadership meeting, and, of course, teaching a class—all of this is teaching, and we are doing it constantly.

Every member of the Church teaches for virtually his whole lifetime. We are teaching when we preach or speak or respond in meetings, for preachers are teachers—at least they generally are, and certainly they always should be. The similarity of the words preach, teach, and speech is not accidental. When we are speaking and preaching, we are teaching.

When we see a list of the verbs that describe teaching, we realize that all of us are doing it most of the time. Such verbs include *instruct, educate, edify, school, tutor, prime, coach, profess, enlighten, inform, direct, guide, show, inculcate, infuse, instill, imbue, impregnate, implant, disseminate, propagate, indoctrinate, expound, explain, interpret, lecture, hold forth, preach.* And there are others, each of them being just another way to say "teach."

We have teachers serving in all the organizations of the Church. A great deal of teaching is done in the priesthood quorums; indeed, all priesthood holders are eligible for appointment as priesthood home *teachers.* The title "teacher" has been given to one of the offices in the Aaronic Priesthood. The auxiliaries are staffed with teachers and with officers, all of whom train or teach.

The prophet is a teacher; his counselors are teachers; the General Authorities are teachers. Stake presidents and mission presidents are teachers; high councilors and quorum presidents are teachers; bishops are teachers; and so through all of the organizations of the Church.

3

The Church moves forward sustained by the power of the teaching that is accomplished. The work of the kingdom is impeded if teaching is not efficiently done. The growth of the Church depends upon teaching, for missionaries are, above all, teachers. They are constantly teaching the gospel of Jesus Christ. Their testimonies are borne in order that others may be taught, and perhaps the most important verb synonymous with teaching in the Church is the verb *testify*.

Teaching Moral and Spiritual Values

This book is written to help you become a better teacher. The discussions are about the teaching of moral and spiritual values, an area that is much neglected. You won't find much about it in the literature in the field of education.

On the other hand, if you want to teach any one of a myriad of other subjects, such as English or mathematics, history or geography, you can get help from almost any library, and certainly from any college or university library. The teaching of such subjects has been taken over by the public schools. Parents, for instance, are only indirectly involved in teaching their youngsters the basic mathematical skills. Nor do parents need to do too much about teaching youngsters how to construct sentences. If they can teach them good study habits, the children will learn the rest in the public schools.

When we want to teach honesty, chastity, obedience, reverence, humility, kindness, and citizenship, however, we must search for help, for not much has been written about how to teach these virtues.

Over the years I have thought constantly about the teaching of moral and spiritual values. I have been assigned to do some of it myself and to supervise others who were

4

either called or hired to teach, and I want to share with you some of the lessons I have learned.

You won't find much academic jargon in the chapters that follow. A few professional terms will be introduced to help you become acquainted with them, and simple definitions of them as they are used in textbooks on education will be included. You can get more information from those other sources if you wish.

This, rather, is a collection of ideas and suggestions and experiences and illustrations that may be helpful to anyone who has the responsibility to teach—suggestions particularly on how to teach moral and spiritual values.

Some of the examples illustrate teaching in the family, some are from classroom experiences, and others relate to training and administration. But all are about teaching, and the principles apply to all of us in all of our teaching.

If we apply these principles, we can respond to the Lord's instruction when he said, "I give unto you a commandment that you shall teach one another the doctrine of the kingdom. Teach ye diligently and my grace shall attend you, that you may be instructed more perfectly in theory, in principle, in doctrine, in the law of the gospel, in all things that pertain unto the kingdom of God, that are expedient for you to understand." (D&C 88:77–78.)

CHAPTER TWO

Don't Leave It to Chance

While everybody in the Church is a teacher, was a teacher, or will be a teacher, if you have children or grandchildren you are continuously a teacher. The principles of good teaching are particularly important to you, perhaps more important in your teaching responsibilities as a parent than in any other teaching assignment you may have. Parents are teachers, for the Lord has said:

> And again, inasmuch as parents have children in Zion, or in any of her stakes which are organized, that *teach* them not to understand the doctrine of repentance, faith in Christ the Son of the living God, and of baptism and the gift of the Holy Ghost by the laying on of the hands, when eight years old, the sin be upon the heads of the parents. . . .
>
> And they shall also *teach* their children to pray, and to walk uprightly before the Lord. (D&C 68:25,28. Italics added.)

This responsibility is repeated in the following:

> The glory of God is intelligence, or, in other words, light and truth.
>
> Light and truth forsake that evil one.
>
> Every spirit of man was innocent in the beginning; and God having redeemed man from the fall,

6

men became again, in their infant state, innocent before God.

And that wicked one cometh and taketh away light and truth, through disobedience, from the children of men, and because of the tradition of their fathers.

But I have commanded you to bring up your children in light and truth. (D&C 93:36–40.)

The obligation rests upon parents to teach their children. In order to fulfill that commandment, in the very beginning a parent becomes a teacher.

It has been said that the responsibility of Church members is divided into three main categories: to provide for the salvation of the living members of the Church, to accomplish the necessary work for our kindred dead, and to preach the gospel to all the world. All of these responsibilities require learning, and all that is learned must somehow be taught. We are among those who must teach it.

To need to teach, to want to teach, and to be called to teach sometimes are not enough, however, and teaching can be a frustrating and disappointing — and sometimes a failing — endeavor.

Feeding a Kitten

An example may illustrate. In the early days of our marriage, I was in the bedroom of our home one day when I heard a loud, screeching noise. Running to the kitchen, I found the refrigerator door standing open, a puddle of milk on the floor, and a trail of milk splashed across the floor to the back door. As I reached the back door, the screeching began again, and I saw an interesting sight.

On the doorstep sat our five-year-old son, feeding his little kitten. Enough milk had stayed in the bowl to more than fill the tiny animal. One hand held the struggling kitten tightly around the throat, while the other one held a back leg. The boy dipped the little kitten head-first into the milk, and the little animal complained loudly and struggled to escape drowning. Finally it maneuvered its free foot to a position where it could scratch the little child on the wrist, and he quickly dropped the animal into the bowl. Before the boy could recover from the pain, the kitten had scrambled out of the bowl and raced around the corner of the house to safety under a woodpile.

Our son didn't notice me watching. Frustrated and disappointed, he began to cry. All his efforts to feed his hungry kitten had failed. The elements of success were all present: He had the kitten; it was hungry; and he had milk, an ideal food for kittens. Nevertheless, something had gone wrong; something about the way he attempted to get the two together had resulted in frustration and failure. The kitten remained hungry and, as our son learned from experience, was all the more difficult to feed the next time. I tried to show him a better way, but it was only after several attempts, and considerable coaxing, that confidence was restored enough that the little kitten would come willingly to a little boy who wanted to feed it.

Surely there are few who have escaped the frustrated, thwarted feelings of that little boy. Such feelings come often — probably more often than necessary — to the teacher. Almost every day, on every turn, we are confronted with someone who is in need of instruction, perhaps even hungry for it. As a parent or teacher or leader, we not only can supply it, but it is our obligation to do so. Yet frequently something about the way one tries to do it repels the student, and the teacher ends up scratched or bitten by the very one he hopes to nourish.

The Finest of the Fine Arts

It doesn't have to be that way. We *can* learn to teach. There are some special challenges in teaching the gospel of Jesus Christ. The teaching of faith and repentance and virtue and humility poses challenges not found in teaching most other subjects. Teaching has been described as "the finest of the fine arts." I think this is true, but if we do not know some of the techniques, it can be the most difficult as well.

For instance, compare teaching with composing music. Suppose you are a composer and awake in the night with a beautiful melody lingering in your mind. You ponder it. It is an inspiration — you must record it. You leave your bed, rush to the piano, and begin to set down the notes.

9

The composition has begun. As you finger the keyboard, the melody fits together and you sense the inner excitement of creation. You sense that it is the best you have ever done.

Suppose, however, that you must leave the score on the piano where many pass by, and any of them are free to tamper with your composition. Time after time you come back to find that someone with permanent ink has scratched through a note, sometimes a whole line—changed it, transposed it.

Can you imagine the difficulty of composing under such circumstances? How earnestly you would wish just to be left alone with your composition until it is completely finished, to have others touch your work only if you invite them to do so. Imagine the difficulty of erasing some of those notes to put your arrangement back the way it should be.

Or suppose you are a painter and have a painting appear on the canvas of your mind, as if by inspiration. You do some sketching and marvel at how quickly it falls together as a composition. It is already created now in your mind; only the process of putting the paint down on the canvas remains to create it materially. You work carefully on this piece, for it is to be your very finest. A good many sittings will be necessary for you to do it well. It is a landscape, so you set up your easel in full view of the subject from which you received the inspiration, even though you are near a busy pathway. At times you must leave your easel, the unfinished painting, and your materials where they are. Any passerby has access to your brushes and your painting.

Can you imagine your frustration when some sidewalk superintendents add their little bit to your work? "A very interesting painting," one of them says, "but this tree is

10

out of balance. I think I'll move it over here and paint over the other one."

Another says, "This has too much of the natural look. I think the sky ought not to be blue. Bright red will make it more exciting."

"Much too old-fashioned, too Victorian," another says, as he picks up the brush and works away on your painting.

The least temperamental among us would want to give up in frustration under those circumstances.

A teacher works under circumstances similar to those we have mentioned. That is true particularly of the parent, for always the parent is a teacher. Teaching *is* the finest of the fine arts, and unless we are trained, in many ways it is also the most difficult. Our subjects do not sit still and wait for us to come back and compose a little or paint a little. They do not hold themselves in some kind of suspension until we decide to teach a little.

Many agencies are clamoring for the attention of our members, young and old alike. Providentially, most of these agencies are good and will perhaps contribute much to our teaching. However, some of them are unspeakably perverse, and their influence must be continually erased. The teaching we do must be so indelible, effective, and impressive that it cannot be erased. Then if it is covered over temporarily by falsehoods or wickedness, a good scrubbing will still leave our work intact and perhaps even a little brighter. We must teach and teach well, and teach permanently. As parents, as teachers, as officers in the Church, that is our obligation and our opportunity.

Teaching Is More Than Example

In the home and in the Church, we must teach our children moral and spiritual values. We can do some of this teaching simply by example. Without that, of course, our teachings are counterfeit. But example alone may not

11

be the most efficient way to teach. If we live the gospel fully, chances are our children and others around us will learn much from our example. They may even get a testimony because of us. But why leave it to chance? With proper attention, righteousness can be taught.

A few years ago I had a pointed discussion with the principal of one of our Church schools. No religion classes were being taught in his school; he said the teachers couldn't spare the time for that. He added, "Since all the teachers and most of the students are members of the Church, they will get testimonies just by association. After all," he added, "don't we open all of our assemblies with prayer?"

I asked what he did about teachings in some of the textbooks that could be morally misleading. His answer was that the atmosphere of the school would reinforce the students adequately, and chances are they would gain testimonies from being taught secular subjects in a spiritual environment.

But why leave our teaching to chance? We can teach a child to be honest as well as we can teach him to compute mathematical figures, use correct pronunciation, or read properly. We employ a different set of teaching tools to do so effectively, but it can be done.

CHAPTER THREE

The Gift to Teach

If you have come to the conclusion that you are going to be teaching at home and in the Church, you have made a good start. The next step is to *want* to be a successful teacher. You can become a very good teacher, and you can teach the gospel of Jesus Christ successfully to your own children and in the Church. But you must *want to*.

If you desire to be a successful teacher, and desire it enough to be willing to earn it, you can have your desire. It is a righteous desire. Can you think of anything the Lord would want you to desire more than to be able to teach righteousness successfully?

The scriptures testify that He will grant unto men according to their desires. The prophet Alma bore testimony of this.

> I know that he granteth unto men *according to their desire,* whether it be unto death or unto life: yea, I know that he allotteth unto men *according to their wills,* whether they be unto salvation or unto destruction.
>
> Yea, and I know that good and evil have come before all men; he that knoweth not good from evil is blameless; but he that knoweth good and evil, to him it is given *according to his desires,* whether

he *desireth good or evil,* life or death, joy or remorse of conscience. (Alma 29:4–5. Italics added.)

There is something important about our deciding that we want to be a good teacher—a good parent. There is something equally important about making that desire known to the Lord. Many of us have the desire, but we keep it to ourselves. An important key is turned when we go through the formality of stating our desires to Him who can grant them.

There is no theme in holy scripture more oft-repeated than the simple injunction, "Ask, and ye shall receive." This theme is in the Bible, the Book of Mormon, the Doctrine and Covenants, and the Pearl of Great Price. No theme is repeated in more ways and more often than this simple counsel. Consider these sample references:

Bible

Ask, and it shall be given you; seek, and ye shall find; knock, and it shall be opened unto you:

For every one that asketh receiveth; and he that seeketh findeth; and to him that knocketh it shall be opened.

Or what man is there of you, whom if his son ask bread, will he give him a stone?

Or if he ask a fish, will he give him a serpent?

If ye then, being evil, know how to give good gifts unto your children, how much more shall your Father which is in heaven give good things to them that ask him? (Matthew 7:7–11.)

And all things, whatsoever ye shall ask in prayer, believing, ye shall receive. (Matthew 21:22.)

Therefore I say unto you, What things soever ye desire, when ye pray, believe that ye receive them, and ye shall have them. (Mark 11:24.)

And I say unto you, Ask, and it shall be given

you; seek, and ye shall find; knock, and it shall be opened unto you. (Luke 11:9.)

And whatsoever ye shall ask in my name, that will I do, that the Father may be glorified in the Son.

If ye shall ask any thing in my name, I will do it. (John 14:13–14.)

If ye abide in me, and my words abide in you, ye shall ask what ye will and it shall be done unto you. (John 15:7.)

And in that day ye shall ask me nothing. Verily, verily, I say unto you, Whatsoever ye shall ask the Father in my name, he will give it you. (John 16:23.)

Be careful for nothing; but in every thing by prayer and supplication with thanksgiving let your requests be made known unto God. (Philippians 4:6.)

If any of you lack wisdom, let him ask of God, that giveth to all men liberally, and upbraideth not; and it shall be given him. (James 1:5.)

And whatsoever we ask, we receive of him, because we keep his commandments, and do those things that are pleasing in his sight. (John 3:22.)

And this is the confidence that we have in him, that, if we ask any thing according to his will, he heareth us:

And if we know that he hear us, whatsoever we ask, we know that we have the petitions that we desired of him. (1 John 5:14–15.)

Book of Mormon

Do ye not remember the things which the Lord hath said? — If ye will not harden your hearts, and ask me in faith, believing that ye shall receive, with diligence in keeping my commandments, surely these things shall be made known unto you. (1 Nephi 15:11.)

Yea, I know that God will give liberally to him that asketh. (2 Nephi 4:35.)

Counsel with the Lord in all thy doings, and he will direct thee for good. (Alma 37:37.)

Ask, and it shall be given unto you; seek, and ye shall find; knock, and it shall be opened unto you. (3 Nephi 14:7.)

And whatsoever ye shall ask the Father in my name, which is right, believing that ye shall receive, behold it shall be given unto you. (3 Nephi 20:18.)

And now I go unto the Father. And verily I say unto you, whatsoever things ye shall ask the Father in my name shall be given unto you.
Therefore, ask, and ye shall receive; knock, and it shall be opened unto you; for he that asketh, receiveth; and unto him that knocketh, it shall be opened. (3 Nephi 27:28–29.)

. . . O Lord, thou hast given us a commandment that we must call upon thee, that from thee we may receive according to our desires. (Ether 3:2.)

Whatsoever thing ye shall ask the Father in my name, which is good, in faith believing that ye shall receive, behold, it shall be done unto you. (Moroni 7:26.)

Doctrine and Covenants

Ask, and ye shall receive; knock, and it shall be opened unto you. (D&C 4:7.)

Therefore, if you will ask of me you shall receive;

if you will knock it shall be opened unto you. (D&C 6:5; 14:5.)

And, as it is written—Whatsoever ye shall ask in faith, being united in prayer according to my command, ye shall receive. (D&C 29:6.)

Therefore, he that lacketh wisdom, let him ask of me, and I will give him liberally and upbraid him not. (D&C 42:68.)

But ye are commanded in all things to ask of God, who giveth liberally. (D&C 46:7.)

Behold, I say unto you, go forth as I have commanded you; repent of all your sins; ask and ye shall receive, knock and it shall be opened unto you. (D&C 49:26.)

Lay your hands upon the sick, and they shall recover. Return not till I, the Lord, shall send you. Be patient in affliction. Ask, and ye shall receive; knock, and it shall be opened unto you. (D&C 66:9.)

Let them ask and they shall receive, knock and it shall be opened unto them, and be made known from on high, even by the Comforter, whither they shall go. (D&C 75:27.)

Draw near unto me and I will draw near unto you; seek me diligently and ye shall find me; ask, and ye shall receive; knock, and it shall be opened unto you.
Whatsoever ye ask the Father in my name it shall be given unto you, that is expedient for you. (D&C 88:63–64.)

Behold this is my will; ask and ye shall receive. (D&C 103:31.)

Be thou humble; and the Lord thy God shall lead

thee by the hand, and give thee answer to thy prayers. (D&C 112:10.)

Pearl of Great Price

. . . asking all things in his name, and whatsoever ye shall ask, it shall be given you. (Moses 6:52.)

While I was laboring under the extreme difficulties caused by the contests of these parties of religionists, I was one day reading the Epistle of James, first chapter and fifth verse, which reads: If any of you lack wisdom, let him ask of God, that giveth to all men liberally, and upbraideth not; and it shall be given him. (Joseph Smith 2:11.)

The Initiative Is Ours

It is clear that the Lord wants us to come unto Him and ask Him for whatever we need. The simple invitation to "ask, and it shall be given you; seek, and ye shall find; knock, and it shall be opened unto you" was repeated by the Lord on many occasions. He gave this message to the people He taught while He lived on earth. He repeated it twice to the people of the New World at the time of His visit to them following His resurrection, including His last words He gave them before returning to His Father in heaven. Interestingly, the Lord repeated the same invitation seven times in the Doctrine and Covenants. In varying ways throughout the scriptures, He has invited us to ask Him for whatever we need in righteousness, that He might give it unto us.

The initiative, then, is ours. We must ask and pray and seek, and then we will find.

There are several paintings depicting Christ at the door, illustrating a New Testament scripture: "Behold, I stand at the door, and knock: If any man hear my voice, and open the door, I will come in to him, and will sup with him, and he with me." (Revelation 3:20.) In the more famous paintings He is shown holding a lantern as he knocks at the door.

The story is told that a little girl once remarked to one painter that his painting of Jesus at the door was not finished. "You have left something out," she said. "You have left out the door latch." The artist replied, "The painting is complete. That door represents the door of the human heart. It opens only from within."

The ability to teach successfully as a missionary, as a parent, as an officer, or as a teacher in the Church is well worth learning. It is well worth asking for. And it can come to each of us.

It is often said of someone who is successful as a teacher that he is talented or that he has the "gift." However, this gift must be developed and earned. There is much truth in these lines by an unknown writer:

> He worked by day and toiled by night;
> He gave up play and all delight.
> Dry books he read, new things to learn,
> And forged ahead, success to earn.
> He plodded on with faith and pluck,
> And when he won, men called it luck.

There is substance to the thought that one can receive a gift to teach. This is promised in the scriptures:

> Deny not the power of God; for he worketh by power, according to the faith of the children of men, the same today and tomorrow, and forever.
>
> And again, I exhort you, my brethren, that ye deny not *the gifts of God,* for they are many; and they come from the same God. And there are different ways that these *gifts* are administered; but it is the same God who worketh all in all; and they are given by the manifestations of the Spirit of God unto men, to profit them.

19

For behold, to one is given by the Spirit of God, that he may *teach* the word of wisdom;

And to another, that he may *teach* the word of knowledge by the same Spirit; . . .

And all these *gifts* come by the Spirit of Christ; and they come unto every man severally, according as he will. (Moroni 10:7–10, 17. Italics added.)

I have thought that the last phrase, "every man severally, according as he will," refers to the man himself. If a man wills that the gift should come to him, and he desires it, the gift shall be his.

A Supreme Gift

Many years ago I read this scripture and pondered it. I thought that among the gifts one might have in order to make himself useful to the Lord, the gift to teach by the Spirit would be supreme. The gift to teach the Word of Wisdom and to teach the word of knowledge by the Spirit is much to be desired. Why should such a gift not come to us if we desire it? If we desire to succeed as a teacher and we're willing to earn that ability, why should it not come to us? If we're willing to ask for it and pray for it, and we believe with sufficient faith that we can possess it, why should it be withheld from us?

Where would we turn to develop such a gift? Where do we go for an example? That, of course, brings us to Him who is the Master Teacher, Jesus Christ, the Son of God, the Only Begotten of the Father. In the scriptures He is addressed constantly as "Master," which by interpretation means "teacher." He is the Master Teacher, and from Him and His example, we also may learn to be master teachers.

CHAPTER FOUR

Jesus the Christ as a Teacher

Jesus has been described as a philosopher, an economist, a social reformer, and many other things. But above all, He was a teacher—a teacher of religious doctrine. If you were to ask, "What did Jesus have as an occupation?" there is only one answer. He was a teacher. That single fact, more than any other, lends great dignity to the subject of teaching and establishes a great ideal for all who teach.

Jesus was a teacher. The Gospels say so. Of some ninety times He is addressed in the four Gospels, sixty times He is called "Rabbi," which means "teacher." He is also referred to as "Master," which comes from the Greek word *didaskalos,* defined as "one who teaches concerning the things of God and the duties of man." This word is sometimes translated as "teacher," at other times as "master."

There is a clearer reason for describing Jesus as teacher than for describing Him as a social reformer, philosopher, or any of the other names He has been called. He *was* a teacher. That is how He accomplished the things He was sent to do. He taught.

The fact that His followers were referred to as disciples is of great significance, for disciple literally means "pupil" or "scholar," and the disciples were literally His students.

The word *discipline* is defined as "instruction imparted to disciples or scholars; teaching, learning, education, schooling."

It is also defined as "a particular course of instruction to disciples." In our day the word is used commonly in education as "a branch of instruction or education; a department of learning or knowledge; a science or art in its educational aspect." Further, it is defined as "instruction having for its aim to form the pupil to proper conduct and action; the training of scholars or subordinates to proper and orderly action by instructing and exercising them in the same; mental and moral training; also used figuratively of the training effects of experience, adversity, etc." (*Oxford English Dictionary.*) To the disciples, Jesus was their Lord and their Rabbi or Master, or, in other words, their Teacher, and they were His disciples, pupils, or scholars. If we will, He likewise is our teacher, and we are His disciples.

Jesus: Our Model as a Teacher

When we begin to analyze ourselves and look to improve ourselves as teachers, what better model could we find? What finer study could we undertake than to analyze our ideals and goals and methods and compare them with those of Jesus Christ?

The Gospels are recorded in 153 pages. One can read them leisurely in an evening and study them carefully in something more. We can compare what we are trying to accomplish with what Jesus accomplished by reading the four Gospels and seeking to find *how* He did what He did. However important the message He presented, the manner in which He presented it also has great meaning for us. There is no information in print on how to teach moral and spiritual values more important nor, if properly approached, more helpful than is found in the Gospels. They

22

constitute a treatise on teaching technique surpassed by none.

Some may be hesitant to make that comparison, thinking that in every way He is beyond reach. Consider, please, that He has declared, "What manner of men ought ye to be? Verily I say unto you, even as I am." (3 Nephi 27:27.) He has enjoined us to be perfect, even as He and the Father are perfect. (See 3 Nephi 12:48.) Would this not relate to teaching as well as, or perhaps more than, anything else that we might do?

I do not hesitate to admit that I desire to teach as He taught. Though that may be far beyond my capabilities, He is, nevertheless, the ideal, and the Gospels are the finest help in print anywhere for solving the problem of how to teach moral and spiritual values.

Except for a few references indicating that He taught in the synagogue (Matthew 4:23, 9:35, 13:54; Mark 1:39, 6:2; Luke 4:15; John 18:20), we do not have any evidence that He taught in what might be termed formal teaching situations. His teaching was done to multitudes or to smaller groups gathered about Him.

That He employed principles of instruction recognized and acknowledged by professional educators in our own day is evident. He recognized those principles that lent themselves to teaching and learning and those that did not. As we proceed through the following chapters, we will point out many examples of this.

Some years ago Ferrot R. Glover wrote a study of Jesus as a character in history and found himself dwelling on Jesus as a teacher. He observed: "I have been treating Him almost as if He were an authority of pedagogy. Fortunately, He never discussed pedagogy, never used the terms I have been using. But He dealt with men, He taught and He influenced them, and it is worth our study to understand

23

how He did it—to master His methods." (*The Jesus of History,* New York: Association Press, 1930, p. 84.)

Although Jesus did not discuss the subject of teaching procedures, we can learn a great deal about how to teach moral and spiritual ideals by studying the accounts of His ministry in the Gospels. It is not untoward for any of us to aspire to teach as He taught. It is not untoward for any of us to aspire to be like Him. He was not just a teacher; He was *the* teacher. Through the centuries and through translation from language to language, His teachings have remained simple and compelling and direct, because they were designed to do just that. In our minds we can go back to that day when He ministered among men. We can pay careful heed to what He is teaching. We can also watch how He did it so that when the commission comes to feed His sheep, we can go and do likewise.

CHAPTER FIVE

Apperception

When we study how Jesus taught, we might note that He employed one principle of teaching more than any other. If we also understand this principle and employ it, it will improve us as teachers of religion perhaps more than any other thing that we could learn about His teaching techniques. Educators refer to it as *the principle of apperception.*

Understanding Through Previous Experience

Apperception is defined as "the process of understanding something perceived in terms of previous experience." This means that if we have something difficult to teach, such as honesty or reverence or love, we should begin with the experience of the student and talk about the things he already knows. Then when we make a transfer or comparison with what we want him to know, he will perceive the meaning.

Jesus was indeed the master of this process. To analyze how He used the principle and to understand why He used it so frequently is enlightening for anyone who desires to teach successfully in the home or in the Church. We will explain this principle in very elementary terms, because it constitutes such a fundamental part of the teaching of Jesus.

Man Uses Symbols for Communication

The most conclusive certification of man's intelligence is his ability to recreate in symbolic form the world in which he lives. He has produced the alphabet of the language, which is a system for sound. Through it, he is able to write and then to read his writing. He can also verbalize the symbols and write, read, and speak—all in symbols.

For instance, the letters C-A-T are the symbols for cat. Yet they look nothing at all like a cat.

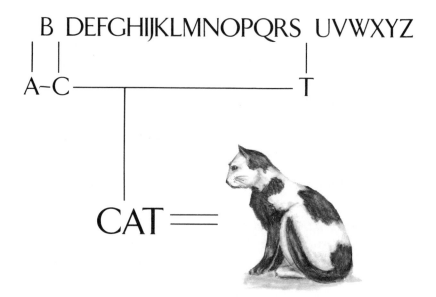

They are not the size of a cat, nor the shape of a cat, nor the anything else of a cat. Nevertheless, a little youngster soon can be taught that those symbols represent cat. They can be vocalized; we can say the word. We can say all of the parts of it separately (C-A-T) or we can put the letters together and say the word in one syllable (CAT). There we have it. In one word only, we can convey the idea: cat.

With the twenty-six letters of the alphabet rearranged into various words, we can convey a great deal about cats. We can "create" sitting cats, sleeping cats, running cats and jumping cats, spotted cats, and striped cats, all with words alone.

If we say it is a large cat, we have introduced size. We can describe just how large the cat is. If we say it is eight inches high at the shoulder, we know that it is a small cat. If we say that it is thirty-four inches high at the shoulder, then we know that it must be a lion or a tiger or one of the very large cats.

In addition to size, we can also talk about color. We can say that it is a brown cat or a black-and-white cat. If we already know that it is a large cat and we say that it is striped with black and orange and some white, we know that it is a tiger.

Shape

With both size and color we have become more specific, but we are by no means through with the tools at our disposal. We can also talk about shape. With a few words, we could teach a youngster to identify the silhouette of a lion from the silhouette of a tiger of the same size simply by pointing to the shape.

The lion has a mane and a tassel at the end of its tail. That difference in shape would be enough to tell the two apart.

We can also say that the cat has fur and that it is very soft fur, and texture has been introduced to further describe the cat.

Once we have created a word — a noun — we can convey much information about it by using size and shape and color and texture. But that is just the beginning.

Another example: Suppose we have a youngster who has no idea in his mind what an elephant is. He has not seen one, nor has he seen a picture of one. With words, how might we put into his mind the idea of an elephant?

First of all, we would start with something he already knows. He has seen some kind of an animal, of course. We would begin by saying that an elephant is an *animal*.

Immediately we have taught him a great deal. Now he will not confuse a tree with an elephant, or a mountain with an elephant, or a house with an elephant, or a river with an elephant. He will know it is an animal.

Then we might use the other tools previously mentioned that are available to the teacher. We could tell him what size animal it is—very large—and then compare it to something else he already knows. We could show him how large by saying that an elephant, even a half-grown elephant, could not possibly walk through the door in the room; it is just too big to get through such a small opening.

We could compare it with something else he knows.

We might say that a large elephant is so large that its back would touch the ceiling of the room. Now the youngster has size in mind. Even if that is all he knows about elephants throughout his life, it isn't likely that he will ever see a cat, a mouse, a dog, or even a horse, and make the mistake of saying, "There goes an elephant."

An elephant has a unique shape. With words alone we might describe that shape.

Then there is color. Ordinarily elephants come in only one color. In teaching color, we might show the child something that is gray, something that he knows and can see to compare it with. If we wanted to be very technical, we could tell him about albino elephants; however, white elephants are so rare that this is a technicality. I have been to Africa and have seen wild elephants, hundreds of them, and I have seen them at the circus and in zoos, but I have not seen a white one, and more than likely neither have you — so that is probably being too technical. We'll discuss the matter of being too technical later.

Texture

There is yet another tool to use, and that is texture. Once we say that an elephant has no fur, that it is not soft like most animals, but has a rough-textured skin, we add to the child's knowledge about an elephant. We can describe the skin as wrinkled and then find something like it that he can see, something he knows; then we will make a comparison with an elephant's skin, saying, "It is like this."

Now our lesson in words is nearly completed, for we have described the size, the shape, the color, and the texture of an elephant. Those things put together set an elephant apart from every other animal on the earth.

There are other steps, such as showing the child a drawing, a small carving or sculpture, or, even better, a photograph of an elephant. And if we could show him a motion picture of an elephant or take him to see an elephant in a zoo, then he would know what an elephant is.

Now that is a lot to say about cats and elephants. I have gone to such length for a significant reason. Most of the things we are obliged to teach can somehow be taught by using the tools we have just discussed. We can recreate the tangible, material world around us in symbols, utilizing some useful tools in making those symbols descriptive. We can convey from one person to another the idea *cat* or the idea *elephant* by describing these in terms of size, shape, color, texture, weight, position, and a number of other features.

Teaching Intangible Principles

The reason the teaching of the gospel ofttimes is so difficult is because it is our responsibility to teach such intangible principles as faith, repentance, love, humility, reverence, and modesty. In teaching the gospel, we do not recreate the material world around us; we deal with the intangible world within us, and there is a big difference. None of the ordinary tools are available to us. To convey to a youngster the idea of a cat is much simpler than to convey the idea of faith; faith is very difficult to describe.

For instance, how big is faith? We soon learn that size is not helpful. Only vaguely can we talk to a youngster who knows nothing about faith by talking about an amount, such as much faith, or little faith. We can't tell him what color it is. We can't tell him what shape it is. We can't tell him what texture it is. And that is the point! When teaching moral and spiritual values, most teachers do not realize that the basic tools—the hammer and the saw and the ruler, common basic tools for building material images in other people's minds—are not used in the same way as they are used to teach anything else. They cannot be used directly. A whole new set of tools, designed in a different way, must be employed.

It is far, far easier to recreate the visible, tangible world around us in alphabetical symbols than to recreate the intangible, invisible world within us and have it understood.

For example, consider a scriptural definition of faith: "Now faith is the substance of things hoped for, the evidence of things not seen." (Hebrews 11:1.)

How much do we know after we have read these words? One would almost have to know what faith is in order for that definition to mean something; then it means very much. It is clarified in the Book of Mormon: "Faith is not to have a perfect knowledge of things; therefore if

31

ye have faith ye hope for things which are not seen, which are true." (Alma 32:21.)

That helps, but if we are starting from a meager knowledge of faith, we still can't talk about it much after pondering over those two scriptures. If a student were to hear them, or even memorize them, he still may not know or understand what they mean or what faith is. As a teacher, we still may not have conveyed the concept of faith.

What do we do, then, if we cannot use the regular basic tools of teaching to convey moral and spiritual values? What do we do with the intangibles? How do we teach them? Well, of course, there is a way. We can tell stories about people and their actions that demonstrate faith. This is helpful and may put the idea of faith in the mind of a student. But it is not the most effective way. A more effective way is to tie the invisible idea of faith to some tangible object the student already knows about and then build from that knowledge. This way will be emphasized in the next chapter.

In the first chapter we mentioned the lens grinder who finally discovered that one little step meant the difference between success and failure in being able to grind the perfect lens. It is like that with teaching.

Use Tangibles to Teach Intangibles

If somehow we might associate faith with something the student already knows about, something that is tangible and measurable in dimensions, then the teaching about it would become much easier. Then we can form words to describe it and create stories about it. We can measure it. Better still, we can draw pictures of it. We can make slides or flannelboard presentations of it. We can show it in color or present it as an object lesson. Then we are on solid ground with the students because students, generally speaking, are more interested in what they know about than in those things they don't know about.

The letters in the alphabet can be arranged in words, which in turn become symbols for objects in the tangible world about us. We can open a book full of such symbols and read them, and in so doing, we can "see" the things the symbols represent. In a similar way, commonplace things that we already know about can be made to represent intangible, invisible ideals. We can learn to "read" these symbols, and in so doing we can "see" the things that they represent, such as faith, love, charity, and obedience.

That is how Jesus taught. Each of us may learn to teach that way also, and in the next chapter is a formula to make it easier. If we learn to teach as Jesus taught, we can then teach our own children and the other children of our Heavenly Father "all things that pertain unto the kingdom of God, that are expedient for them to understand." (D&C 88:78.)

CHAPTER SIX

Is Like Unto . . .

There is a practical way in which faith or any other intangible ideal can be transposed into something tangible and teachable. In fact, there is a formula we can use. This procedure can help teachers, especially teachers of religion, immeasurably. It can also help parents in teaching some difficult things to children.

At first the formula may seem too simple to be useful. But as we study it a bit and begin to experiment with it, we find it very useful.

I remind you that this method of teaching comes from the New Testament. And I remind you also that Jesus as a teacher taught unlettered audiences about the invisible, intangible ideals of the gospel. In teaching faith and love and brotherhood and repentance, he employed the technique of likening the intangible, invisible ideal to a well-known, ordinary object about which His disciples already knew. To relate the unknown to the familiar is known to educators as the principle of apperception. Here is the formula:

_____ is like _____

In the first blank enter the idea or ideal that you must teach. For example, in the first blank write FAITH.

___*Faith*___ is like _____

Now use your imagination and think of a tangible object the student will recognize that might be likened unto faith. The homier, more commonplace, more ordinary it is, the better your illustration. Perhaps you will use this one: FAITH is like A SEED. Faith really is like a seed—at least Alma thought so:

> Now, we will compare the word unto a seed. Now, if ye give place, that a seed may be planted in your heart, behold, if it be a true seed, or a good seed, if ye do not cast it out by your unbelief, that ye will resist the Spirit of the Lord, behold, it will begin to swell within your breasts; and when you feel these swelling motions, ye will begin to say within yourselves—It must needs be that this is a good seed, or that the word is good, for it beginneth to enlarge my soul; yea, it beginneth to enlighten my understanding, yea, it beginneth to be delicious to me.
>
> Now behold, would not this increase your faith? I say unto you, Yea; nevertheless it hath not grown up to a perfect knowledge. (Alma 32:28–29.)

Notice that you have reduced faith to a tangible object the students know. Now you have something with dimension. Faith can be compared to a seed. Jesus used this illustration: "Verily I say unto you, if ye have faith as a grain of mustard seed, you shall say unto this mountain, remove hence to yonder place; and it shall remove; and nothing shall be impossible to you." (Matthew 17:20.) In

35

using the mountain for the comparison, He introduced size, making the lesson more understandable and impressive.

Once you have likened faith to something tangible, you can form word pictures of it, describe it, measure it; you can tell the size, the shape, the color, the texture; you can draw it on the chalkboard, find a picture, make a slide or a flannelboard cutout. You might show some actual seeds as an object lesson — perhaps displaying a seed from a vegetable packet or a stone from a fruit.

The young students could be given some corn seeds to plant in containers. The teacher could water a plant and let other plants wither, to demonstrate, as Alma did, that faith must be nourished.

When the teacher uses comparisons such as these, students soon begin to "see" what faith is like and come close to knowing and understanding a gospel principle.

Apperception
— Relating the Unknown to the Familiar —
Is a Key to Teaching the Gospel

Apperception can work in many lessons to teach such intangible concepts as faith, hope, charity, love, reverence. They can be taught very effectively and with great meaning even to young minds. Knowing this principle is of great value to the teachers at home or in the Church. It really is not necessary to falter and stumble and half-teach these virtues when they can be successfully taught. To know this one thing is a very important key in teaching the gospel of Jesus Christ.

Suppose we use another illustration. Take the subject *repentance.*

Repentance is like _____

What commonplace thing familiar to everyone could be likened to repentance? Suppose we use soap.

Repentance is like _____ *Soap* _____

A lesson to explain this idea might be developed as follows:

Repentance is the soap of life. When properly used it can cleanse us from our transgressions; yet some people stay dirty. Why? Why do so many individuals not use repentance when it is individually, immediately, and constantly available to everyone?

You could illustrate the misuse of the ideal in this way. Describe a beautiful, white handkerchief, pure and untouched, that is dropped in the mud. If it can be carefully washed, it will be clean once more. But suppose it is dropped in the mud again and washed again; then into the mud and washed again many times. The handkerchief soon becomes gray and ingrained with dirt, and it is much harder to get it clean, even with strong soap.

On one occasion I sat with a group of seminary teachers, presented this formula, and asked them to put their minds to work on the subject of teaching repentance. In an hour of discussion we produced a dozen or more life situations that might be used.

Use Imagination

It is important to understand that if you are too literal or too technical, no comparison or reference or "liken unto" will satisfy, not even those the Lord used. You must use imagination.

I remember one teacher arguing that repentance really

isn't like soap. For that matter, the kingdom of heaven really isn't like a net, nor are the Pharisees like unto the whited sepulchre. Some creative imagination is necessary. If you don't try to develop that, then you will be a very dull teacher, not an interesting one. If you are determined to be too literal, no apperceptive reference is quite good enough.

Let me illustrate how likening repentance to soap can be used to teach this important gospel principle.

"My! What Filthy Men!"

During World War II, I was being transferred overseas from Langley Field, Virginia. The group I was with was transported in boxcars that had been made into makeshift sleeping cars by attaching bunks to the walls so they could be folded up during the day to allow room for us to move around. We referred to the accommodations as cattle cars. Our meals were served from a camp kitchen and cooked over an open fire in one of the cars. The fire was built on a six- inch layer of dirt.

Our luggage was separated from us the first day, so for six days and six nights we traveled across the southern United States wearing the same uniforms without the possibility of bathing or changing or washing our clothes. Since it was July, the heat added to a very sweaty situation.

We arrived in Los Angeles on Sunday morning and were told we were free until afternoon; then we would report back to the train and continue to a military base in northern California preparatory to going overseas. The ten members of our bomber crew got together in the station and pooled our money. We determined that the one thing we wanted most was a good meal.

We went to a fine restaurant and stood in line waiting to be seated (there were always long lines at restaurants during the war). The civilians in line were in their Sunday best. I was in front of our crew, and in front of me were several distinguished-looking ladies. They could tell we were there without turning around: our unbathed condition announced that. Finally one woman did turn around. She studied me carefully from head to toe and then announced in a voice loud enough to attract the attention of everyone in the restaurant, "My! What filthy men!"

We endured the humiliation silently, but oh, how I wanted to be clean! How soap would have helped! I will never forget how I determined never to go before the Lord spiritually filthy. If repentance is like the soap of life, I want to use it frequently and properly.

These two examples—likening faith unto a seed as is done in the scriptures, and likening repentance to soap—may provide a lesson for our day, demonstrating how tangible, familiar things from the world about us can be employed as symbols for the intangible, invisible ideals that sometimes are difficult or impossible to describe with words alone.

CHAPTER SEVEN

It's in the Book

Now that you have some idea how the principle of apperception operates, it will be helpful to look again into the scriptures to see many illustrations of this method of teaching. In His teachings, Jesus always dealt with familiar objects and experiences. By studying the examples He presented, one will recognize that many are very ordinary illustrations. In presenting the familiar example, Jesus began where the people were in order to provide a learning experience.

One thing Jesus had in common with most of those whom He taught was basic life experience. From the information we have concerning His personal life, we conclude that He might have been regarded as an ordinary individual of His day. His teachings reflect and portray for us the world of His earlier days.

He related directly to the background of his listeners. He referred often to the basic religious instruction that was paramount in the life of every youngster in that day in His expression, "Ye have heard that it was said by them of old. . . . " (See Matthew 5:21, 27, 38; Matthew 12:3, 5, etc.) Or, if he was not referring to something they had heard, He said, "Ye have read. . . . "

Common, Ordinary Things

The Sermon on the Mount is perhaps as productive an example as any particular teaching episode. Note the many illustrations He draws into the instruction in one chapter, Matthew 5. Here we list phrases and sentences that have reference to commonplace things.

> Ye are the **salt** of the **earth;** but if the salt have lost its savour, wherewith shall it be salted? It is thenceforth good for nothing, but to be cast out, and to be trodden under**foot** of men.

Ye are the **light** of the **world.** A **city** that is set on an **hill** cannot be hid. Neither do **men light a candle,** and put it under a **bushel,** but on a **candle-stick;** and it giveth light unto all that are in the **house.**

One **jot** or one **tittle** shall in no wise pass from the law.

Except your righteousness exceed the righteousness of the **scribes** and **pharisees.**

Ye have heard it said by them of old times.

Whosoever is angry with his **brother.**

Whosoever shall say, thou **fool.**

41

Leave thy **gift** at the **altar.**

Lest at any time the adversary deliver thee to the **judge,** and the judge deliver thee to the **officer,** and thou be cast into **prison.**

Thou shalt by no means come out thence till thou has paid the uttermost **farthing.**

Whoso looketh on a **woman** to lust after her.

Whoso shall put away his **wife** shall give her a **bill** of divorcement.

Again, Ye have heard that it hath been said. Swear not at all.

Ye have heard it hath been said.

An **eye** for an eye and a **tooth** for a tooth.

If any man sue thee at the law and take away thy **coat.**

And whosoever compels thee to go a **mile.**

For he maketh his **sun** to rise on the evil and on the good, and sendeth **rain** on the just and the unjust.

Do not even the **publicans** the same.

And if ye salute your **brethren** only.

This familiar chapter was selected because it is well known and is representative of what might be found anywhere in the teachings of Jesus. Other chapters have additional examples.

The references in this and the other chapters are, you will note, directed at the experience of the listeners. Garbage disposal in the cities of that age consisted of refuse dumped into the streets. Therefore, savorless salt would literally be trodden under feet of men. Jerusalem was referred to as the city on the hill, a reference full of meaning to the people. A Roman soldier could legally compel any Jew to carry his burdens a full mile. These and other references were familiar things to Jesus' disciples.

Quite as rich a source of obvious apperceptive material can be found in a study of the parables. In these stories He refers to experiences common to the average life in

42

Palestine in His day or refers to Judaic history for references to well-known regulations from the Law of Moses.

He speaks of hens, chickens, birds, flowers, foxes, trees, burglars, highwaymen, sunsets, the rich and the poor, the physician, patching clothes, pulling weeds, sweeping the house, feeding pigs, threshing grain, storing into barns, building houses, hiring help, and dozens of other things. None of them is mysterious or obscure, and all are from the real-life, everyday experiences of those whom He taught.

" . . . Is Like . . .

He was always comparing the tangible world about us with the intangible world within us. Time after time after time He used the expression "is like" or "I will liken."

Read through these sentences from the Gospels and from other books of the New Testament:

Matthew	11:16	It *is like* unto children sitting in the markets
	13:31	The kingdom of heaven *is like* to a grain of mustard seed
	13:33	The kingdom of heaven *is like* unto leaven
	13:44	The kingdom of heaven *is like* unto treasure
	13:45	The kingdom of heaven *is like* unto a merchant man
	13:47	The kingdom of heaven *is like* unto a net
	13:52	*Is like* unto a man . . . an householder
	20:1	The kingdom of heaven *is like* unto a man
	22:39	The second [*is*] *like* unto it, Thou shalt love
Mark	12:31	The second [*is like*] . . . this, Thou shalt love
Luke	6:47	I will shew you to whom he *is like*
	6:48	He *is like* a man which built an house
	6:49	*Is like* a man that . . . built an house upon
	7:31	And the Lord said . . . to what are they *like*?
	7:32	They *are like* unto children sitting in the market place
	12:36	*Like unto* men that wait for their lord
	13:18	Unto what is the kingdom of God *like*?
	13:19	It *is like* a grain of mustard seed, which
	13:21	It *is like* leaven, which a woman took

44

| John | 8:55 | I shall be a liar *like* unto you; but I know |
| | 9:9 | Others said, He *is* *like* him . . . he said, I am |

Other scriptures also reflect the same method of comparison:

Acts	17:29	That the Godhead *is* *like* unto gold, or
Galatians	5:21	Drunkenness, revellings, and such *like*
1 John	3:2	We shall be *like* him; for we shall see him
Jude	7	The cities about them, *in like* manner
Revelation	1:13	*Like unto* the Son of man, clothed with
	1:15	His feet *like unto* fine brass, as if they
	2:18	the Son of God . . . his feet [are] *like* fine brass
	4:3	he that sat was to look upon *like* a jasper
	4:3	a rainbow . . . in sight [*like*] unto an emerald
	4:6	a sea of glass *like* unto crystal
	4:7	*like* a lion, and the second beast *like* a calf
	4:7	and the fourth beast . . . *like* a flying eagle
	9:7	locusts . . . *like* unto horses prepared unto
	9:7	as it were crowns *like* gold
	9:10	they had tails *like* unto scorpions
	9:19	their tails . . . *like* unto serpents
	11:1	there was given me a reed *like* unto a rod
	13:2	the beast which I saw was *like* unto a leopard
	13:4	Who is *like* unto the beast?

13:11 He had two horns *like* a lamb, and he spake

14:14 one sat *like* unto the Son of man

16:13 I saw three unclean spirits *like* frogs

18:18 What city is *like* unto this great city

21:11 her light was *like* unto a stone most precious

21:18 the city . . . pure gold, *like* unto clear glass

The Book of Mormon too is rich in similar references:

1 Nephi   2:9   O that thou mightest be *like* unto this river

2:10 O that thou mightest be *like* unto this valley

12:1 in number as many as [*like*] the sand of the sea

15:12 the house of Israel was compared unto [*likened to*] an olive-tree

17:45 he has spoken unto you *like* unto the voice of thunder

2 Nephi   5:21 they had become *like* unto a flint

7:7   Therefore have I set my face *like* a flint

8:6   the earth shall wax old *like* a garment

8:8   the moth shall eat them up *like* a garment

8:8   the worm shall eat them *like* wool

26:6 they shall be as [*like*] stubble

Mosiah   12:5 they shall be driven before *like* a dumb ass

12:12 thou shalt be as [*like*] the blossoms of a thistle

14:6 All we, *like* sheep, have gone astray

Alma	32:28	compare the word unto [*liken to*] a seed
3 Nephi	7:8	*like* the dog to his vomit
	7:8	*like* the sow to her wallowing in the mire
	10:4	as [*like*] a hen gathereth her chickens under her wings
Ether	2:16	*like* unto the lightness of a fowl upon the water
	6:7	their vessels being tight *like* unto a dish

Notice also these samples from the Doctrine and Covenants:

49:24 shall blossom as [*like*] the rose
121:45 shall distil upon thy soul as [*like*] the dews from heaven
128:19 as [*like*] the dews of Carmel
130:9 will be made *like* unto crystal
133:48 his garments *like* him that treadeth in the wine-vat

In section 88 the Lord revealed celestial laws governing earth and planets and said: "*Unto what shall I liken these kingdoms,* that ye may *understand?*" (D&C 88:46.)

And finally we find these samples in the Pearl of Great Price:

Moses	7:28	shed forth their tears as [like] the rain upon the mountains
	7:62	to sweep the earth as [like] with a flood
Abraham	3:14	the number of sands, so shall be the number of thy seeds
Joseph Smith	1:38	a parable of the fig-tree . . . *likewise,* mine elect
	1:47	if the good man of the house had known in what watch the thief would come
	2:37	the day cometh that shall burn as [*like*] an oven

2:37   all that do wickedly shall burn
       as [like] stubble

These are but a few of the many references that we find in scripture, a rich source for illustrations on how the principle of apperception is employed to teach difficult-to-teach subjects.

To Make the Lesson Clear

Keep in mind that Jesus was not merely talking to the people of His day about their experiences and the things in their environment. He was not teaching them about hens and chickens. He was using the hen and the chickens to teach them about something else. He related and interrelated these experiences in the visible world to the unseen world within. He made the application, the comparison, so that the lesson was obvious.

If we were to subtract from the discourses of Jesus the applications He made, we would end up with something of a disjointed commentary on peasant life in ancient Palestine. It is the teaching of the gospel that makes the illustrations come alive. The illustrations, in turn, make the meaning of the lessons clear to people of all ages.

The application in each discourse was the important thing. In the reference to salt (Matthew 5:13), for instance, He was not interested in reminding His listeners of the common table condiment—so common, in fact, as to be almost uninteresting if mentioned in other ways. The word *salt* as used in His teaching was not used to tell them how to eat, but rather, was a steppingstone to relate and interrelate the past experience of His students into larger, more meaningful, more inclusive learning patterns.

We mentioned earlier that such concepts as faith, repentance, and humility are hard to teach because we cannot picture them. They have no size, no shape, no texture, no color; therefore, it is difficult to make word pictures of

48

them. By using the method Jesus used, however, we can teach them well.

How often would I have gathered thy children together, even as a hen gathereth her chickens under her wings (Matthew 23:37).

How oft will I gather you as a hen gathereth her chickens under her wings (3 Nephi 10:6).

I will gather them as a hen gathereth her chickens under her wings (D&C 10:65).

will gather his people even as a hen gathereth her chickens under her wings (D&C 29:2).

How often would I have gathered you together as a hen gathereth her chickens under her wings (D&C 43:24).

CHAPTER EIGHT

The Gospel Is Like a Keyboard

On one occasion in General Conference I wanted to talk on the subject "The Only True and Living Church" and use as the basic text Doctrine and Covenants 1:30.

> And also those to whom these commandments were given, might have power to lay the foundation of this church, and to bring it forth out of obscurity and out of darkness, the only true and living church upon the face of the whole earth, with which I, the Lord, am well pleased, speaking unto the church collectively and not individually.

I did not want to say that all of the other churches were without truth, for they have some truth — some of them a great deal of it. They have a form of godliness. Often the clergy and adherents are not without dedication, and many of them practice remarkably well the virtues of Christianity. They are, nonetheless, incomplete, and the Lord has declared: "They teach for doctrines the commandments of men, having a form of godliness, but deny the power thereof." (Joseph Smith 2:19.)

How could I get the idea across that all churches perhaps have an element of the truth, but there is only one with the fulness of the gospel?

50

In using the formula for *likening,* I determined that the gospel is like a piano keyboard. After finding something with which to compare the gospel, something that would be familiar to everyone who would be listening, it was much easier to prepare the talk, part of which I will quote:

Like a Keyboard

"The gospel might be *likened to* the keyboard of a piano. A full keyboard with a selection of keys on which one trained can play a variety without limits—a ballad to express love, a march to rally, a melody to soothe, and a hymn to inspire—an endless variety to suit every mood and satisfy every need.

"How shortsighted it is, then, to choose a single key and endlessly tap out the monotony of a single note, or even two or three notes, when the full keyboard of limitless harmony can be played.

"How disappointing when the fulness of the gospel, the whole keyboard, is here upon the earth, that many churches tap on a single key. The note they stress may be essential to a complete harmony of religious experience, but it is, nonetheless, not all there; it isn't the fulness.

"For instance, one taps on the key of faith-healing, to the neglect of many principles that would bring greater strength to faith-healing itself.

"Another taps on an obscure key relating to the observance of the Sabbath — a key that would sound different indeed, played in harmony with the essential notes on the keyboard. A key used like that can get completely out of tune.

"Another repeats endlessly the key that relates to the mode of baptism and taps one or two other keys as though there were not a full keyboard. And again, the very key they use, necessary as it is, just doesn't sound complete when played alone to the neglect of the others.

"There are other examples, many of them, in which parts of the gospel are endlessly stressed and the churches build upon them, until alone they sound nothing like they would if blended with the full measure of the gospel of Jesus Christ.

"We don't say that the key of faith-healing, for example, is not essential. We not only recognize it, but we also rely on it and experience it; however, it alone is not the gospel, nor its fulness.

"We would never hold that baptism was not essential, absolutely essential, for it constitutes the official enrollment in the Church and kingdom of God. If that key, however, is played alone, without the counterpart key of authority, the fulness and the harmony are gone and it becomes dissonant. Without the key of faith and of repentance, it is meaningless, and perhaps worse, it is counterfeit. This happens when the authority we speak of is lacking.

Power and Authority

"Now we do not say other churches are wrong so much as we say they are incomplete. The fulness of the gospel has been restored. The power and authority to act for Him is present with us. The power and the authority of the priesthood rest upon this church. The Lord revealed:

> This greater priesthood administereth the gospel and holdeth the key of the mysteries of the kingdom, even the key of the knowledge of God.
> Therefore, in the ordinances thereof, the power of Godliness is manifest.
> And without the ordinances thereof, and the authority of the priesthood, the power of Godliness is not manifest unto men in the flesh. (D&C 84:19–21.)

A Single Key

"It is not unusual to find people who take an interest in The Church of Jesus Christ of Latter-day Saints but give only casual attention to the ideal that the fulness of the gospel is here.

"They become attracted by a single key, a doctrine. They investigate it by itself alone. They want to know all there is about it without reference — in fact, with specific objection and rejection — to anything else.

"They want to hear that key played over and over again. It will give them little knowledge unless they see that there is a fulness; other complementary ideals and doctrines that present a warmth and a harmony and a fulness, that draw at the right moment upon each key, which if played alone might seem discordant.

"Now, that danger is not limited to investigators alone. Some members of the Church who should know better pick out a hobby key or two and tap them incessantly, to the irritation of those around them. They can dull their own spiritual sensitivities. They lose track that there is a fulness of the gospel, and they become as individuals, like many churches have become. They may reject the fulness in preference to a favorite note. This becomes exaggerated and distorted, leading them away into apostasy." (General Conference address, October 1971.)

Just as an Illustration

It should be very clear that although I likened the gospel to a piano keyboard, I was not interested in teaching about pianos or keyboards. I was just using the keyboard as an illustration. I do not play the piano, and I know relatively little about a keyboard. Yet that did not make the comparison or the "likening" less meaningful, either to me or to those who heard the sermon. I know from the response that many could "see" what I was trying to teach. I might have talked at length trying to describe the ideas, quoting from many sources, including scriptures, and yet I would not have been successful in teaching what I desired.

There is one other very important point that must never be overlooked. When you successfully employ the principle of apperception, or liken something from the unseen world within you to the real world around you, the lesson can repeat itself. You can understand why someone would tell me, "Often when I see a piano keyboard I think of the fulness of the gospel." It is as though the lesson is repeating itself in the mind of that individual. That is one reason why the more commonplace and close to everyday life the comparison is, the more powerful your lesson.

That is why the Lord, when He was teaching, used such illustrations as He did. They were close to the people. We can use the very same method, as illustrated in the following story.

Thoughts Are Like Water

When I was about ten years old we lived in a home surrounded by an orchard. There never seemed to be enough water for the trees. The ditches, always fresh-plowed in the spring, would soon be filled with weeds. One day, in charge of the irrigating turn, I found myself in trouble.

As the water moved down the rows choked with weeds, it would flood in every direction. I raced through the puddles trying to build up the bank. As soon as I had one break patched up, there would be another.

A neighbor came through the orchard. He watched for a moment, and then with a few vigorous strokes of the shovel he cleared the ditch bottom and allowed the water to course through the channel he had made. "If you want the water to stay in its course, you'll have to make a place for it to go," he said.

I have come to know that thoughts, like water, will stay on course if we make a place for them to go. Otherwise our thoughts follow the course of least resistance, always seeking the lower levels. I was told a hundred times or more as I grew up that thoughts must be controlled. But no one told me how.

In an attempt to tell the youth of the Church how to control their thoughts, the principle of likening was useful again:

The Stage of Your Mind

"The mind is *like* a stage—the curtain is always up except when we are asleep. There is always some act being performed on that stage. It may be a comedy, a tragedy, interesting or dull, good or bad; but always there is some act playing on the stage of the mind.

"Have you noticed that without any real intent on your part, in the middle of almost any performance, a shady little thought may creep in from the wings and attract your attention? These delinquent thoughts will try to upstage everybody.

"If you permit them to go on, all thoughts of any virtue will leave the stage. You will be left, because you consented to it, to the influence of unrighteous thoughts. If you yield to them, they will enact for you on the stage of your mind anything to the limits of your toleration. They may enact a theme of bitterness, jealousy, or hatred. They may be vulgar, immoral, or even depraved.

"When they have the stage, if you let them, they will devise the most clever persuasions to hold your attention.

They can make it interesting all right, even convince you that it is innocent—for they are but thoughts.

"What do you do at a time like that, when the stage of your mind is commandeered by the imps of unclean thinking? Whether they be the gray ones that seem almost clean or the filthy ones that leave no room for doubt?

"If you can control your thoughts, you can overcome habits—even degrading, personal habits. If you can learn to master them, you will have a happy life.

A Favorite Hymn

"I would teach you this. Choose from among the sacred music of the Church a favorite hymn, one with words that are uplifting and music that is reverent, one that makes you feel something akin to inspiration. Go over it carefully in your mind. Memorize it. Even though you have had no musical training, you can think through a hymn.

"Now, use this hymn as the place for your thoughts to go. Make it your emergency channel. Whenever you find that these shady actors have slipped from the sidelines of your thinking onto the stage of your mind, put on this record, as it were.

"As the music begins and as the words form in your mind, the unworthy thoughts will slip shamefully away. The hymn will change the whole mood on the stage of your mind. Because it is uplifting and clean, the baser thoughts will disappear, for while virtue, by choice, *will not* associate with filth, evil *cannot* tolerate the presence of light.

"In due time you will find yourself, on occasion, humming the music inwardly. As you retrace your thoughts, you discover that some influence from the world about you has encouraged an unworthy thought to move on stage in your mind, and the music has almost automatically begun.

"Once you learn to clear the stage of your mind from unworthy thoughts, keep it busy with learning worthwhile things. Change your environment so that you have things about you that will inspire good and uplifting thoughts. Keep busy with things that are righteous.

"Young people, you cannot afford to fill your minds with the unworthy hard music of our day. It is *not* harmless. It can welcome onto the stage of your mind unworthy thoughts and set the tempo to which they dance, and to which you may act." (General conference address, October 1973.)

It is easier, so very much easier, when we take such elusive things as thoughts and compare them with something the students already know about, in this case the actors on a stage. It is more interesting, particularly to the young people. They remember it, and teaching has taken place.

CHAPTER NINE

A World of Examples

Some years ago I was on a plane bound for Seattle, Washington, from Spokane. I had been attending a religious emphasis week at the University of Idaho at Moscow, Idaho, and was on my way to Seattle to meet with the stake leaders regarding the seminary program. There were not many passengers on the plane and I found a seat alone, hoping to sleep during the trip, which would take something more than an hour.

I was momentarily irritated when someone sat next to me, and willingly consented to his request to borrow the newspaper I had on my lap. This will keep him busy, I thought. But he soon began to mutter, "Awful, miserable, terrible," and when I responded, he pointed to the front page of the newspaper, a typical city paper with the sordid, the ugly, and the tragic openly reported on the front page.

He said the newspaper was typical of humanity and of life—miserable, meaningless, and in all ways useless and futile. Finally I had to protest and insist that life was purposeful, that there lives a God who loves His children, and that life is good indeed.

An Atheist

The young man introduced himself as an attorney. When he learned that I was a minister he said, with some emphasis, "All right, we have one hour and twenty-eight minutes on this flight, and I want you to tell me what business you or anyone else has traipsing about the earth saying that there is a God and that life has any substantial meaning."

He then confessed himself to be an atheist and pressed his disbelief so urgently that I finally said, "You are wrong, my friend. There is a God. He lives. I know He lives."

I then bore testimony to him that God lives and that Jesus is the Christ and that I knew it to be so. This testimony fell on doubtful ears. "You don't know," he said. "Nobody knows that. You can't know it."

I would not yield, and the attorney finally said, condescendingly, "All right, you say you know, then [inferring, 'if you are so smart'] tell me *how* you know."

I felt helpless at this, perhaps the ultimate of questions. I said, "The Spirit of the Holy Ghost has borne witness to my soul."

The attorney said, "I don't know what you are talking about."

I found that the words *prayer, discernment,* and *faith* were meaningless to him, for they were outside his experience.

Seeing me helpless to explain how I knew, he finally said, "You see, you don't really know. If you did know, you'd be able to tell me how you know." (The implication of his words was that anything we know we can readily explain with words alone.)

The Taste of Salt

I felt that I may have borne my testimony unwisely, and I prayed in my heart that if the young attorney could not understand my words, he could at least feel the sincerity of my declaration.

"All knowledge is not conveyed in words alone," I

said. I then asked this question: "Do you know what salt tastes like?"

"Of course I do," was his reply.

"When did you taste salt last?"

"I had dinner a short time ago and I tasted salt then."

"You just think you know what salt tastes like," I said.

"I know what salt tastes like as well as I know anything," he insisted.

"If I gave you a cup of salt and a cup of sugar, and let you taste them both, could you tell the salt from the sugar?"

"Now you are becoming juvenile," was his reply. "Of course I could tell the difference. I know what salt tastes like!"

Then I asked one further question. "Assuming that *I* have never tasted salt, can you explain to me in words just what it tastes like?"

After some thought the attorney ventured, "Well, it is not sweet and it is not sour."

"You've told me what it isn't," was my answer, "not what it is."

After several attempts he admitted failure in the little exercise and found himself quite as helpless as I had been to answer his previous question: how I know the gospel is true.

As we walked into the terminal I bore testimony once again and said, "I claim to know there is a God. You ridiculed that testimony and said that if I did know I would be able to tell you exactly how I know. My friend, spiritually speaking, I have tasted salt. I am no more able to convey to you in words how this knowledge has come than you are able to perform the simple exercise of telling me what salt tastes like. But I say to you again, there is a God. He lives. Just because you don't know, don't try to tell me I don't know, for I do."

Techniques and Tools

This confrontation is an illustration of how difficult it is to teach the very things that we are commissioned to teach in the Church. When we teach moral and spiritual values, we are teaching things that are intangible. Perhaps no teaching is so difficult to accomplish, nor so rewarding when successfully done.

There are techniques to employ and tools to use. There are things that teachers can do to prepare themselves and their lessons so that their students, whether it be their own children or those whom they are called to teach in classrooms or whom they are leading as officers in the Church, can be taught, and their testimonies can be conveyed from one to another.

I would like to point out that in the previous experience, while the subject of our conversation was revelation, the discussion for the most part was about salt. It is probable that very little would have been accomplished if I had continued to speak of inspiration, of the Spirit of the Holy Ghost, or of testimony. Those terms were totally out of his experience, and if we made a point at all, it was because we began with something he knew — salt.

Incidentally, as we walked into the terminal he muttered, over and over again, speaking softly and to himself, "I don't need your old religion for a crutch, understand; I don't need it."

Subject ideas for comparisons and references are everywhere, and there are many of them in our surroundings if only we can see them. Consider the following illustration.

A New World

During World War II, I was in cadet training at Thunderbird Field near Scottsdale, Arizona. We would on occasion go into Phoenix on the weekend, and on Sunday afternoon we would be finding a way back to our base.

Scottsdale, Arizona, in those days was a rural suburb of Phoenix and consisted of not much more than an intersection.

One Sunday several of us were not able to get a ride, so we began the long walk back to the base. As we were hiking along, an old car drew up and a gentleman offered us a ride. There were more of us than could get in his old car, but there were running boards on which we could stand, and so he drove slowly along as we chatted. Several complained about the desert and how dry and dead and lifeless it was. Finally he stopped the car and said he wanted to show us something.

He then told us he was a teacher of natural sciences, and we spent some time walking into the desert. He showed us plants and animals and living things and opened our eyes to a new world. He pointed out shriveled and supposedly dead plants.

"All they await is the spring rains," he said. "Take this," he added, pointing to a shriveled lump of dried vegetable matter, "put it in water, and within hours it will unfold and become green. It is really a very beautiful plant if you will study it closely; it is unnoticed because no one really bends over to look at it."

63

The desert never was the same to me after that. Always thereafter it was beautiful and intensely interesting.

Once we understand the principle of apperception, the whole world comes alive like that. We see examples that are meaningful everywhere we turn.

This principle of teaching opens up a world of visual aids. When we are in command of it, we can add the eyes to our means of communication. Using examples our students can literally see, we can then lead them to see invisible ideals. A picture is worth a thousand words.

Once a teacher begins to look about for things to "liken" in his lessons, it becomes a new world. He then knows that to realize an ideal means he must sometimes idealize the real.

CHAPTER TEN

The Question

The simplest way to learn something is to ask a question about it. Questions and answers are essential to any teaching method. They constitute the process most used in teaching in the home. Children are full of questions, and parents need to be equally full of answers.

In all training and teaching and classroom situations we find the question. This was true of Jesus as He taught His disciples or the multitudes. There is something interesting and meaningful about the way He handled questions and answers. He asked many questions. He answered but a few of them.

It is also interesting that the Spirit of the Lord, in teaching Nephi, used many questions:

Behold, what desirest thou? (1 Nephi 11:2.)

Believest thou that thy father saw the tree of which he hath spoken? (1 Nephi 11:4.)

What desirest thou? (1 Nephi 11:10.)

Knowest thou the condescension of God? (1 Nephi 11:16.)

Knowest thou the meaning of the tree which thy father saw? (1 Nephi 11:21.)

Thou rememberest the twelve apostles of the Lamb? (1 Nephi 12:9.)

Answering a Question with a Question

Contrary to what you may suppose, the Lord generally did not answer questions—at least not in the usual way, particularly the questions that came from those who were tempting Him. Generally He did not answer them with a direct answer or an explanation. In fact, He almost always responded by asking a question of those who raised the question in the first place.

Consider the occasion when the tempters asked Him if it was lawful to pay taxes to Caesar. This was a loaded question. If He had answered, "No, it is not lawful to pay taxes unto Caesar," He would have been guilty of treason and subject to death. If He had answered, "Yes, it is legal to pay taxes to Caesar," He would have immediately incurred the wrath of the Jews, who had been conquered by the Romans and detested the heavy taxation. Neither a yes nor a no answer was safe.

Notice how the Savior handled the question asked Him by the Pharisees and the Herodians:

"Tell us therefore, what thinkest thou? Is it lawful to give tribute unto Caesar, or not?

"But Jesus perceived their wickedness, and said, Why tempt ye me, ye hypocrites?

"Shew me the tribute money. And they brought unto him a penny.

"And he saith unto them, Whose is this image and superscription?"

Notice that He is asking them a question; the initiative is with Him now.

"They say unto him, Caesar's. Then saith he unto

them, Render therefore unto Caesar the things which are Caesar's; and unto God the things that are God's.

"When they had heard these words, they marvelled, and left him, and went their way." (Matthew 22:17–22.)

On another occasion He had told the people to love their neighbors as themselves, and so a question came to Him, "Who is my neighbour?"

He might have given a direct answer, "Your neighbor is the one who lives next door to you," or, "Your neighbor is everyone in your block or in your community, or in your nation," or, "Your neighbor in this context is everyone in the world."

But He did not answer the inquiry that way. He began with a narration.

> A certain man went down from Jerusalem to Jericho, and fell among thieves, which stripped him of his raiment, and wounded him, and departed, leaving him half dead.
>
> And by chance there came down a certain priest that way: and when he saw him, he passed by on the other side.
>
> And likewise a Levite, when he was at the place, came and looked on him, and passed by on the other side.
>
> But a certain Samaritan, as he journeyed, came where he was: and when he saw him, he had compassion on him.

And went to him, and bound up his wounds, pouring in oil and wine, and set him on his own beast, and brought him to an inn, and took care of him.

And on the morrow when he departed, he took out two pence, and gave them to the host, and said unto him, Take care of him; and whatsoever thou spendest more, when I come again, I will repay thee. (Luke 10:30–35.)

When the narration was over He asked, "Whom sayest thou was the neighbour?" And when they had answered, He commended them for the correct answer. That brings us to the point: Who answered the question? Well, of course, His listeners answered their own question after some discussion and teaching. They answered their own question by answering *His* question.

Be Careful Lest You Answer

You can employ the same techniques. When a student asks a question, be careful lest you answer it! Or more emphatically, be careful lest the teacher answer it. How easy it is for a teacher to respond quickly to simple questions, to close a conversation that might have ignited a sparkling and lively class discussion.

The wise teacher deftly and pleasantly responds, "That's an interesting question. What does the class think of this?"

Or, "Can anyone in the class help with this interesting problem?"

A simple two-way conversation, and you've involved the whole class and their minds come alive and are open to teaching.

Few things are so agonizing for a new teacher as to want to start a discussion and then have everyone remain silent. The use of discussion, simple question and answer, is one of the basic, useful, and important teaching processes. It often does not go well simply because the teacher does not know how to ask questions or how to respond (or how *not* to respond) to those that are asked by the class.

Good questions to use when teaching moral or spiritual values, when teaching subjective principles, are questions that ask, "Why do you think?"

"In your opinion, what . . . ?"

Or, "In your estimation, how . . . ?"

"Where, do you think?"

"In your mind?"

"When?"

Or, "Would you please explain?"

These questions relate little to factual details to be remembered, but they are thought provoking.

Do you remember when you were in your Sunday School class recently? The teacher asked a question. You started to put up your hand, then hesitated and brought it down. You weren't all that positive that you knew the answer. You were sure you did, but you were not *positive;* and because of the possibility that you might embarrass yourself, you did not respond.

Rescue the Student

Isn't it a pity that in a Sunday School class or a priesthood class we would be so concerned about giving a wrong answer and embarrassing ourselves that we would refuse to participate? And yet that is the way it generally is. It is that way partly because some teachers don't know how to handle questions.

Suppose you are a Sunday School teacher, and in a class of young people you say, "John, please tell us who was the fourth president of the Church."

John blurts out, "Abraham Lincoln."

And of course everyone in the class laughs. They needn't tell him the answer is wrong, or that it's a stupid answer, or that he himself is stupid. All of this is conveyed when they laugh at him.

A teacher can rescue the student if he's alert. We are wise if we never make a student feel he is stupid or wish he had not replied. Experiences like that make us hesitant to participate and reduce our ability to learn. They also reduce the ability and opportunity for many to teach.

Accept the Responsibility

What can a teacher do in such a case? For one thing, he can take the blame himself. "I'm sorry, John, I didn't make the question clear. It was the Church we were talking about, not the country. Perhaps I didn't explain it plainly enough."

In that way, the teacher accepts responsibility. When a student responds to a question and his answer is not right or is only partly right, the teacher can kindly say, "Perhaps I did not make the question clear."

Or, "I had not thought of it in just that way."

Or, "Perhaps you are thinking of this other instance."

Or, "Your answer indicates a point that perhaps most of us have overlooked."

Or, "I'm glad you have brought that up."

Or merely, "Thank you for your response. I'm still looking for another answer to the question."

Imagine a class of Aaronic Priesthood holders or a Sunday School class. The teacher asks the question, "Which president of the Church led the pioneers west from Winter Quarters to the Salt Lake Valley in 1847?"

John responds, "I think it was Heber J. Grant."

The teacher winces, looks around the room, and says with a note of exasperation in his voice, "Isn't there anyone in the class who can give us a *correct* answer?" From then on, John will no longer volunteer an answer. He'll even be hesitant to answer when you call on him, because by your handling of the question and the inflection of your voice you say, "Look, stupid, don't we have enough problems without having dumbbell answers like that in our class?"

John is not the only one who is affected, either. The other students will develop reticence and reluctance. You have only about three chances at something like this, and then it's very difficult to get a class to respond. On the other hand, if John gives an incorrect answer and you rescue him, apologize for the question, and help him out— maybe give him something of a hint—you will find you can do much to encourage participation on the part of the class members.

If we handle questions like this routinely, the class soon develops confidence and class members are willing to respond, even at the risk of giving an incorrect answer; they soon become outgoing instead of withdrawn. The student will not begin to raise his hand and then pull it back for fear of being embarrassed. A teacher must cultivate this method of handling questions. It takes the development of mutual respect.

Reword the Question

There was something else wrong about the first situation. We have talked about the wrong answer, but there is also something wrong with the question. The question, you will remember, was "John, tell us please, who was the fourth president of the Church?" If you frame a question that way, the instant you say "John," the other students in the class relax. They put their minds in neutral and realize that John is on the hook to answer this one. There's no need for them to scratch in their memories to try to remember who was the fourth president of the Church.

If a teacher is alert and wise in posing questions, he

will reverse the order and say, "Tell us please, who was the fourth president of the Church?" Then he will pause briefly and look around the class, at one student or another and yet another. Immediately they are alerted that they may be asked and their minds are thrown into high gear; they begin quickly to think, "Let's see now, Joseph Smith, Brigham Young, John Taylor, Wilford Woodruff. It would be Wilford Woodruff." Then each person in the class is doing something about learning, scratching in his mind to dig up an answer.

After the class members have been working mentally for a minute, the teacher can say, "John," and he will respond, but all of them have participated silently. Remember that the question, "Who is the fourth president of the Church (pause), John?" is a much better question than, "John, who is the fourth president of the Church?"

A Better Question

There is something else about questions that a teacher should keep in mind. Suppose I were to ask you, "Would you please give me the year, the month, the day, and the time of day that the Prophet Joseph Smith was martyred in Carthage Jail?" I doubt if you could answer that. In fact, I think there would be very few who could. Such a technical question is ordinarily not the kind of question that will encourage conversation and participation.

Often a teacher will wonder, "Why can't I get this class to participate? They just don't seem to respond. I will ask a question, and everybody will look blank. Then I'll ask something else, and I don't get a response. Pretty soon the silence is so loud that I read something out of the manual or do something else. I just can't stand the non-participation."

It may be that it's the kind of questions you ask. After all, what does it matter what year it was or what day it was or what time of the day it was? That information is not essential to anyone's salvation.

A much better question would be, "In reviewing Church history, let me remind you that it was in the afternoon of June 27, 1844, that the Prophet Joseph Smith was killed. We know about what time it was because the watch that John Taylor wore was struck by a bullet and stopped at that hour. Tell me, please, *why* was Joseph Smith willing to go to Carthage when he knew what would probably take place?"

Now that's a question to which more people will respond, and you should have no difficulty getting a discussion started, because they would have some idea as to why the Prophet would be willing to go to Carthage.

There's an even better way to phrase that question, and that is to say, "In your opinion, why did Joseph Smith go to Carthage when he knew he would be in danger?" Then there really can be no incorrect answer, because the class members give their opinions. Their opinions may not be accurate or technically perfect, but they are giving them as you have asked them to—"In your opinion." If you phrase your questions like this, you will have much better opportunity to generate discussion in the class.

Sometimes a well-prepared teacher, with much information about the lesson, is frustrated and unable to get class participation started simply because the question he asks is not the kind of question that makes the class comfortable, and the reactions to incorrect answers dampen student participation.

It is important for a teacher to make sure that the students understand there is only one stupid question, and that is the one that is never asked. It is worth a few minutes in class to explain that no one is all-knowledgeable. No one knows everything; everyone is uninformed in one area or another that is known to most people. It is not out of place for members of a class or for parents and children to ask questions.

More than once I have scolded members of a class just a little when they seemed to ridicule in one way or another a question asked by one of the group. And I have repeated with some emphasis the statement that there is only one stupid question: the one that isn't asked. Every student should have an open invitation to ask questions all of the time.

We make it a consistent practice in our family to respond to the questions of our children, and in doing so, we find that they ask many questions. If parents are not careful, they can dam up the quest for knowledge.

"You Are My Friend"

A number of years ago I was in the Southwest Indian Mission and waited some time to meet with the mission president, Alfred E. Rohner, who was in an interview with an Indian brother. Afterwards he told us that this Navajo man had appeared at the office and asked to see him. President Rohner invited the man into his office, and they sat there for a long time and said nothing. President Rohner, familiar with the Navajos, knew that this was the "Indian way," that it wasn't necessary to be talking all the while the man was there, and he sat there for a long time.

After considerable time the Navajo asked President Rohner how to spell a word. I have forgotten what the word was—it was not an uncommon word, but a word of three or four syllables. President Rohner gave him the correct spelling, and then the Navajo brother asked if President Rohner would write it on a piece of paper for him. He did so, and the Indian brother gave an indication that he was going to leave. President Rohner was interested in why the man wanted to know how to spell that word, and

74

after visiting with him, he learned something very interesting.

This Navajo brother was working for the tribal council. He was employed on a road crew and was evidently a dependable worker for the week before he had been made foreman of a crew of workmen. At the end of the week it was necessary for him to fill in some forms. He had a meager education and was able to speak English well and write it to a degree. Filling in forms, however, presented something of a challenge. In doing so, he found that he could not spell one of the words. So he had driven seventy miles to mission headquarters to ask President Rohner how to spell it.

President Rohner then asked him, "Why did you come all the way here? There are many people who could have helped you with the spelling. You could have gone to the trading post or stopped at the service station or gone to one of the schools and saved the long trip."

The Navajo man replied in logic that is very sensible to anyone who is a teacher. "You are my friend, so I came here."

Keep that incident in mind when you're dealing with the questions of your little children, of your teenage children, of those whom you teach or whom you direct as an officer or teacher in the Church, or of those with whom you come in contact in your work. It is so easy to pass off questions, to ignore them, or to give some offhand answer. I repeat that we have made it a practice in our family of always responding to questions and stopping whatever we are doing to make explanations. This keeps the lines of communication open. If your own children can come to you with their questions and know that they will not be belittled in any way, many another serious problem is forestalled. In a class, if a student is able to ask questions, the class will be a successful experience, and the class members will enjoy it and will respond. Keep that in mind.

The Right Answers for Wrong Questions

I learned an important lesson about answering questions from President Henry D. Moyle. We were in Alaska to attend a youth conference and were scheduled for a television interview. For some reason the cameras had been set up at Elmendorf Air Force Base, so we went there for the interview. A member of the Church who was a television star at that time also was scheduled to be at the youth conference but at the last minute had to cancel.

When we arrived at the place of the interview the commentator was obviously disappointed as he looked at President Moyle and me and said, "Is this all there is?"

The mission president indicated that we were the two to be interviewed. "We were given to understand that there would be theatrical luminaries present," the commentator responded.

When the mission president explained that the television personality had canceled her appearance, the commentator was obviously irritated. When he became discourteous to President Moyle, I could restrain myself no longer. I said to him, "I'll have you know this is a member of the First Presidency of The Church of Jesus Christ of Latter-day Saints. And in most places in the world the media are very interested and anxious to have an opportunity to schedule an interview with him."

The commentator settled down a little and finally said, "Well, I suppose we might just as well go ahead." He started the interview with questions that exposed his antagonism.

The interview lasted for over thirty minutes. Later, as we were returning to the car, I said, "President Moyle, that was marvelous, just marvelous. How did you do it?"

President Moyle asked, "What do you mean?"

I said, "All those antagonistic questions he asked you; it was just marvelous the way you handled them. He was so antagonistic and bitter and yet the interview itself was successful."

President Henry D. Moyle

I have never forgotten his answer. He said, "I never pay any attention to the questions—that is, if the interviewer is antagonistic. If he doesn't ask the right questions, I give answers to questions he should have asked."

That short statement from President Moyle held great wisdom, and on a number of occasions I have been rescued in difficult situations by referring back in my mind to his comment.

On one occasion, in Halifax, Nova Scotia, I was invited to appear on a talk show on which people who were thought to be interesting were interviewed. The missionaries had arranged my appearance on the show, thinking it would help the Church. It was obvious to me in the beginning that the commentator wanted to talk about me personally. He asked several questions about my teaching experience, my military experience, and so on, and seemed to be avoiding any questions about the Church.

Remembering what President Moyle had said, I paid little attention to his questions and directed the answers in such a way that I explained the Church program rather than talked about myself.

On another occasion I was scheduled for an interview in Maine. The missionaries who had arranged the radio interview apologized to me beforehand, saying that the commentator appeared to be antagonistic and was intent on embarrassing me and the Church with questions about who could or could not hold the priesthood.

Again I remembered the experience with President Moyle, and when the interviewer raised his first question about the priesthood, I quickly countered with a question: "Do you know anything about the priesthood?"

He said, "No," and I was immediately able to take lead in the interview. "You know about the elders, don't you?" "Not very much," he said. So I began to tell him about the elders who were preaching the gospel in the cities and was able to urge those listening to invite them in and hear their message.

The time allotted for the interview had elapsed before he was able to twist the conversation back to the point where he had hoped to begin.

When Sister Packer and I were touring a mission in South Africa, the branch president in Salisbury, Rhodesia, had arranged a television interview for me with a man who was known to be very brutal to those who appeared on his show. Again there came into my mind the statement of President Moyle: "If they don't ask the right questions, I give answers to questions they should have asked."

On several occasions, in addition to the experiences mentioned, I have been protected in very challenging circumstances by remembering the counsel by the first counselor in the First Presidency of the Church.

Teachers and students, parents and children would also do well to remember this counsel. Sometimes the question that isn't asked but should have been is as important as the one that is actually asked!

CHAPTER ELEVEN

Handling Very Difficult Questions

A teacher must expect to be confronted frequently with difficult questions. Often these are questions to which there is no satisfying or comforting answer. A teacher cannot know everything. The Lord has not yet revealed everything. And yet, to a teacher the questions will come, asking about everything. He should have the humility to say, "I don't know." Often that will be the only true answer. If it is something that he should know, it is well to add, "I should know the answer to that, and I can find out the answer. When I have been able to do so, I will give it to you."

When we are teachers in the Church, we will often find ourselves saying, "I do not know the answer, and I do not know anyone who does know the answer to that." We needn't be afraid or ashamed to say that. It won't hurt the students to know that we're not all-knowing.

There are some things that a teacher can keep in mind when a very difficult question arises — and there *are* some difficult questions that are asked frequently. Sometimes they are asked by those who really do not want to know, but who are antagonistic. Often, however, they are asked by someone who simply doesn't know and doesn't understand and is trying to find an answer. Then we as teachers are obligated to help.

The Principle of Prerequisites

There is a principle of education that we might entitle "The Principle of Prerequisites." Let me illustrate.

Most educational programs require the completion of basic or prerequisite courses before one can register for advanced courses. For instance, one cannot register for Chemistry 171 or 181—advanced courses—until he has completed Chemistry 24, 25, and 26, the basic elementary courses. That is common sense. Without the fundamental principles of chemistry, the 181 course would, at best, be a mistake. To understand it all, even a brilliant mind would need to know about basic elements, about atoms and molecules, about electrons and protons, about valence, compounds, properties, formulas, equations, densities, solutions, suspensions, and mixtures. Chemistry is a vertical field. A foundation of information must be built before one can proceed upward.

Perhaps there may be a genius who could register for the graduate course in chemistry and, without the prerequisite courses or even an introduction to the fundamentals, survive and achieve a top grade. There might be such a student—but there likely isn't. If one should attempt to master the advanced course first, he will end up in confusion and will then learn to dislike the subject and perhaps the teacher, and might wonder about a school that would subject him to such misery.

This elementary principle of prerequisites applies to all disciplines. It relates to all subject matters.

Every student must learn the value of mastering fundamentals. Teachers must know that. There are few things so well demonstrated in the learning process.

If we apply this principle of prerequisites to a very difficult question, we will approach it in an entirely different way. There just isn't much use in trying to answer a difficult question for someone who has not undergone the prerequisite study of faith, repentance, baptism by immersion for the remission of sins, and the laying on of hands for the gift of the Holy Ghost. Unless he knows something about revelation and about authority, whatever answer we give will not be satisfying to him.

I, for one, do not object to having such questions raised anytime, for it immediately gives me the opportunity to deal with fundamental principles of the gospel. Our missionaries try with such effort to get people to listen to the principles and doctrines of the Church, many of whom are not interested. They want to spend the time of day talking about anything but the doctrines. However, when someone asks a difficult doctrinal question, the way is immediately opened to discuss basic doctrines. Consider an approach such as this: "If you really want to know the answer to that, there are some things I'll have to explain first, or you will never understand the answer when I give it to you. You will have to know that God lives. I know that He lives. [Now you are bearing testimony.] You will have to know that He reveals His mind and will to prophets."

When, as teachers, we are confronted with difficult questions, we must keep in mind the principle of prerequisites, and if the inquirer has not had the prerequisite courses, then we should start there and give him a brief course in fundamentals. He will learn the answer in no other way.

When we are confronted with a difficult question on plural marriage in pioneer days, or why the general public can't enter our temples, or any of a number of others, we must meet the question head-on with forthright candor and not try to avoid it. We must not apologize for the position of the Church. We must not "do battle" for it. We must not try to "convert" the questioner to it. We should explain the reason, but explain it on the basis of the prerequisites. It is a waste of time to try to discuss the question politically or philosophically or sociologically or ethically; we must get to the point and begin to discuss it theologically. If the questioner won't listen to the prerequisites, he'll not obtain the answer. If he does, he'll not have a problem.

There is another important matter we should discuss. A teacher naturally wants everyone to be satisfied and in agreement with him. That is not always to be. Often in the best teaching someone is left unsatisfied, perhaps even upset. Particularly is this true if we have an encounter with someone who is antagonistic. A mature teacher will know from the beginning that when the conversation is over, someone will be unsettled and upset. Let it not be the teacher. If the student has not had the prerequisite courses nor the basic understanding on which to get an answer, and won't be patient to be taught them, he will end up unsettled and disturbed. But we shouldn't be embarrassed or unsettled or disturbed about his being disturbed.

I think it not unkind to say that if a teacher is uneasy or disturbed about such questions, perhaps the place he needs to look is at the basic courses. Did he skip some of them? Is he uneasy about these questions? A peace of mind about them, of course, is to be found only on his knees. If we are sincere and open, humbly and spiritually tuned, we'll be all right. If we want to be popular and have everyone in agreement with everything we teach, we want something that never will be.

Master the Fundamentals

Now one other illustration on prerequisites. Let's suppose that I am stricken physically and collapse in an area with no nearby hospital. Suppose the first person to my side and without his satchel is my doctor. Suppose he diagnoses that except for immediate surgery my life will be over.

83

I can conceive of my consenting to his finding an old rusty spoon, sharpening it on a curbstone, boiling it in an old can, and then, with whatever else he might gather to assist him, proceeding with the surgery. At least I'd rather submit to him under those circumstances than be rushed into the operating room of a large hospital, with all its modern equipment, its sterilized atmosphere and precision instruments, and have a nonmedical person proceed to operate.

I'd like to know that the one who is going to operate on me has at least some idea of what he will be looking for when he has me opened up. I don't think I'd be too anxious for my doctor to operate either if he had skipped all the prerequisite courses and had taken, as his initial course, advanced surgery, with me as one of his first patients.

There is good reason to ensure that a medical doctor begins with basic courses in physiology and that it is a long time, indeed years, before he finally touches a scalpel to living flesh. There are some things that he just must know before he arrives at that point.

This ought to be sufficient to fix in our minds the advisability of putting first things first, of mastering the fundamentals and then moving on to more advanced achievement.

Anyone can ask a difficult question. Anyone can tune in from the outside and want to know all about statistical analysis, for example, before he has learned to add and subtract. To attempt to satisfy him on that level is to confuse him.

Reassure Him

The most important thing we as teachers can do with our students is to assure them that we are at peace, to understand difficult, even controversial, issues, we must realize there are some things that we can't answer. I don't have the slightest embarrassment or hesitancy to say that I do not know why the Lord has done some of the things He has done.

But there are some things I do know. I do know that we will never be without some of these difficult questions. I do not feel that they have ever hurt the church and kingdom of God. I do not think we have lost an honest convert because of the position of the Church on controversial matters. I do know that the more arrogant and academic and self-centered a person is, the less likely he is to be satisfied with an answer that has spiritual implications.

I had the privilege of doing missionary work in an area where there were many investigators with advanced academic degrees. Many of them had great admiration for the Church and perhaps would have joined for the social benefits they observed in it, but some of the difficult questions we have talked about became stumbling blocks for them. Those who sought the answers spiritually, who approached them theologically, and who humbled themselves found sufficient answers and came into the waters of baptism. Others did not. The strait gate and the narrow way repelled them and they proved themselves to be not ready.

Too Sacred to Discuss

I hope these comments will lead you, as a teacher, to face difficult questions without anxiety and without fear. There is one other thing I should add. There may be times when you are asked a question—perhaps about the temple—and you know the answer but you are not authorized to respond, simply because he who asks has not completed the prerequisite courses. The prophet Alma declared:

It is given unto many to know the mysteries of God; nevertheless they are laid under a strict command that they shall not impart only according to the portion of his word which he doth grant unto the children of men, according to the heed and diligence which they give unto him.

And therefore, he that will harden his heart, the same receiveth the lesser portion of the word; and he that will not harden his heart, to him is given the greater portion of the word, until it is given unto him to know the mysteries of God until he know them in full.

And they that will harden their hearts, to them is given the lesser portion of the word until they know nothing concerning his mysteries; and then they are taken captive by the devil, and led by his will down to destruction. Now this is what is meant by the chains of hell. (Alma 12:9–11.)

All teachers are, of course, themselves students. While as teachers there are some difficult questions that we can hardly attempt to answer, likewise as students there are some questions that we could not in propriety ask.

One question of this type I am asked occasionally, usually by someone who is curious, is, "Have you seen Him?" That is a question that I have never asked of another. I have not asked that question of my Brethren in the Council of the Twelve, thinking that it would be so sacred and so personal that one would have to have some special inspiration—indeed, some authorization—even to ask it.

Though I have not asked that question of others, I have heard them answer it—but *not* when they were asked. I have heard one of my Brethren declare, "I know, from experiences too sacred to relate, that Jesus is the Christ." I have heard another testify, "I know that God lives, I know that the Lord lives, and more than that, I know the Lord." I repeat: they have answered this question not when they were asked, but under the prompting of the Spirit, on sacred occasions, when "the Spirit beareth record." (D&C 1:39.)

There are some things just too sacred to discuss: not secret, but sacred; not to be discussed, but to be harbored and protected and regarded with the deepest of reverence.

There are many difficult questions, including some that we will not be able to answer, and many things are to be taken on faith. As a teacher, therefore, do not let difficult questions create difficult problems for you or for those you teach.

CHAPTER TWELVE

We Are Children of God

In many churches of the world a doctrine is taught that holds that men are basically evil; that they are earthy and carnal and devilish, conceived in sin and possessed of a tendency to be wicked. This doctrine holds that the corrupt and evil nature of man must be conquered. It holds out the meager hope that by an extension of grace man may, on occasion, be lifted from his evil, carnal, and groveling state. In simple terms it avers that man is, by his very nature, inclined to be bad.

That is false doctrine. I could not accept it to be true and still be a successful teacher. The doctrine is not only false; it is also very destructive. Should one accept it, the assignment of a teacher to discipline his class or of parents to discipline their children would be hopeless indeed.

Good, Not Evil

How glorious it is to have the revealed word of God, to know that we have a child-parent relationship with Him. If we are of His family, we have inherited the tendency to be good, not evil. We are sons and daughters of God.

The word *God,* with one letter added, can be changed very quickly to *good.* The word *devil,* with one letter deleted, becomes *evil.* The central message of all revelation is that God is our Father. We therefore are inherently good.

It is essential for a teacher to understand that people are basically good. It is essential to know that their tendency is to do the thing that is right. Such an exalted thought is productive of faith. It makes all the difference when we stand before our own children or go before a class of young people to teach them.

I am fully aware that in the world there are individuals whose basic motivation seems to be contrary and disruptive and evil. I know this exists, but it is against their nature. If we are to teach, we must constantly remind ourselves that we are dealing with the sons and daughters of God and that each, being His offspring, has the possibility of becoming as He is. It is encouraging for a teacher to keep in mind the statement, "As man is, God once was, and as God is, man may become." This ideal was beautifully framed in verse by Lorenzo Snow in his poem "Dear Brother," written in January of 1892, three verses of which I quote:

> As Abra'm, Isaac, Jacob, too.
> First babes, then men—to gods they grew.
> As man now is, our God once was;
> As now God is, so man may be,—
> Which doth unfold man's destiny.
>
> The boy, like to his father grown,
> Has but attained unto his own;
> To grow to sire from state of son,
> Is not 'gainst nature's course to run.
>
> As son of God, like God to be,
> Would not be robbing Deity;
> And he who has this hope within,
> Will purify himself from sin.

I am aware of those scriptural verses that speak of the fallen state of man. I know that some verses describe man's depravity. However, when we take the revelations as a whole, that idea is balanced and overshadowed by the constant message that the word *father* in scripture means *father*.

A Spark of Divinity

Years ago I determined that if I were to be a teacher, a belief in the goodness of man must be fundamental to my philosophy of life. The day I made that decision, things began to change rapidly. Thereafter there was always hope. No matter how fractious or difficult or lawless others appeared, I knew that somewhere within them was a spark of divinity to which we can appeal.

Such basic love and respect are essential to those who would teach. It is essential to the parent as he looks at his children. It is essential to the teacher as he looks at his class. Although at times it is hard to maintain that belief, it nonetheless is true. A fundamental quality of good discipline is the ability to love those whom you are to teach and to maintain a desire to be a servant.

I repeat, I believe that the tendency in the human family is to be good and to do the thing that is right. I believe it is the desire of men to want to possess the noblest virtues. Men, women, and children, given the opportunity, have within them the disposition to do that which they ought to do. Furthermore, it is natural with men to want to learn.

It takes great searching and often great generosity to see the good and the divine in students. Yet such a search will be rewarded. Let me tell you of two experiences.

When I was teaching seminary I frequently heard the name of a boy, a junior in high school, who was the bane of all the faculty. Somehow I had never seen him. "You are not a teacher until you've had him in class," was the expression.

One day during fourth period, the door flew open. In came a young man, about five feet eight, well built, with heavy shoes. He stomped down the aisle to where I was standing at the chalkboard and thrust an admittance slip at me. In what I thought to be the mimic of a stutterer he said, "I am K-K-K-K-Kenneth."

He needn't have said his name. I knew who it was when he was two steps into the room; his reputation had preceded him. I thought, "What have I done to deserve this?"

I wish I could tell all that happened in the next few months. That would be worthy of a book in itself. Kenneth came from a broken home. He had a major speech impediment. He was a show-off, an interrupter, and a disrupter of the first order. He was something of a natural comedian and was admired and despised by the students at the same time.

Constantly I reminded myself that somewhere inside this boy was the disposition to want to learn.

A month or two later, in an after-school conversation, I was aware that he had not stuttered. He was able to talk to me in an unhesitant flow of words. When I mentioned it he said, "I didn't use to stutter. With a few people I can talk without that. But when I get up in front of a class and try to say something, it's just like somebody puts a steel collar around my throat. The harder I try to talk, the tighter they cinch it up."

Some months later early on a Friday evening he telephoned me at home. There was to be a dance after the basketball game that night, and he was wondering what he ought to wear. "Would a sweater be all right?" His question was incidental and easily answered. I'll not soon forget how I felt after that conversation when I realized the confidence that had been rewarded when he was willing to call me, his teacher, to ask a question like that.

Remember that a fundamental part of discipline is to know and to understand and to believe that all men are basically good; that we are children with heavenly parentage; that all men are instructed sufficiently that they know good from evil; that there is hope for everyone.

A Lesson Learned

The second such experience occurred during my first year of teaching. In my class was a teenage girl who disturbed me a great deal by a seemingly insolent attitude. She wouldn't participate and she disturbed the class continually. On one occasion I asked her to respond in class with something that took no previous preparation. She said, with some impudence, "I won't."

With some pressing I insisted, but with increased impudence she refused. I said something very foolish to the effect that "students who are not willing to respond are not to be given grades or credit." And under my breath I said, "We'll see. You'll either conform or else."

A few weeks later in a parent-teacher visiting session her mother described her as being shy and retiring and hesitant to participate. Shy and retiring conduct would not have disturbed me; it was the impudence and insolence that had concerned me.

Fortunately, before I could describe her impudence to her mother, her mother added, "That's because of her speech impediment."

In surprise I asked what that was. The mother said, "Oh, haven't you noticed?" I hadn't noticed! "She will do almost anything to keep from participating in groups," her mother informed me. "Her speech impediment is such an embarrassment to her."

After the conference with her mother I felt about two inches tall! I should have sensed that there was some reason for her to react the way she had. I spent that year making my repentance complete. I counseled with the girl and drew her out. "We will work together on this," I told her.

Before the end of the year she was responding in class and participating often, with the help and cooperation of the other students. She had success experiences many times in appearing before them.

I am still ashamed of my first handling of that situation. But I learned so much from it that I am glad it happened. I think in the long run she came out none the worse, and I came out much the better as a teacher.

Fundamental to the discipline of any child or any class or any organization, fundamental to the success of any teacher, is a knowledge that each one he teaches is a child of God. Fundamental to teaching the gospel is the conviction that men are basically good.

An incident from pioneer days illustrates a successful search for good in the youth of the Church.

Out of Order

In the days of the pioneer settlements it was not uncommon to have a ward marshal whose assignment, under the direction of the bishop, was to maintain orderly conduct among the teenagers.

On a Sunday evening after sacrament meeting, the ward marshal at the little settlement of Corinne came upon a buggy with some teenagers. Since it was his responsibility to check on the young people, he stealthily crept near the buggy to see what was going on.

He managed to reach a rather insufficient tree close to the buggy just as the moon came out. He had to stand more or less at attention to keep from being seen, but he could easily hear all that was transpiring in the buggy.

Later, in reporting to the bishop, he told what had gone on. There had been some jokes told, much laughter, and the usual teenage chatter. He said they sang several songs. The bishop interrupted with the question, "Well, was there anything out of order in that situation?" His answer: "Yes! Me, behind that _____ tree!"

How often have we scolded our children with "You are a bad boy," or "You are a bad girl"? We do better if we believe that there is no bad boy or bad girl. There are bad things and bad actions. Do not say, "You are a bad boy." Say, "It is a bad thing that you have done." The better approach is, "It is too bad that a good boy like you would do a bad thing like that."

The relationship of an adult to a child is little different from the relationship of an adult to an adult. The feelings of the children are honored. There is little difficulty in control, and the child develops dependability. Little children at an early age can develop a responsible relationship with their parents.

I Will Trust Everyone

A few years ago I indulged on one occasion in some introspection and found there were reasons why I didn't like myself very well. Foremost among them was the fact that I was suspicious of some I met. I had in mind this thought: "What's his angle? What's he going to try to do?" This came about because I had been badly used by someone I trusted. Cynicism and bitterness were growing within. I determined to change and made a decision that I would trust everyone. I have tried to follow that rule since. If someone is not worthy of trust, it is his responsibility to show it—not mine to find it out.

"A" Grade—Number One

Students, including our own children, will rise to our high expectations of them. When I was a teacher, I always made a certain speech on the first day I met a class. I made it to each new group of missionaries that arrived in the

94

mission field. I have also always tried to convey to others around me the same message. It is a message of confidence. The speech goes something like this:

> I assume that you are mature. I look upon you as being old enough to be able to learn and sensible enough to want to. Right now I may not know who you really are or where you have been or what you have done. Most of that, depending on you, will not matter. I take you just as you are and stamp you "A-Grade, Number 1." You can prove yourself to be less than that, but you will have to work at it. I will be very reluctant to believe it. If there is something about yourself that you do not like, now is the time to change it. If there is something in your past that has been disabling, spiritually or otherwise, now is the time to rise above it.

I have found that with remarkably few exceptions the response has been for people to want to rise above themselves. This has a stabilizing effect. It helps immeasurably with discipline and creates an environment where learning can take place.

As I begin a new relationship with anyone — students, missionaries, or those with whom I associate or whom I supervise — it is on the basis of confidence and trust. I have been much happier since. Of course, there have been times when I have been disappointed, and a few times when I have been badly used. I do not care about that. Who am I not to be so misused or abused? Why should I be above that? If that is the price of extending trust to everyone, I am glad to pay it.

I have come to be much less afraid of that possibility than I was before. It is sometimes painful when one is misused or when trust or confidence is not honored. That kind of pain, however, is not unbearable, for it is only pain; it is not agony. The only agony I know is when I discover that inadvertently I have misused someone else. That is torture; that I will *avoid*.

An Exercise in Confidence

On one occasion when I was teaching seminary, I marked a report card with a B grade. It was the highest grade on the card. All the others were C–, D, or F. When I passed out the card, the boy studied it carefully for a few minutes and then came up, hesitantly, and said, "Brother Packer, I think you have made a mistake. You have given me someone else's grade."

I looked at him with some compassion and said, "No, I think I have not." He showed me his card, and I said, "Yes, that is what I intended to write down." He looked at me quizzically. "If there has been a mistake," I said, "it has been a mistake in timing. Perhaps I have given it to you a little before you have earned it, but I think it is not a mistake."

When the next reporting period came by, I gave him a higher grade — this time by calculating test scores and measuring responses in class and evaluating his performance precisely as I did for all of the other students. I noticed as time went on that the other grades on his report card began to move up also.

It has been my experience that when you approach with such an attitude those whom you teach, whether they be children, students, or persons whom you supervise, they respond in kind. Many who perhaps were not initially worthy of such trust soon earn it. It gives them something to reach for, and they deserve it, for they are children of God.

CHAPTER THIRTEEN

On Teachers "Learning" Students

W hen we are teaching moral and spiritual values, we should understand that children have a well-developed sense of right and wrong. It can be appealed to. There are many things that they know simply because they know them. It is important for teachers, including parents, to study those whom they teach. Young people have well-defined guidelines in their minds on what is fair and what isn't fair. Sometimes these even become exaggerated.

We need to understand whom we are teaching. We must remember that they came from a preexistent state, and while much is not remembered, there still can be considerable spiritual maturity.

The following statement from President J. Reuben Clark, Jr., is important for teachers:

"Our youth are not children spiritually; they are well on towards the normal spiritual maturity of the world. I say once more there is scarcely a youth that comes through your door who has not been the conscious beneficiary of spiritual blessings, or who has not seen the efficacy of prayer, or who has not witnessed the power of faith to heal the sick, or who has not beheld spiritual outpourings, of which the world at large is today ignorant. You do not have to sneak up behind this spiritually experienced youth and whisper religion in his ears; you can come right out, face to face, and talk with him. You do not need to disguise religious truths with a cloak of worldly things; you can bring these truths to him openly, in their natural guise. Youth may prove to be no more fearful of them than you are. There is no need for gradual approaches, for 'bed-time' stories, for coddling, for patronizing, or for any of the other childish devices used in efforts to reach those spiritually inexperienced and all but spiritually dead." ("The Charted Course of the Church in Education," pp. 8–9. This article is reprinted in the appendix of this book.)

Children Already Know

We do not often give credit for the spiritual maturity of children, particularly little children. There are some things they know. They need not be taught them; they just know them to begin with.

Let me give you an example. While our children have been growing up, we have purposely lived in a rural setting where we could keep some animals and birds about, for several important reasons. One is that we have chores, regular responsibilities that cannot be put off and that must be attended to on at least a daily basis. From this our youngsters have learned to work and to be dependable.

On one occasion a hen had hidden a nest away under a manger in the barn. The nest was discovered by our little girl. When the chickens were hatched, the tiny ones began to peep. She wanted to see them and hold them but was confronted by a very angry hen protecting her chicks. When I came home in the evening, she came running to the car and excitedly told me of her discovery, pleading with me to let her hold some of the baby chicks. It was not easy to get the hen to cooperate, but finally I had a double-handful of little chicks. There were black ones, white ones, striped ones, and spotted ones, and as the children gathered around, admiring them with childish expressions, I let our little girl hold one.

"That will make a nice watch dog when it grows up, won't it?" I said. She wrinkled up her little nose and looked at me quizzically. It was obvious that she didn't believe what I said, so I hurriedly corrected myself. "It won't turn into a dog, will it?" As she shook her head, I said, "It will make a nice horse, won't it?" She looked at me as though I did not know very much. She knew and wondered why I didn't seem to know that the little chicken would never grow up to be a dog or a horse or an elephant or even a turkey, but when it grew up it would be a hen or a rooster; it would follow the pattern of its parentage.

How did she, a four-year-old, know that? We had never taught it to her. She knew it as children know many things. Many lessons, basic and sacred in life, children know and understand without being taught.

It is easy, then, to explain that when we reach our full development in the eternities ahead, we will be gods. We too will follow the pattern of our parentage. God has created us to address him as Father!

I have always been interested in the fact that little children know what dreams are. It would be impossible to show them, and it is difficult to describe what a dream is. But there really is no need to do so, for children seem to know.

Another scripture is very important for a teacher to understand: "All men are instructed sufficiently that they know good from evil." (2 Nephi 2:5; Helaman 14:31.)

Parents and teachers need to know that a youngster can tell right from wrong. This knowledge may be distorted or perverted or covered up in unfortunate life experiences, but intuitively, as a part of the spiritual endowment of all humanity, there is a knowledge of right from wrong.

99

That gives me great hope, for then I understand that every child of God, however reprobate he may have become, however degenerate he may seem to be, has hidden within him the spark of divinity and a sensitivity to that which is wrong as compared to that which is right.

It is important for a teacher to understand that little teaching will be accomplished, little learning will take place, unless a one-to-one relationship exists between the teacher and each student. Emerson, in his essay "Of Spiritual Laws," stated: "There is no teaching until the pupil is brought into the same state or principle in which you are; a transfusion takes place; he is you, and you are he; there is a teaching; and by no unfriendly chance or bad company can he ever quite lose the benefit."

The teacher immediately responds, "How can there be a one-to-one relationship if I have thirty students in the class?" In that case the teacher must simply have a one-to-one relationship repeated thirty times over. That one-to-one relationship can exist in your mind. You can create it and maintain it and sustain it and not lose it—this often by great conscious exertion. Students can feel it when it is there. It means you take the time to learn thirty names, to check out thirty backgrounds, to draw thirty students into class discussions, to pass out thirty words of encouragement, all personalized.

"Watch Out for February"

For six years Elder A. Theodore Tuttle and I supervised the seminaries under the direction of William E. Berrett, who was the administrator. We held conventions about the Church, meeting with seminary teachers and stake presidents. After a year or two we discovered something interesting about February. We might schedule a convention in Phoenix for February and then find out that a teacher in Idaho Falls or Logan was in such difficulty that one of us had to visit him. This occurred so often at that time of the year that we eventually did not schedule conventions between the middle of January and the middle of March. That was when we had the largest outcropping of discipline problems.

It was not too difficult to determine why. The answer is helpful to both parents and teachers. School begins in the fall. There's a certain excitement and interest on the part of all the students. Athletic activities and many other activities go on into the holidays. The Christmas and New Year's holidays are full of excitement, but when they are over, the school routine settles down to a long grind, looking toward spring activities and graduation. The days are short, the nights are long, and the weather is often cold and disagreeable. If anyone is going to have the blahs, that's an ideal time for it.

We began to alert the teachers in the preschool conventions to "watch out for February." We told them to plan their year with some interesting activities and their very best teaching scheduled for January and February. If a teacher (or a parent) is forewarned, he can prepare himself and lift the young people just a little bit more to compensate for the tensions and pressures of that seasonal dreariness.

I have come to believe that this is worth knowing, not only for teachers, but for everyone. If you get a little depressed during those dreary days, do not begin to think that you're psycho-something-or-other.

For missionaries, this was well worth knowing. Occasionally a missionary told me in an interview, "I'm not doing very well. I just seem to be depressed and discouraged." Unless there was an unusual reason for these feelings, my answer was, "Well, I'm glad to hear that. At least now we know that you're normal. Enjoy the feeling—it

probably won't last. And the first sunny day will do won-
ders for it."

We know from the Book of Mormon that there must
be opposition.

"For it must needs be, that there is an opposition in
all things. If not so, my first-born in the wilderness, righteousness could not be brought to pass, neither wickedness, neither holiness nor misery, neither good nor bad."
(2 Nephi 2:11.)

It helps a great deal if we realize that there is a certain
healthy element in getting the blues occasionally. It is quite
in order to schedule a good, discouraging, depressing day
every now and again just for contrast.

"You Miss Your Horse, Don't You?"

Shortly after I was called as an Assistant to the Council
of the Twelve, I was a member of the Missionary Committee and was working in the Missionary Department. I
had a call from a mission president in New York who said
that a missionary had run away and they had found he
had taken a bus west, no doubt heading for his home in
Idaho.

The mission president said the missionary didn't like
missionary work. He didn't like anything about it. He had
gone into the mission field the previous September and
had enjoyed it up until early spring; then he could stand
it no longer. He decided he would just quit and go home.
The mission president counseled with him, but that made
little difference.

With a little checking of the schedules, we were able
to meet the missionary at the bus station and take him to
the office for a chat. We talked about his life and his activities, and it didn't take long to discover what the problem
was. Finally I said, "You miss your horse, don't you?"

Tears welled up in his eyes, and he said, "You're going to laugh at me, aren't you?"

"No, my boy, I won't laugh at you," I said, "because I understand! Isn't it true that this roping horse you have mentioned frequently in your conversation was the center of your life? Isn't it true that you'd hurry home after school so you could change clothes and get out to the corral and work with your horse? Those were choice hours to you, weren't they? And isn't it true that there was something about the days of early spring that made it glorious to get home from school and work with that beautiful animal before the sun went down? And isn't it true that when missionary work was slow, every now and again a day would remind you of home? Finally you could stand it no more, and you just had to go home."

Then he knew I understood. After a long talk we went to lunch and then to the airport so he could catch the next plane back to his mission. Because he understood a few things about himself, there was no question now that he could finish his mission.

Know Yourself

If you want to know about students, learn as much as you can about yourself. As you begin to gain deep insights into your own reactions and feelings and sensitivities, you will come to know much about your students. There is an expression, "Go to your bosom and ask your heart what it doth know." If we make this inquiry, we will come to know much about our students. We can come to know it by knowing ourselves.

One of the most significant statements in the discourses of President Brigham Young was on this subject:

"The greatest lesson you can learn is to know your-selves. When we know ourselves, we know our neighbors. When we know precisely how to deal with ourselves, we know how to deal with our neighbors. You have come here to learn this. You cannot learn it immediately, neither can all the philosophy of the age teach it to you; you have to come here to get a practical experience and to know yourselves. You will then begin to learn more perfectly the things of God. No being can thoroughly know himself, without understanding more or less of the things of God; neither can any being learn and understand the things of God, without knowing himself; he must know himself, or he never can know God." (*Discourses of Brigham Young*, selected and arranged by John A. Widtsoe, Deseret Book Company, 1946 ed., p. 269.)

Know Your Students

Teacher, someday put your class to work filling in forms or reading or writing a treatise on some subject, and then stand at the head of the class and study each student intently for a few moments. The good teacher has already studied the lesson. The superb teacher also studies the students; he studies them seriously and intently.

Two things may well occur. First, if you look at your students and wonder why they think and act and feel as they do, you may learn many, many things, and you will be more keenly equipped to help them. Second, as you study carefully their features and expressions, there may well up in your heart a warmth of Christian compassion that comes all too infrequently even to a dedicated teacher. The feeling is akin to inspiration, a feeling of love. This love will compel you to find the way to do well the work of the Lord: feeding His sheep.

CHAPTER FOURTEEN

The Ego

I would like to discuss one aspect of physiology and then use it to make a comparison—which, incidentally, is a perfectly respectable principle of teaching. While we will not consider at length the principle of transfer of learning, it is important in the learning process.

Through transfer of learning, experience we have gained in any field of learning can be transferred and made important in any other field. Something a boy learned on a farm may serve him well as an executive in a corporation. Something a man learns on his job as a mail clerk may be useful to him in his Sunday School class. And, of course, all that we teach members of the Church in Sunday School, priesthood quorums, sacrament meetings, conferences, and socials should have application in their life activities.

In this case I simply want to talk about the physical body, which is tangible and visible, and then draw an analogy with the invisible part of our being in order to make an important point.

In the body are ductless glands that regulate and integrate the body through chemical means. The brain, on the other hand, regulates and integrates the body through the nervous system. The secretions of the ductless glands stimulate or depress; they activate or retard various parts of the body as it reacts to the circumstances around it. These important glands can be as important as the nervous system in influencing behavior.

The hormones produced in the glands govern the development and action of the body in many ways. They determine the growth pattern and the development of the individual. If they are disturbed, the results can be far-reaching and sometimes permanent. Some of them are so essential to life that an individual could not live for long if they were completely lacking. For example, hormones of the pancreas and parathyroids are essential to sustain life.

Although we know much about the glands and the organs of the body and their interrelationship, there is much that we do not know.

In our unseen emotional body are also controls and influences that can stimulate or depress the emotional and spiritual behavior of an individual. These unseen "glands," if not healthy, can cause maladjustment in behavior and development. In this part of us that is not physical are things that are quite as important as the effects of the ductless glands upon the physical body.

Somewhere in the invisible part of us is a center of influence. The word most closely describing it is *ego*. Among the dictionary definitions for the word *ego* is self-esteem.

It has a marvelous effect on that part of us that is not physical and an apparent effect on our physical well-being also.

If I were to draw a picture of an ego—a normal, healthy one—I would draw it similar to a small, round balloon.

An ego can be deflated with an action, with an expression, with words, or even with a glance.

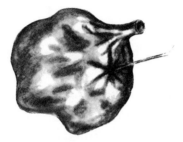

The words that work best for puncturing an ego include: "Stupid, can't you do anything right?" "Wrong again." "When will you ever get some sense?" "Get lost." And you, of course, know many others that you have experienced.

Most of us have had our egos deflated, and we know that it can be a painful experience. A story is told of a boy who was six years old before he knew what his last name was. Until then he thought it was Johnny Stop!

If a student's ego becomes deflated, it has a disturbing effect on him. It produces some very apparent effects in him. This type of disorder in the ego is generally fairly easy to correct. It can be inflated with air in the form of words, which are inexpensive and easy to supply. Words that inflate a depressed ego and round it out in a good, healthy image include these: "That was well done." "You are important." "We think highly of you." "Thank you for your contribution." "It is important that you are here."

We know how grateful we are when someone pumps our ego up a bit. A deflated ego, after all, need not really be a serious disorder, and a parent or a teacher can ordinarily correct the disorder in a moment or two. If it has been deflated several times, it may be a little more difficult, but a treatment of genuine compliments and kind words and encouragement extended over a period of time does the trick.

An Unhealthy Substitute

There is a very serious disorder or disease affecting the ego that is much more difficult to cure. Teachers would do well to diagnose it early. This disease develops when the ego is deflated frequently over a long period of time. It becomes flattened out to the point that it becomes very painful to the individual. If no one inflates it with words of encouragement and kindness, a serious condition sets in. The individual himself begins to inflate his own ego — an artificial process that is not satisfying. It is an unhealthy substitute.

When an individual goes for long periods of time without hearing words of praise, such as *"You* are someone," he will try to fill in for himself and say, *"I* am someone." If this becomes habitual, he becomes an egotist. It is pathetic to see an individual with a bad case of egotism.

A wise teacher knows that the treatment for egotism is precisely the same as for a deflated ego. It just has to be administered a little more carefully, over a longer period of time. While the over-inflated ego must never be punctured too abruptly, it sometimes needs to be pierced just a bit to get it down to normal size.

Encouragement and Love

Teachers should be generous in their praise and encouragement. They can do more to govern behavior through that channel than in any other way. This manner of encouraging good behavior is not new in education.

In 1558 Roger Aschcam, who had been a tutor to Queen Elizabeth in her youth and enjoyed some favors from the royal court, was dining one day with Sir William Cedric and Sir Richard Sackville. The conversation centered around the report of several boys who had run away from Eton because of much beating there. Sir Richard Sackville, who was largely silent during the meal, listened to Aschcam's views on education. Later he drew him aside and proposed that he would finance an educational experiment for his own son and others based on encouragement and love. The two became lifelong friends, and this conversation inspired Roger Aschcam's immortal book *The Scholemaster.*

In his book he states:

> I will now declare at large why, in mine opinion, love is fitter than fear, gentleness better than beating to bring up a child rightly in learning.
>
> With the common use of teaching and beating in the common schools of England, I will not greatly contend. I do gladly agree with all good schoolmasters in these points: To have children brought to good perfection in learning, to all honesty in manners, to have all faults rightly amended; to have every vice severely corrected. But for the order and way that leadeth rightly to the points we somehow differ.
>
> For commonly many schoolmasters . . . be so crooked a nature as when they get a hard witted scholar they rather break him than bow him, rather mar him than mend him. . . . But this will I say, that even yet the worst of your great beaters as oft punish nature as correct faults.

An example of what parents can learn about discipline is found in a comment of President David O. McKay at Merthyr-Tydfil, Wales, in 1963:

> I was reminded of a visit I made home when I was in college. Mother was sitting on my left at the dinner table where she always sat. I said, "Mother, I have found that I am the only member of your children whom you have switched." She said, "Yes, David O., I have made such a failure of you, I didn't want to use the same method on the other children!"

A Child of God

It is important for a teacher to understand that each of his students, whether they be his own children or those assembled in class, is a child of God. The Lord has not revealed much about our premortal state, but the knowledge that we had one is monumentally significant to parents and teachers. Those things that we do know — that we were individual, that we were intelligent, that some were more intelligent than others, and that we have a parent-child relationship to God the Father — are valuable revelations. For one thing, this concept means that some spiritual ideals that otherwise would be difficult to teach may be caught as well as taught, and are found as a natural possession of even little tiny children.

CHAPTER 15

Individual Differences

Presiident David O. McKay once said:

> From birth to death men differ. They vary as
> much as do flowers in the garden. In intellect, in
> temperament, in energy, and in training. Some rise
> to one level and some to another. A successful
> teacher is one who with the spirit of discernment
> can detect, to a degree at least, the mentality and
> capability of the members of his class. He should
> be able to read the facial expressions and be re-
> sponsive to the mental and spiritual attitudes of
> those whom he is teaching. It is written that he
> who governs well leads the blind, but that he who
> teaches gives them eyes.

That the Lord was such a teacher and recognized in
His teaching the individual differences of those whom He
taught is very evident in the parable of the sower.

> And he spake many things unto them in par-
> ables, saying, Behold a sower went forth to sow;

And when he sowed, some seeds fell by the way side, and the fowls came and devoured them up:

Some fell upon stony places, where they had not much earth: and forthwith they sprung up, because they had no deepness of earth:

And when the sun was up, they were scorched; and because they had no root, they withered away.

And some fell among thorns; and the thorns sprung up, and choked them:

But other fell into good ground, and brought forth fruit, some an hundredfold, some sixtyfold, some thirtyfold. (Matthew 13:3–8.)

The interpretation of the same parable recognizes the differences when one is trying to teach:

When any one heareth the word of the kingdom, and understandeth it not, then cometh the wicked one, and catcheth away that which was sown in his heart. This is he which received seed by the way side.

But he that received the seed into stony places, the same is he that heareth the word, and anon with joy receiveth it;

Yet hath he not root in himself, but dureth for a while; for when tribulation or persecution ariseth because of the word, by and by he is offended.

He also that received seed among the thorns is he that heareth the word; and the care of this world, and the deceitfulness of riches, choke the word, and he becometh unfruitful.

But he that received seed into the good ground is he that heareth the word, and understandeth it; which also beareth fruit, and bringeth forth, some an hundredfold, some sixty, some thirty. (Matthew 13:19–23.)

No principle of education has received so much attention from professional educators as the principle of individual differences. No teacher will succeed without knowing something about this principle. One cannot get a group together without noting that each person is individually different. That is true of a family. It is true of any class or congregation.

The Difference in the Apostles

The Twelve Apostles who were chosen by the Lord while He was upon the earth is an interesting example of a class in which the individuals differed greatly. The Twelve were apprenticed to Him and were trained to carry on His work after He was gone. There was great variety in them.

In Peter we see the impulsive, impetuous man, maybe a little erratic to begin with. There is evidence that he may

115

also have been a bit profane. In Thomas was the doubter. "Seeing is believing" seemed to describe him. John and James, sons of Zebedee, were also called Sons of Thunder. They seemed to be quick-tempered enough to want Him to call down fire from heaven to destroy a village because the inhabitants rejected the Lord. Matthew was a publican and likely to be despised because of his occupation.

Sometimes the Savior taught His disciples in small groups. At the Transfiguration (Matthew 17: 1, 8), for instance, three were with Him. Likewise at the healing of the daughter of Jairus, "He suffered no man to follow him, save Peter, and James, and John the brother of James." (Mark 5:37.)

There is the account of Nicodemus, a member of the Sanhedrin, who came to Jesus by night and received individualized instruction. That the instruction was effective is indicated by the fact that Nicodemus later defended Jesus before the Sanhedrin (John 7:50), and after His death Nicodemus provided costly herbs used in the embalming of His body (John 19:39).

Peter also had a personal interview with Jesus after the Resurrection (Luke 24:34).

The parable of the talents (Matthew 25:14–30) has a lesson on individual differences. Note one very meaningful statement:

"For the kingdom of heaven is as a man travelling into a far country, who called his own servants, and delivered unto them his goods.

"And unto one he gave five talents, to another two, and to another one; *to every man according to his several ability;* and straightway took his journey." (Matthew 25:14–15. Italics added.)

Every One Is Different

Those of us who teach, both as parents and in the Church, should remember those revelations that tell of our

116

premortal existence. We are told that the intelligences differed one from another.

One of the great miracles of life is that no two individuals are exactly alike. We know that fact from various measurements that can be taken of the physical body — fingerprints, for example, where no two are ever the same — and also from measurements of intelligence and from emotional reactions. It is helpful for a teacher to understand that many of those whom he teaches, his own children or those in the Church, just do not see things the same way he sees them.

"You Mean, No Quotations?"

I recall being in a graduate class at Brigham Young University taught by a visiting professor. The course was on instruction. The professor was preoccupied with individual differences and spent most of his time emphasizing the significance of this principle to teachers. We were assigned a term paper. I thought, "Since this teacher emphasizes individual differences, here is my opportunity to write the kind of a term paper that will help me best. I will be individually different. I will write a paper that will help me discover what I know, and therefore what more I need to know about a subject."

We had an interview with the professor before we proceeded with our projects. I told the professor the subject I had chosen and my desire to do it different than it is usually done. I proposed that I would survey the literature of the field and then write, in my own words, without reference to any other authors and without including any quotations, the subject according to *me*. I indicated to the professor that I did not care how carefully she edited it or how severe she was in her judgment. Her appraisal would be the more helpful. Then I expressed myself as being willing to read references and cite any number of references as a bibliography, but *not* to include quotations.

I say here that I question the practice, often imposed upon students, of racing to the library to look through books, trying to find something that somebody has said in approximately the direction they themselves desire to speak, extracting the quotations, tying them together with a few meaningless connecting sentences, and then handing it in as a term paper. Thus my proposal to the professor.

The professor considered the proposal carefully and then said, "You mean, *no* quotations?"

"Exactly."

"You mean, spin it out of whole cloth?"

"I do."

Then she pondered rather deliberately and said, "Oh, no. I don't think we could let you do that."

Before I left the office I had been assigned one book and several articles from which I could quote.

"How foolish," I thought. "Here is a college professor spending a summer emphasizing individual differences but unable to accommodate a student who wishes to be individually different and write a different kind of term paper." The professor insisted upon expert opinion.

We are always looking for the so-called "expert opinion." While I'm not critical of the use of expert opinion, I think it is often misused. This idea of trying to find quotations where others have said something that approximates the way you want to say it, tying it together with sentences, and handing it in as research is, I think, often a waste of time. I think it is a waste of time because the student ends up without really knowing what he himself thinks or how he feels about the subject.

In the course of always looking for what others have done and what others have thought and what others have felt, we never learn what we think or feel about a subject.

We overlook learning what is in our own hearts, and in so doing we never make the most important of all discoveries. That is, How do I feel about the subject? What do I think about it? That introspection or exploration is perhaps the most important kind of study in which we can engage.

This process of putting term papers together from somebody else's quotations is a clerical process. It robs a student of the thinking process.

Search Our Own Minds

It is important to know the gospel, for instance, according to the leaders of the Church. But an even better starting place is to know the gospel according to one's own self; that is, to take a subject such as the Word of Wisdom and really search our own minds as to how we feel about it. We should read what we can find in the scriptures about the subject and then write down our feelings. Then we may compare those feelings against what leaders of the Church have written or said.

If we are sincere, we will find our conclusions being sustained by their conclusions. If we are searching inside ourselves in the right way, and we have included prayer as part of that search, we are tapping the same source of intelligence that the leaders of the Church are tuned-in upon.

Then we may become independent witnesses of that principle from our own inquiry. Then our obedience is not blind obedience. Then our agency is protected and we are on the right course. Then we will do things because we know they are right and are the truth. We will know this from our own inquiry, not simply because someone else knows it.

Like the professor who preached about individual differences but could not really make allowances for them, some parents make major mistakes in trying to raise a

119

family of children as though they were all alike. They assume each child to be a duplicate of the parent and expect that he will respond precisely as the parent responds.

May each of us, in all our teaching experiences—at home as well as in the formal classroom setting—be aware of the individual differences of those whom we teach.

CHAPTER SIXTEEN

How Individuals Are Alike

Since no principle of education has received more attention from educators than individual differences, the beginning teacher especially may be in a quandary. It is not uncommon for him to suffer a sense of frustration when he considers the problems associated with this principle. While the importance of giving attention to individual differences could hardly be ignored in preparing him for his assignment, too much emphasis on the differences may disarm him.

Much has been done in educational testing and measurement to determine the extent of these differences. General norms have been established. Teachers often overlook the fact that if norms can be established, individuals are very much alike also.

In dealing with problems relating to the principle of individual differences, there is a compensating principle that is almost entirely neglected. We will refer to it as the principle of *likenesses*. This principle can be very helpful indeed to the teacher.

Teacher-training institutions require courses in educational psychology and tests and measurements. In such courses prospective teachers become acquainted with the vast amount of research that continually goes on in the measuring of intelligence and the development of norms of growth and behavior.

Scholastic aptitude and achievement norms for students are highly developed. Standardized tests give reasonable assistance in placing individual students with relation to such norms as percentile norms, grade-level norms, and age-level norms.

In all of this, some of the most useful likenesses are almost universally ignored. Few practical applications of these important similarities are ever discussed.

Different and Alike

I have known teachers who have been revitalized when they have realized that although individuals differ in many respects, they are also very much alike in others. It is a revelation to them to learn there is another side to the question of how individuals differ; that other side is how individuals are alike.

While it is important to know that every individual differs from every other individual, it can be even more helpful to a teacher to know that there are always likenesses. The following verse of scripture attests to this likeness: "We have learned by sad experience that it is the nature and disposition of *almost all men,* as soon as they get a little authority, as they suppose, they will immediately begin to exercise unrighteous dominion." (D&C 121:39. Italics added.)

The teacher can recognize many such tendencies. Some of them are so nearly universal that the exceptions are hardly worth considering.

Everybody isn't *exactly* alike; we can find exceptions to every similarity. Nevertheless, we will get further in our teaching, both with our own children and in the classroom, if we'll look for likenesses and appeal to them, rather than concentrating solely on differences. This has application in administration also, as the following example illustrates.

When I was president of the New England Mission, we were trying to get the Relief Society organized in the mission. We had sixty branches and about sixty different kinds of organizations, everything from study groups to gossip circles. We wanted Relief Societies.

The mission Relief Society president was a lovely little lady who was a convert to the Church. Following our instructions, she set about to announce that hereafter the organizations would shift to the Relief Society pattern, including the time of the meeting, the length of the meeting, the courses of study, and all of the rest.

We knew there would be some objection on the part of the sisters in some of the small branches. They had been following the same pattern for a generation or more and would not be anxious to change. But if they were to have the full power of the program, those changes must come.

The Rule First, Then the Exception

I attended the Relief Society conference where Sister Baker, our Relief Society president, was to make the announcement. After the explanation, most of the sisters accepted the direction in good spirit and committed themselves to cooperate. However, one sister stood up and challenged Sister Baker.

"You don't understand," she said. "We're different in our branch. We want to do it the way we want to do it. You've got to realize there are exceptions, and we are an exception."

Sister Baker was taken aback by the vigor of this challenge, and she turned to me, her eyes pleading for help. I thought she was doing fine and just nodded for her to continue. After a moment she answered with a sentence that is so simple and yet so profound that I afterwards told

123

her I would be quoting it all over the Church. She said, "Dear sister, we'd like not to consider the exception first. We'd like to consider the rule first, and once we have that established, then we'll take care of the exception."

That is good counsel for teachers. Concentrate on likenesses, not differences. Discover how people are alike. Use that knowledge; then take care of the exceptions as you must. Many teachers are so concerned with all of the exceptions that they concentrate and specialize on the differences and end up failing.

If you have a group to teach and it is a large group, determine beforehand how the members of that group are alike. If you have a congregation to instruct and they range from little children to the very old, remember that in many ways they are all alike. In spite of age differences and in spite of all the other differences, in many ways they are similar. If you keep that in mind, you can teach them all. The Lord did.

For example, take the expression "everyone loves a story," and you may see what I mean. If you have a point to put across and can illustrate it with a story, all can be taught. If you tell it in simple terms, a youngster can understand it; at the same time the oldest person may draw a great lesson from it. That is one of the reasons the Lord taught in parables. By so doing, He was teaching everybody at once, but not all of them the same lesson.

Some time ago in a meeting the Brethren were discussing motion pictures, specifically those that would strengthen the family. Someone mentioned one featuring President Harold B. Lee. "Which one?" someone asked. "There were many produced in which he appeared." One of the Brethren identified it simply by saying, "You know, the one about apricots."

Everyone nodded. That identified the film from all of the others. Why? Because in it President Lee had told an incident about his daughter canning apricots. Not wanting to be interrupted, she had almost put off her little boys who wanted help with their prayers. "But, Mommy, what is more important," one of them had asked, "prayers or apricots?"

In that film President Lee had lectured forcefully on strengthening the home, but the film is remembered as the "apricot" film. We may have missed other things, but we all got that message. Each of us was alike in remembering that.

As We Love Ourselves

There is significant insight in the following incident in the New Testament: "And, behold, one came and said unto him, Good Master, What good thing shall I do, that I may have eternal life?" (Matthew 19:16.) Among the things the Lord said in reply was: "Honour thy father and thy mother: and, Thou shalt love thy neighbour as thyself." (Matthew 19:19.)

He said a similar thing to a lawyer who came tempting him, asking:

"Master, which is the great commandment in the law?

"Jesus said unto him, Thou shalt love the Lord thy God with all thy heart, and with all thy soul, and with all thy mind.

"This is the first and great commandment.

"And the second is like unto it, Thou shalt love thy neighbour as thyself." (Matthew 22:36–39.)

The Lord might have answered, love your neighbor as you love your husband or your wife, or love your neighbor as you love your parents or your best friends. But He knew something. He knew that while there are many exceptions to any rule as to who loves whom, there is virtually no one who does not love himself. In this we are all alike.

We acclaim a teacher who is successful with group

dynamics and is able to establish a spirit in a classroom in which everybody participates and everybody learns. Sometimes we credit that to his being a "born teacher" or someone who has a "real knack" or "a talent to teach," when in fact it may be that he uses basic principles anyone can apply if he is willing to learn about them and then to apply them.

In each class it is possible to illustrate this principle. Every student is different in some way from all the others.

While class members are similar in at least two aspects (that is, they are all in the class and they are all people), no two of them are just alike. How then will we teach them?

First we can think of ways in which they are all alike. We've already mentioned that everybody loves a story.

When we apply that similarity to the class members, we don't take away their individuality; we don't make them cease to be different, but we do appeal to the similarities, to the likenesses, to make it possible to do the same thing with all of them at once with fairly uniform results.

Let's illustrate another likeness: humor. Everybody responds to that. When you tell a humorous anecdote or a story or a joke or comment, everyone responds with laughter.

Again the class members have not ceased to be different, and yet they are all welded together as a class. Humor draws similar responses from all members of the class. The teacher who systematically develops the ability to sense how people are alike has at his command a unifying influence. It can be powerful in maintaining a relaxed mood in which the students can learn. This is true in the family as well as in the classroom.

There are other examples. Visual aids, for instance, fall in that category. The saying, "A picture is worth a thousand words," is generally true. We are alike in that if we see a picture, a graph, a chalkboard sketch, an object lesson, we will pay more attention than when we just hear words. We are all alike in many ways. Everybody responds to sincerity, to integrity, to love. Once you know that, use them.

In the Church we open our meetings with a hymn. Everyone is doing the same thing together as the meeting begins. Our differences in mood, in attitude, in a lot of other ways, are temporarily set aside as we all do the same thing at the same time. We are welded together as a congregation or as a class, ready to be taught as a unit. We become more alike.

When we keep in mind that in many ways we are very much alike, then teaching individuals, families, groups, classes, or congregations need not be difficult.

A concluding story from the New Testament illustrates this point.

He That Is without Sin

That the Lord knew how much His students were alike is found in the incident of the woman accused of adultery who was brought before Him. Witnesses were available and the law prescribed the death penalty, which in such cases amounted to being stoned to death.

Jesus had been teaching mercy. His adversaries wanted to trap Him. He must either forsake His teaching on mercy or speak against the law, a dangerous thing to do. But He knew them and knew how they were all alike.

When they asked if they should stone her, He appealed to the one thing wherein His questioners were all alike, not the ways in which they were different. "He that is without sin among you, let him first cast a stone at her." (John 8:7.)

There was no difference among them! And the scrip-

127

ture records that from the oldest to the youngest, they all departed. (John 8:9.)

While there is considerable difference in the teaching of young children as compared to teaching adults, and a group of teenagers differs much from a group of grandfathers and grandmothers, nevertheless I have come to believe that the basic principles of teaching apply across the board. A five-year-old will respond to respect and courtesy quite as quickly as will an older person.

If a teacher is a good people-watcher, he can soon observe likenesses. If he will study himself and his own deep feelings, he will find a kinship with all of humanity and be able to teach them.

"Ready or Not, You Will Be Taught"

When I was a little boy, one of the favorite games played in our neighborhood was "Kick the Can." Usually it was played at dusk with all of the children in the neighborhood gathered in one of the yards or orchards where there were many hiding places. The game began with the one who was "it" standing over the tin can with his eyes tightly closed, counting, while all the other youngsters fled to hiding places. He concluded his counting, "Ninety-six, ninety-seven, ninety-eight, ninety-nine, one hundred!" And then he would shout in a loud voice, "Here I come. Ready or not, you will be caught." And so the game began.

I have thought when observing a teacher struggling with a disinterested class, or watching a parent trying to give an untimely lesson to a youngster, that teaching is something of a game in which we announce through our actions, "Here I come. Ready or not, you will be taught."

If teaching is to be effective, it must capitalize on the readiness of the students to learn. A number of years ago when I was teaching seminary, a student was killed in an automobile accident on the way to school. There was a pall of gloom and shock over the whole school that day. The students came to class more serious and ready to learn than I had ever seen them before. I was teaching Church history, and we were bringing the pioneers West. But that was not the time for a lesson on pioneering. That day they were ready for a lesson on the atonement of Christ, the Resurrection, life after death.

A good teacher will be alert and will seize upon the opportunity to teach when the youngster is ready. Many lessons that we have been anxious to teach our own children have had to wait until they were ready.

Too Much Too Soon

One of the major difficulties, and one of the monumental dangers, of sex education courses in public schools is that they disregard this significant principle of teaching. They tell all before the youngster is ready, and in so doing, they often wreak havoc with the spiritual, emotional, and moral stability of the students. They open them to great jeopardy. Things should be done in the season thereof, and there is a time for all things. A wise teacher and a wise parent will be alert to that fact.

Likewise, in programming Church activities we should use great wisdom in considering the maturity and readiness of our members to be taught the basic principles of morality. If we teach the basic principles too soon, they may be meaningless to the youngsters. The matter of teaching morality may be necessary, but the framework in which it is set should recognize the degree of maturity and readiness.

For instance, when the youngster is too young to have been subjected to the urging of physical desires, he must be taught about the subject in an entirely different way than will be appropriate when he is older. There will come a time for some more mature discussion later, but this must always be with reverence.

Information presented to a student must be palatable

to him and of such a nature that his learning constitution can digest it. Unfortunately, there is no series of charts or graphs or measures or tests available that will enable the parent or the teacher to gain an accurate profile of maturation of each student and thereby tailor his teachings accordingly. This means that we must be careful and must be quiet observers of each youngster in order to be able to understand when he is ready. This is true of many subjects.

One reference in the New Testament that might be illustrative is the incident in the home of Mary and Martha.

> Now it came to pass, as they went, that he entered into a certain village: and a certain woman named Martha received him into her house.
>
> And she had a sister called Mary, which also sat at Jesus' feet, and heard his word.
>
> But Martha was cumbered about much serving, and came to him, and said, Lord, dost thou not care that my sister hath left me to serve alone? bid her therefore that she help me.
>
> And Jesus answered and said unto her, Martha, Martha, thou art careful and troubled about many things:
>
> But one thing is needful: and Mary hath chosen that good part, which shall not be taken away from her. (Luke 10:38–42.)

In Mary and Martha we see two individuals, two different degrees of readiness—Mary, of course, being the responsive and eager student while her sister Martha was encumbered with sundry household tasks that served to distract her from the learning situation. Similar lessons can be drawn from the parable of the Ten Virgins:

Five Were Ready

> Then shall the kingdom of heaven be likened unto ten virgins, which took their lamps, and went forth to meet the bridegroom.

And five of them were wise, and five were foolish.

They that were foolish took their lamps, and took no oil with them;

But the wise took oil in their vessels with their lamps.

While the bridegroom tarried, they all slumbered and slept.

And at midnight there was a cry made, Behold, the bridegroom cometh; go ye out to meet him.

Then all those virgins arose, and trimmed their lamps.

And the foolish said unto the wise, Give us of your oil; for our lamps are gone out.

But the wise answered, saying, Not so; lest there be not enough for us and you; but go ye rather to them that sell, and buy for yourselves.

And while they went to buy, the bridegroom came; and they that were ready went in with him to the marriage: and the door was shut.

Afterward came also the other virgins, saying, Lord, Lord, open to us.

But he answered and said, Verily I say unto you, I know you not.

Watch therefore, for ye know neither the day nor the hour wherein the Son of man cometh. (Matthew 25:1–13.)

This parable, of course, teaches something else also, but in the illustration we can easily see the difference in the response of the five who were mature and ready compared with the five who were not ready or receptive.

Elsewhere in His teachings, the Lord indicated that "all men receive this saying, save they to whom it is given" (Matthew 19:11), which means those who are ready to receive. On one occasion He reminded His disciples that "unto you it is given to know the mysteries of the kingdom of God: but unto them that are without, all these things are done in parables." (Mark 4:11.)

132

To the Master came one who was sick with palsy, and the Lord evidently recognized some were there who were ready to be taught, for He healed the man, "and seeing their faith, said unto the sick of palsy: son, be of good cheer; thy sins be forgiven thee." (Matthew 9: 12.)

The record in John indicates that Jesus knew "there are some of you that believe not. For Jesus knew from the beginning who they were that believed not. . . . " (John 6:64.) Jesus seemed to realize that on some occasions He was teaching *at* the people rather than instructing them. "But whereunto shall *I liken* this generation? It is like unto the children sitting in the markets, and calling unto their fellows, And saying, We have piped unto you, and ye have not danced; we have mourned unto you, and ye have not lamented." (Matthew 11: 16–17. Italics added.)

It is interesting that some of the verses we quote are used likewise to illustrate other principles of education. Note the word *liken* in this reference, and consider it in the light of the chapter on apperception.

There is a lesson on readiness in the parable of the Prodigal Son:

One Became Teachable

A certain man had two sons:

And the younger of them said to his father, Father, give me the portion of goods that falleth to me. And he divided unto them his living.

And not many days after the younger son gathered all together, and took his journey into a far country, and there wasted his substance with riotous living.

And when he had spent all, there arose a mighty famine in that land; and he began to be in want.

And he went and joined himself to a citizen of that country; and he sent him into his fields to feed swine.

And he would fain have filled his belly with the

133

husks that the swine did eat: and no man gave unto him.

And when he came to himself, he said, How many hired servants of my father's have bread enough and to spare, and I perish with hunger!

I will arise and go to my father, and will say unto him, Father, I have sinned against heaven, and before thee.

And am no more worthy to be called thy son: make me as one of thy hired servants.

And he arose, and came to his father. But when he was yet a great way off, his father saw him, and had compassion, and ran, and fell on his neck and kissed him.

And the son said unto him, Father, I have sinned against heaven, and in thy sight, and am no more worthy to be called thy son.

But the father said to his servants, Bring forth the best robe, and put it on him; and put a ring on his hand, and shoes on his feet.

And bring hither the fatted calf, and kill it; and let us eat, and be merry:

For this my son was dead, and is alive again; he was lost, and is found. And they began to be merry.

Now his elder son was in the field: and as he came and drew nigh to the house, he heard musick and dancing.

And he called one of the servants, and asked what these things meant.

And he said unto him, Thy brother is come; and thy father hath killed the fatted calf, because he hath received him safe and sound.

And he was angry, and would not go in: therefore came his father out, and intreated him.

And he answering said to his father, Lo, these many years I do serve thee, neither transgressed I at any time thy commandment: and yet thou never gavest me a kid, that I might make merry with my friends:

But as soon as this thy son was come, which

hath devoured thy living with harlots, thou hast killed for him the fatted calf.

And he said unto him, Son, thou art ever with me, and all that I have is thine.

It was meet that we should make merry, and be glad; for this thy brother was dead, and is alive again; and was lost, and is found. (Luke 15:11–32.)

The son did not respond to the father's teachings to begin with, but he was anxious for them at the conclusion of the incident.

Such expressions as "if any man have ears to hear, let him hear" (Mark 4:23) are common to His teachings. On one occasion, as a reaction to the power evidenced in His miracle, the people "besought him that he would depart. . . . " (Matthew 8:34.) They were not ready for such forceful instructions.

The Time Is Now—Right Now!

The principle of readiness is important when teaching our own children. Parents are with their children almost constantly and can observe when they are ready to be instructed. From questions or behavior, or because of experiences in their own lives, they can sense that it is time to teach. Parents must know when the time for the lesson is *now*, right now, for their children are ready for it.

My wife and I have made it a practice as parents never to put off a question from one of our youngsters. Regardless of how unimportant the question seems or how busily we are involved, we have always been willing to interrupt anything to respond to the question of a youngster. That is because the question is an indication that he is ready; he wants to know—now.

There is yet a more difficult policy to follow that has to do with this matter of readiness. Little youngsters have the tendency to want to help and to want to get involved in what grownups are doing. Often this seems to bother the parent. They always seem to want to help at just the wrong time!

I am painting a wall. Along comes my five-year-old and says, "Daddy, can I paint?" I always let him do it. I know that the interest span of children is very short. If I spread some papers and give him the brush and let him work for a few minutes, he soon loses interest, soon finds it is too difficult and not as much fun as he thought it would be. He hasn't interrupted me very long. Then I can praise him for having helped and cooperated, and it becomes a success experience for him. That is much different from being put off.

Let Them Help

I think one of the major mistakes in teaching children is the tendency for parents to be bothered when children want to participate and to learn something. If we let them help, it is amazing how quickly they become accomplished. How eagerly they learn, for they are ready.

We do a little woodwork around our home, and our boys have all wanted to get involved. We have let them and encouraged them. When I have been working on a project and a youngster wants to do the same thing, I let him try — always.

On those rare occasions when I've found an opportunity to work on an oil painting, one of our little youngsters would come along and say, "Daddy, let me paint." So I have let him do it. Generally I have shown him a corner and said, "Will you paint this for me?" When children are young, of course, their coordination is not good. Sometimes they've smeared across the painting. Philosophically I've said, "So what?" It's easy to repaint with oil paints; it can be covered up. Besides, my objective is rearing children, not painting masterpieces.

136

Our children were allowed to help when they were little, urged to help when they grew a little older, and sometimes ordered to help when they were teenagers. They have, accordingly, learned to do many things for themselves, and very expertly. They know how to work.

When we were living in Cambridge, Massachusetts, one of our sons completed a project for an elementary school unit. He carved a Viking ship out of wood, hollowed it out, made a little dragon's head to glue on the front of it, and then sawed end sections from a large pencil and glued them along the side as shields. He came home brokenhearted because the teacher would not accept the project, saying he did not do it himself, that he could not at his age have done work that good. That called for a parent-teacher conference in which the parent took a very leading part.

Feed Them When They Are Hungry

We have learned something about feeding that intangible, invisible appetite within by comparing it with physical hunger. While our children have been growing up we have made it a practice to feed them when they are hungry. Now that may seem like a very strange and reckless thing to do, but it has been very successful.

Soon after our children come home from school, a hot dinner is waiting for them. About four-thirty or five o'clock they eat. They have been in school all day; their blood sugar is low; they are restless and tired; and when they come home they are hungry.

There are two courses that could be followed. Their mother could serve them cookies and milk or bread and jam in order to tide them over until dinner time, in which case their appetite is usually dulled and they don't eat as well as they should at dinner. The other course is to feed

137

them the dinner when they are most hungry. They eat heartily, and then the snack comes a little before bedtime.

It is interesting to see them, after they have had a good meal, go about their chores or settle into studying or peacefully play or take care of any other activities.

The question is immediately raised: Well, doesn't father eat with the children, then? Father has his dinner when he comes home. Often the children sit around and visit. And with a snack served later, it is like family home evening virtually every night.

This has contributed much to the peace and tranquillity of our home because the children are fed when they are ready.

There is, of course, a comparison to teaching in this. Sometimes we give students little off-hand answers, little tidbits that really spoil their appetite for learning, and they come away without being given the nourishment spiritually and intellectually that they need.

The cry from the childhood game, "Ready or not, you will be taught," is poor advice for any teacher or parent.

CHAPTER EIGHTEEN

Objectives

Some gardeners
Slash frantically
At the weed's
Offending shoots—

And others
Labor steadily,
Loosening
Its roots.*

Suppose you are in a home and notice a beautiful statue of a child, one with angelic proportions that seem so alive, a supreme example of the sculptor's art.

"How beautiful," you might remark. "Where did you get it?"

Can you imagine a response such as this?

"I was carrying this piece of material up a long flight of stairs when it slipped out of my hands. As it bounced down the stairs, it was chipped in every way. At the bottom of the stairs it rolled into the street and was run over by a large truck. The wheels of the truck flipped it across the street into the park, where it lay for months in the weather

---

*Carol Lynn Pearson, *The Search* (Provo, Utah: Trilogy Arts, 1970), p. 29. Used by permission of the current publisher, Doubleday.

139

until it was mangled by a lawnmower. When I went to get it, it was as you see it now."

Ridiculous! The statue would take careful planning, and the sculptor would have to see the end from the beginning. He would have to know where to start chiseling on the rough block of marble, and how to "find" the child that was hidden in it.

In much of the teaching at home and in the Church, the teachers are doing just that—teaching. They are not quite sure where they have been, and they haven't planned ahead enough to know where they are going. They are something like Alice in Wonderland, when she approached the Cheshire Cat.

Alice: "Would you tell me, please, which way I ought to walk from here?"

Cheshire Cat: "That depends a good deal on where you want to get to."

Alice: "I don't much care where."

Cheshire Cat: "Then it doesn't matter much which way you walk."

Alice: " — so long as I get *somewhere*."

Cheshire Cat: "Oh, you're sure to do that, if you only walk long enough!"

In teaching we have a specific "somewhere" to get to, and there must be a plan. We must give careful attention to objectives. Fortunately much is done in preparing lesson materials in the Church. The objectives are carefully considered, and the plans are carefully organized so that with reasonable attention to the lesson manual, one can formulate objectives.

The Overview

I have always thought it helpful to the student to have an overview of the entire course to begin with. If he has an overview of the course or of the subject, then the teacher can go back and fill in the details and a lot more will be taught.

For instance, in teaching Church history there is a great advantage in giving what might be called a "mini course" in Church history the first few class periods. In brief overview form, with a map included, the Apostasy might be discussed, the restoration of the gospel, the organization of the Church, the movement of the Church from place to place, and the establishment of the Church headquarters in the Salt Lake Valley. All of that could be briefly covered as an overview of Church history.

Then the teacher can start over again and go over the same material, but this time take the full time of the course to develop it. The students then know where they are going and will be collecting information along the way. The class will be much more meaningful to them. They will, in other words, have an objective in mind.

There is a tendency on the part of speakers, and sometimes of teachers, to assume that since an idea is clear to them, it is clear to the audience or class. There is the tendency also to assume that the student is learning, putting each piece in place, because the teacher has a plan.

Let Them See the Plan

If I were a contractor building an office building or a shopping center, I would make very certain that all the men who worked on it saw a copy of the plans. Perhaps some of the detailed plans and specifications wouldn't be interesting to anyone but the journeymen. I would nevertheless want everyone to see the architect's drawing of the building so they would know what it was going to look like. Then they would know at least a little bit about how their work fitted into the whole.

In the mission field I interviewed an elder who had spent the first several months of his mission in Canada sitting in his apartment doing telephone contacting. He had a lazy senior companion who didn't like to get out in the cold weather, and this nearly ruined his mission. He said, "I didn't know but what that was all there was to missionary work."

We developed thereafter an introductory program in which the senior companion took the first week with a new missionary and gave him an overview of his mission. He introduced him to each type of proselyting and gave him a short course on what he would be doing for the next two years.

This proved to be very worthwhile. Some of the experiences would not be realized for many months, perhaps even toward the end of the mission, but the missionary had something of the feel of what was ahead.

142

This principle is well known by good leaders. You'll remember Brigham Young seeking an interview with Jim Bridger on one occasion in order to talk with someone who had been over the road the Saints were to follow. While the principle is well established in many activities of life, it is often overlooked by a teacher. If used, however, a preview and an overview become another example of the repetition that is essential to learning.

Definite Objectives

A wise teacher, in preparing any lesson, will have definite objectives in mind. He will decide beforehand what he wants to teach and why he wants to teach it. For instance, a Church history lesson on the martyrdom of the Prophet Joseph Smith and the succession of Brigham Young to be president of the Church can be taught without having any noticeable application to the life of the student. If the teacher has established definite objectives, however, he can make the lesson meaningful to his students.

It is important that the lessons be likened unto ourselves.

> Wherefore I spake unto them, saying: Hear ye the words of the prophet, ye who are a remnant of the house of Israel, a branch who have been broken off; hear ye the words of the prophet, which were written unto all the house of Israel, and *liken them unto yourselves,* that ye may have hope as well as your brethren from whom ye have been broken off; for after this manner has the prophet written. (1 Nephi 19:24. Italics added.)

So What?

Unless the message is likened unto ourselves, young people, particularly, may not see much meaning in it. For example, young people often have difficulty seeing much relationship between things that happened in Old or New

143

Testament times or in Church history and the here and now. If the lesson is taught using the likening technique, they can more readily see the application to their lives.

One teacher had a "so what" test that he used in preparing each lesson. He would imagine in his mind one of his students saying, "So what?" Then he would find some explanation as to why the teaching or the lesson was pertinent to the here and now. It changed both his preparation and his presentation.

If we can bridge the then and there to the here and now, the lives of young people can be changed for the good.

There is value to a teacher—whether it be in a class, the family, a sermon, or a talk—in writing an objective with the following little formula.

First determine what you want to teach and then add:

_____ in order that _____

In the blank space, write something that you want the class members to *do* about what you told them.

For instance, suppose you are teaching teenage girls and the lesson is on the restoration of the priesthood. The formula could be filled in something like this:

Lesson title: The Restoration of the Priesthood

Objectives: To show that the priesthood was restored by heavenly messengers with authority

In order that: The girls will encourage the young men with whom they are associating to place regular attendance at priesthood meeting high on their list of priorities.

If you have this worked out, you will say different things in class than you would otherwise. You will have something that the girls can do to implement the message of the lesson.

This brings us to the *here* and *now*. In the class you are going to mention something about the young men with whom the girls are associating. You will discuss how a young woman can encourage a young man to attend priesthood meeting. Real-life circumstances and examples that exist in their lives today can be brought into the lesson, not just history.

On the other hand, a teacher might follow the lesson manual and get the historical facts correct, and still have the young sisters sitting in class with "what does that matter to me?" complacency. If you add "IN ORDER THAT" to your lesson, somewhere in the discussion you're going to mention things of interest to the students.

Most textbooks on instruction treat teaching students rather than teaching subjects. There are some very competent people who possess great knowledge of subject matter but have no ability to share what they have. A ten-gallon teacher may hardly get two pints of information conveyed to someone else. On the other hand, a two-quart teacher may, with some consistency, get six pints conveyed to those he teaches. The difference is in the teacher's making the lesson relevant to the student's here and now.

Suppose the lesson is on the Beatitudes, and the basic objective is to teach the Beatitudes. Using the formula, you could add "IN ORDER THAT" and have this as an objective: to teach the students that good things must be earned, that their privileges must be paid for in advance, and that blessings, including the inheritance of the kingdom of heaven, come only to those who are qualified.

A Noisy Class

Let me describe the experience of a teacher trying to teach that subject. On one occasion, while supervising seminaries, I visited a seminary one afternoon. It was the last period of the day, when teenage students have a tendency to be restless. They've had a long day of intense activity, often their blood sugar is low, and they're just plain restless.

From the foyer it was easy to pick a class where there was trouble. You could hear the voice of the teacher straining to rise above all that was going on in the classroom. So noisy was it that I was able to step in and take a seat behind the students without the teacher even knowing I had entered.

The course was on the New Testament, and the day's lesson was on the Beatitudes. The teacher was reading, without looking up, a scholarly treatise on the Beatitudes in which he seemed to be very interested. Only occasionally did he look up to scold one student or another. The article was professional in its language, and the students didn't have the slightest interest in it.

The teacher finally stopped reading when a student nearly fell from his chair trying to pass a note to a girl in the second row from him. With some irritation the teacher said, "You're not helping the class very much. Don't you think about anything but girls?" "Yes," was the reply, "basketball." Of course the class was on the side of the boy, and they all enjoyed his rebuttal.

It was then that the teacher noticed me. His face turned pale, and I was a little embarrassed for being there. He introduced me and asked if I would like to say something to the class. I was not anxious to sit there any longer watching the teacher and the students trying to torture one another, so I was happy to respond.

The Here and Now

The lesson, I remind you, was on the Beatitudes, but they did not seem to be very meaningful in the lives of the students. Looking at the boy who had caused the last disturbance, I said, "Evidently you're a basketball player." "Yes." "How did you get elected to that?" "I wasn't elected. The coach chose me." "That isn't very democratic, is it?" For this he didn't have an answer.

I then gave a little lecture on living in a democracy and said that we ought to be elected to the team, not appointed to it. Pretty soon a hot debate was going, with the students in the class insisting that was no way to have a good team. It was not easy to be on a team. Membership was a position to be earned through work and practice and skill and endeavor. I argued the point for a few minutes and then shifted to the pep club, just to get the girls involved. A similar discussion resulted.

"Why not organize the pep club by random chance?" They weren't interested in that. Again they defended the fact that one has to put something into membership, to work, be responsible, attend the practices, etc.

I finally agreed with them. "There are many things you must earn in life or you just don't get them. To half earn them is not enough. Did you know that the Lord has said something about that? There are some rewards He has promised on condition that we earn them."

We turned to the Beatitudes and read them with some emphasis, with every student listening carefully and thoughtfully. Then for the rest of the period we discussed the Beatitudes and their meaning in our lives. Somewhere along the way basketball and pep club were forgotten, and so was any inclination to disturb.

Being "chosen" to enter the celestial kingdom is something like being "chosen" for the main string in a basketball team or to belong to the pep club. The celestial kingdom and the Beatitudes they know not of, but basketball and pep club they know, and it is useful for a teacher to begin in the world with the students and then lead them carefully to the brow of a hill where he can point them to the worlds beyond.

A teacher who knows young people and is teaching lessons in order that the young people may understand them can teach under circumstances that would otherwise be impossible.

An Unsuccessful Competitor

I recall on one occasion visiting a seminary class in Pocatello, Idaho. Sister Heaps was the teacher. The class met in a new building, with fairly large windows all along one side of the classroom. The students could see what was going on outside.

A building across the street was being demolished by a crane with a large metal weight. As I slipped into the back of the classroom, the sound of the heavy machines was, of course, quite audible, and I thought how terribly distracting for Sister Heaps to try to teach a class with a distraction like that just across the road.

I was focusing my attention on the demolishing of the building until it suddenly occurred to me that I was the only one doing so. Sister Heaps had so captivated the interest of the class that none of them was paying any attention to what was going on across the street.

This became a marvelous demonstration to me of teaching ability, and for the rest of the class period, I was captivated by a teacher with students vitally interested in her lesson. The construction crew across the street just wasn't competition enough for her. She was feeding her students.

In 1938 seminary and institute teachers of the Church were gathered at Aspen Grove near Provo, Utah, for a special summer session. President J. Reuben Clark, Jr., spoke on the subject "The Charted Course of the Church in Education." He opened his address by referring to a schoolboy experience.

He indicated that Daniel Webster "seemed to invoke so sensible a procedure for occasions where, after wandering on the high seas or in the wilderness, effort is to be made to get back to the place of starting." He then set forth, in an almost scriptural statement, the objectives of those who teach in the Church:

President J. Reuben Clark, Jr.

The Church is the organized Priesthood of God; the Priesthood can exist without the Church, but the Church cannot exist without the Priesthood. The mission of the Church is first, to teach, encourage, assist, and protect the individual member in his striving to live the perfect life, temporally and spiritually, as laid down in the Gospel, "Be ye perfect, even as your Father which is in Heaven is perfect," said the Master; secondly, the Church is to maintain, teach, encourage, and protect, temporally and spiritually, the membership as a group in its living

150

of the Gospel; thirdly, the Church is militantly to proclaim the truth, calling upon all men to repent, and to live in obedience to the Gospel, "for every knee must bow and every tongue confess."

In all this there are for the Church and for each and all of its members, two prime things which may not be overlooked, forgotten, shaded, or discarded:

First: That Jesus Christ is the Son of God, the Only Begotten of the Father in the flesh, the Creator of the world, the Lamb of God, the Sacrifice for the sins of the world, the Atoner for Adam's transgression; that He was crucified; that His spirit left His body; that He died; that He was laid away in the tomb; that on the third day His spirit was reunited with His Body, which again became a living being; that He was raised from the tomb a resurrected being, a perfect Being, the First Fruits of the Resurrection; that He later ascended to the Father; and that because of His death and by and through His resurrection every man born into the world since the beginning will be likewise literally resurrected. This doctrine is as old as the world. Job declared: "And though after my skin worms destroy this body, yet in my flesh shall I see God, whom I shall see for myself and mine eyes shall behold, and not another." (Job 19:26, 27.)

The resurrected body is a body of flesh and bones and spirit, and Job was uttering a great and everlasting truth. These positive facts, and all other facts necessarily implied therein, must all be honestly believed, in full faith, by every member of the Church.

The second of the two things to which we must all give full faith is: That the Father and the Son actually and in truth and very deed appeared to the Prophet Joseph in a vision in the woods; that other heavenly visions followed to Joseph and to others; that the Gospel and the holy Priesthood after the Order of the Son of God were in truth and

151

fact restored to the earth from which they were lost by the apostasy of the Primitive Church; that the Lord again set up His Church, through the agency of Joseph Smith; that the Book of Mormon is just what it professes to be; that to the Prophet came numerous revelations for the guidance, upbuilding, organization, and encouragement of the Church and its members; that the Prophet's successors, likewise called of God, have received revelations as the needs of the Church have required, and that they will continue to receive revelations as the Church and its members, living the truth they already have, shall stand in need of more; that this is in truth the Church of Jesus Christ of Latter-day Saints; and that its foundation beliefs are the laws and principles laid down in the Articles of Faith. These facts also, and each of them, together with all things necessarily implied therein or flowing therefrom, must stand, unchanged, unmodified, without dilution, excuse, apology, or avoidance; they may not be explained away or submerged. Without these two great beliefs the Church would cease to be the Church.

Any individual who does not accept the fulness of these doctrines as to Jesus of Nazareth or as to the restoration of the Gospel and Holy Priesthood, is not a Latter-day Saint; the hundreds of thousands of faithful, God-fearing men and women who compose the great body of the Church membership do believe these things fully and completely; and they support the Church and its institutions because of this belief.

I have set out these matters because they are the latitude and longitude of the actual location and position of the Church, both in this world and in eternity. Knowing our true position, we can change our bearings if they need changing; we can lay down anew our true course. And here we may wisely recall that Paul said:

"But though we, or an angel from heaven,

preach any other Gospel unto you than that which
we have preached unto you, let him be accursed."
(Galatians 1:8.)

This statement by President Clark, speaking for the
First Presidency, is to me the position paper for teachers
in the Church. Never a year goes by but that I reread it
carefully. Every teacher in the Church should read it in its
entirety. I have quoted but part of it here; however, I regard
it as being so important that I am including his sermon in
its entirety in the appendix.

May each of us, as parents and as teachers in the
Church, follow the sound counsel and wisdom given here
and thus improve our teaching of important gospel principles.

CHAPTER NINETEEN

Discipline

*D*IS'·CI·PLINE, verb. To sub-
*ject to discipline; in earlier use, to instruct, educate, train; in
later use, more especially, to train to habits of order and subor-
dination; to bring under control.*

The word *discipline* comes from the word *disciple,* meaning pupil or student. It also means follower, particularly
a follower of Jesus Christ. The New Testament and the
Book of Mormon speak of His "disciples." As we talk of
the discipline employed by a teacher, it shall be in this
context: "those actions which cause a person to become a
disciple or follower, only incidentally of the teacher, but
particularly of Jesus Christ."

Prevention — The Basis of Discipline

During the years I supervised teachers, one thing
puzzled me. That was the inability of most successful teachers — those who might have been termed master teachers —
to explain how to solve serious discipline problems. Occasionally I asked, "We have a teacher who is having great
difficulty. The class has just about come apart. What would
you do?" The question generally brought inconclusive answers even from successful teachers.

I was puzzled at first. However, I soon came to realize that the teachers didn't know how to *correct* such problems; they knew only how to *prevent* them. They used procedures that prevented such things from happening. Things just didn't ever get that far out of hand. Though these teachers had their good days and their bad days, and occasionally terrible days, such days were incidents, not patterns, in their teaching. Prevention is the basis of discipline.

A good beginning is very important. It is half the battle. If the teacher employs discipline consistently, from the beginning, the class will be successful.

Silence

Ordinary procedures for discipline are the most powerful. Take, for instance, the use of silence. Make it a rule that when someone else in the classroom is talking you will stop. That's all, just stop, until the guilty party has been silenced. Usually that doesn't take very long. You don't even need to look at the person in the initial encounter. Just look at the floor or pause and wait a minute. Ordinarily it takes only a few seconds, though it may sometimes seem like an eternity.

In the chapter on likeness, we referred to the incident recorded in the eighth chapter of John in which a woman brought before Jesus was accused of adultery. The Lord seemed to look away from her; He stooped down and wrote on the ground, so as to let her accusers' consciences, rather than His piercing look, condemn them. He said nothing to them. Finally, when they continued asking Him, He said, "He that is without sin among you, let him first cast a stone at her." (John 8:7.)

Beginning teachers seem to be afraid of that silence. It ought to be practiced. Once it works well, that generally is all the teacher ever has to do.

At times you will have to stop right in the middle of a sentence without even ___ ___.

Better still, you can stop right in the middle of a wo_ _.

This technique, the simple use of silence, can be employed in classrooms, in meetings, in council meetings. It's wise to employ it in the home. Parents would do well to keep that in mind: when someone else is talking, stop.

Another value we have not mentioned yet is that what is being said may well be worth hearing. It may be the most important thing the teacher hears that day. If he has not learned, he has not taught, and in a class or in a family the teacher learns from his students, the parent from the children.

What do you do if silence doesn't work? What is the next step? A foolish teacher will employ direct verbal correction with an expression such as, "John, I wish you would be quiet so that we can go on with the lesson." Mistake!

The fewer times you call a person's name in class and subject him to verbal correction before his peers, the more powerful you will be. If you're alert enough, you might know that John is having some deep personal problems and is really seeking attention. It is very satisfying to him when you say, "John, — — —." He has been singled out, and perhaps it is the only prestige and attention he gets. He will ask for this and invite it many times again if you are foolish enough to begin that way. There is a much better way.

If silence doesn't work, you can make a casual comment, such as, "Someone in class is not cooperating." You need not look at the offender. The class will do that for you. Peer group pressure is therefore applied. Often class members will single out the noisy one and discipline him themselves. (There is more about peer group influence in a later chapter.)

That is also a kind thing to do, because the outstanding member of the class may be so full of something that he simply must talk to his friends about it. It may really be innocent enthusiasm, not rebellion. If you handle the situation in an indirect way, the student has a chance to repent and to slip back into acceptable conduct without the embarrassment of having his name called out.

Easier to Prevent Than to Rescue

The successful teacher will not overreact. He will start with gentle elements of discipline and move to the more powerful and persuasive types. Actually they are not more powerful. The more powerful ones are the very gentle ones we've talked about.

The wise teacher does not kill a fly with a sledgehammer or try to adjust a watch with a crowbar. He takes control of the class at the beginning and then keeps that control. It is so much easier to maintain control than it is to try to rescue the situation once it has gotten out of hand.

Every teacher, I suppose, must face a skirmish or two with class members. Sometimes he will foolishly use the heavy artillery when small-arms fire would have won the battle. Or he will mount a full cavalry charge when just a small scouting party would have saved the day.

Most situations can be controlled with even a slight gesture. If the gesture does not work, the teacher can always apply something a little more intense. On the other hand, if he fires his heavy artillery first, there's little left to do, if the students will not respond.

If at the first challenge of discipline the teacher rolls out the twenty-millimeter cannon and fires it, when the encounter calls only for a show of weapons, it is very difficult for him to know what to do when things really get out of order. Students will have long since become used to cannon fire, and thereafter they are likely to ignore it.

Years ago I had an experience with one of our children that taught me not to overreact.

He Didn't Know

When our oldest son was a little fellow, he came in one day and in the course of conversation used, matter-of-factly, a profane word. It was worse than profane—it was a filthy word. I have always been grateful I restrained myself from spanking or punishing him in such a way that he never would forget the incident.

Fortunately I said, "Hey, where did you learn that word?" He told me he had heard it from one of the boys in the neighborhood. I said, "That's not a good word." He looked up at me in innocent surprise and said, "It isn't? I didn't know that." And he *didn't* know.

There was a chance for me to quietly explain to him not only about that word, but also others like it, with him listening, an eager student. I've never heard him profane in all of the years since. Now he teaches children of his own.

There's a certain courtesy that is the obligation of a teacher in administering discipline. Perhaps this can best be illustrated by talking about parents. Often it is difficult to wait until some private time can be arranged for special discipline. A teacher or a parent must remember that overreaction on the scene generally makes things worse.

On one occasion Brother Van Valkenberg came to shoe a horse for us. We brought the horse up on the driveway, near the garage. Of course all of the children were there, and the excitement of seeing a horse shod brought an audience from the neighborhood also. It was a hot day, the horse was somewhat uncooperative, and Brother Van

Valkenberg was perspiring freely. One of our little young-sters asked if he liked to shoe horses. He said that he did. "But it's harder than hell, isn't it?" asked the little fellow.

It was an interesting situation. The General Authority and his family and the neighbors. I managed to cough and sputter a little, and observed quietly to our little boy that we'd have something to talk about later. The conversation was then diverted to something else about shoeing horses.

It is a good idea to make sure children understand why they are being punished. Sometimes we administer pun-ishment for an infraction of the rules and the young person has not been really aware of what he has done. That, in his mind, then becomes some kind of persecution. It is a good idea to have enough of a conversation to make sure children understand why they are being punished. Parents who follow this rule are often quite surprised when they readily submit and understand that they deserve just what they are getting.

We have one boy who has a twinkle in his eye and all that goes with it. He is constantly full of humor and in-nocent mischief. I came home one day to discover there had been an infraction of family discipline. Circumstantial evidence was complete, so I disciplined him. He protested his innocence, but I knew he was guilty because this was so typical of his mischief.

That night I learned that he was innocent, so I went to his room to apologize. I told him I was sorry and asked forgiveness. Then I added another lesson. I said, "Son, I hope you're big enough to take this, because life has a way of doing things like this to us. Life has a way of serving up some judgments that we may not deserve or think we do not deserve. If you're not big enough to face a few of those in life, you've got a mighty long row to hoe, and there are some mighty big clods in it. So, your great concern, my boy, isn't when you're misused now and again. Your great concern ought to be when you hurt or offend another."

When I taught seminary I used to begin the first day of each school year by saying, "In this class there are no 'have to's.' " I would usually wait until some student with sophomoric enthusiasm would raise his hand and say, "Brother Packer, do we have to do this or do we have to do that?" That was my cue to say, "There are no 'have to's' in this class. You don't have to come to class. If you do come, you do not have to come on time. If you do come on time, when you are here you do not have to study. You do not have to listen." I would then add a very meaningful and menacing, "But if you don't!"

React to the Right Thing

I have a rule that I made for myself and have always tried to follow. It is this: Never correct a serious problem by reacting to the incident that brings it to my attention.

When I was a mission president, an elder called and requested permission to play the wedding march at a wedding in one of our chapels. There were two things about the request that were out of order. One, we don't encourage worldly type weddings in our chapels, with such pomp as candles and wedding marches. And second, a missionary is a missionary, and ought to be about his ministry. Thus, I forbade him to do it.

It wasn't long until I had a tearful mother on the phone explaining that the wedding was just a day or two away and it had already been announced. They had counted on the elder, and she didn't know what she would do without him.

I then realized I had not followed the rule I had set for myself, so I authorized the elder to play for the wedding, and all went well.

Several weeks later, independent of that incident, directives were sent with full instructions on the subject from the handbook. All weddings planned thereafter could fit the pattern that was approved. Another directive went to the missionaries giving them some guidance on their responsibility to stay with their ministry.

When you want to control the behavior of others and administer correction, you ought to have some reason for doing something about it as compared to doing nothing about it. There ought to be a very good reason for doing something right now as compared with doing something later when the atmosphere is less tense.

Scientific neglect can be a respectable procedure in discipline.

One missionary came into the mission field with some serious physical deformities. He was withdrawn, self-conscious, and retiring, particularly around girls. I had him examined by several doctors. Then I wrote to a friend of mine and told him I needed a substantial amount of money. He responded immediately with a check, the only condition being that he remain anonymous. With the cooperation of some able professional help, the deformities were corrected and the missionary was transformed in his appearance. Immediately his behavior changed.

Then I began receiving reports that he was breaking mission rules. I did not show much interest in the reports, although inwardly I was delighted. A few weeks later the problem came to a head when my missionary assistants reported that at a stake conference this missionary had left his companion and had gone up to the balcony to sit with a girl. There had been other times also, they said, when he had left his companion to go talk with the girl.

I was not disturbed by the report, and some time later my assistants returned to the office for something of a confrontation. They said, "You are not fair. This elder can get away with anything and you don't do anything about it. Ordinarily nothing would make you act so fast as a report that an elder was leaving his companion to visit a girl. Yet in this case you won't do anything about it. Why?"

It was only after a long discussion that they understood I was doing something about the matter. I was treating it with scientific neglect. When the right times comes, I told them, the elder will either return voluntarily to observing the rules or he will be pulled back to observe the rules — but that "pulling" will be ever so gentle.

In a short time, when he was convinced that the transformation was permanent and that there would be time for all of the things he had been kept from enjoying during his earlier years, the elder did return to being a missionary. During his period of breaking the rules it took some faith to believe that he would not overreact and get himself into difficulties so serious we would be required to apply severe punishment. But my faith in him was justified.

I repeat and emphasize that a lot of little things are

much better than one big thing when it comes to discipline. Discipline is a constant effort — many little skirmishes, but few battles. If a teacher or a parent will constantly do the little things, the big things will automatically be taken care of.

CHAPTER TWENTY

The Eyes Have It

When it comes to controlling a child or a class, the eyes have more power than a club has. Expressive, friendly, demanding, appealing, forgiving, commanding—the eyes have it. The direct, unwavering, piercing look has called many a student back to the classroom, leaving broken conversations to be gathered after class and put together in surroundings more appropriate for chatter. The alert and sensitive teacher can discipline a student more effectively with his eyes than the clumsy teacher can ever do with accusations or ultimatums or pressure of any kind.

The eyes of the alert teacher move constantly back and forth across the class, taking in each movement, recording each expression, responding quickly to disinterest or confusion. They read immediately a puzzled expression or sense at once when learning has taken place. Just as the conductor of a symphony orchestra controls a complicated and magnificent organization and yet himself is silent, so the master teacher directs the workings of the class by gesture, inflection, expression, and, most of all, the use of his eyes.

Much of our communication takes place with the eyes. You can look at a person and convey meaning without a word being said. A teacher ought to use his eyes constantly. Class arrangement can help enhance use of this teaching technique.

The Long Room

On one occasion I visited a seminary teacher who was having a discipline problem. I found he was teaching in a long, narrow room in a much-remodeled old building, and this makeshift classroom, pressed into service, was really in no shape to be a classroom. The chalkboard was placed in the center of one of the long walls, with the students stretched out on either side to the narrow walls at the end of the room. They were sitting in three rows, about twelve students to the row, all facing the wall with the blackboard. Those on the ends could see the blackboard only at an angle. The teacher could not possibly look all of the students in the eye at once. He would have to start at one end of the room and move back and forth as he talked. Never did he have more than a third of the class within his direct sight at once.

165

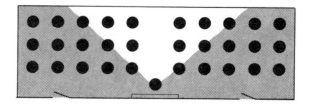

The beginning of the solution was to change the arrangement of the room and simply have the students face the end of the room. Arranged that way, they could be four abreast with nine in a row. The chalkboard was moved to that end of the room, and the teacher could see all of the students at once. That simple move helped solve the discipline problem, for all the students were constantly under the eye of the teacher. There was great improvement in the discipline.

I have noticed that in many of our church buildings, particularly in Relief Society rooms, the chalkboard is placed on the long wall with the chairs set in a semicircle or in long rows two or three deep facing that wall. I find it difficult to teach in such a situation.

Often when I have leadership meetings in such a room I invite the group to rearrange the chairs and put a portable chalkboard at one of the narrow ends of the room so we can work from that end. Then I have everyone in eye contact, and everyone can see the chalkboard, even though some of them may be a little farther away from it than otherwise.

166

I don't care for the informal arrangement of seating in classes. Putting the students in a semicircle or arranging them so the situation is informal and loose and "comfortable" is an invitation for the class to behave that way. In my experience, a more formal arrangement of the class with the informality in procedure is the better way. I am not able to do very well sitting or standing in the middle of a semicircle where I am unable to have everyone in sight all of the time. Others are able enough to control such an informal class, but I need the formality to set the order of discipline.

The Aisle

There is another point a teacher should keep in mind. The best teaching space is directly in front of the teacher, directly in front of the chalkboard, or directly in front of the pulpit. How foolish we are in many of our classrooms, even large classrooms, to arrange the aisle right in the middle. That means that the best teaching space is used for walking but not used at all during the teaching periods. In a large chapel this is not so critical if the teacher or speaker is elevated above the audience. But in a classroom situation, the best teaching space is wasted if the aisle is in the center where otherwise students would be directly visible to and able to see the teacher or speaker.

Please the Eye Also

The classroom, besides being orderly in its arrangement, ought to be neat and orderly in its furnishings and appointments. We tend to have more orderly behavior when we are in orderly surroundings. A teacher can create a comfortable, inviting atmosphere through pictures on the wall, by the way books are arranged on the desk, and by a number of other things. It doesn't help discipline to have a bunch of old manuals stacked in the corner or the scenery from a drama leaning along one wall, and a lot of other things that should be in closets scattered around. It's worth the effort to do something about making the place where we are going to teach as well organized as possible. That's true also of our own homes.

A number of years ago a seminary teacher was assigned to go out to a little community in a ranching area. It was a small high school, and the seminary building was an old one-room frame building that had been neglected for years. No teachers had stayed very long in that community. The students would run them out. The little high school was known for its lack of discipline, and the seminary — which was really not an inviting place — was no better.

The new teacher who was assigned there arrived in the early summer. He knew the history of the problem, so he set about to solve it. The first thing he did was to clean the building up as much as possible and get some fresh paint on it. There wasn't enough money to buy new furnishings, but he did dig around the foundation and plant petunias.

When fall came and the students returned to school, there stood the little frame seminary building painted white, with flowers growing all around it. The teacher had also done everything he could do at the time to make the inside inviting, and the seminary had been transformed. During the year he did one other thing that others would not have thought to do. He bought a canary and hung the cage in the classroom. It was just another touch that added something that needed to be added there.

The teacher taught there for several years and each year made some improvements. He touched the lives of everyone who came into the seminary, and his example with the building soon began to find its influence in the homes and the other little community buildings in the area. He built a little greenhouse and sent flower starts home with the students. To this day he is remembered in that community and in every place to which his students have scattered over the years.

When you as a parent or a teacher need to discipline someone, remember that the eyes are more powerful than a club, more compelling than a loud voice, more persuasive than an action to discipline those whom you are called to teach.

CHAPTER TWENTY-ONE

Ultimatums

The teacher and the parent ofttimes get themselves into a corner by issuing ultimatums: "If you do not do this, I will do such and such." "If you do this, I will do such and such." Sometimes we can be emotional and vigorous and make declarations and threats and give ultimatums that really cannot be fulfilled.

For instance, the ultimatum "If you do not be quiet, we're going to expel you from the class" corners the teacher. If the student doesn't conform, to follow through may be unwise. If a teacher gives a foolish ultimatum to a class (or if we do it to our children), there are perhaps two alternatives: He can carry through with the declaration and thus lose the respect of the students, or if he doesn't carry through with the ultimatum, he will also lose the respect of the students.

It is unwise to give ultimatums! If you make declarations, make them vague. Just talk about measures that can be employed to get cooperation; then you're not forced to save face by taking measures that will not be productive. Keep that in mind as a teacher and as a parent.

It's generally better for the teacher to handle a serious problem by saying, "Robert, I will talk to you later." There is a chance that there may be some justifiable reason for

Robert's behavior. When you talk to him alone about it, you might just learn a valuable lesson from him.

While breaches of deportment almost always happen in public — that is, in the classroom or a family situation — the correcting of them generally can be handled and usually is much better handled privately.

It is helpful for a teacher to know that a student who is a discipline problem ofttimes is a student trying to get attention. You can have better control over such a student if you are indefinite in your disciplinary measures. We have already mentioned that you should not call his name out in class to begin with. In successive steps you should:

1. Stop talking and wait.

2. Observe, without singling out anyone, that "someone" in the class is not cooperating.

3. Look at that "someone" — generally silently. (If you finally call him by name, you are moving into a major encounter. In such encounters the teacher, more frequently than the student, is the loser.)

Indefinite Punishment

A teacher has to be wise in what he threatens to do in order to get cooperation in a class. For instance, if he says, "Robert, if you don't cooperate in class, I'm going to report to your father," that may be no threat at all to Robert. He may know his father doesn't care.

It is much better to say, "If I can't get cooperation, I feel very sad about the measures I will have to employ." In this situation the students invent for themselves the punishment. Usually they will come up with something compelling enough to induce them to change their behavior. Whatever you might choose and express verbally as punishment generally is not as powerful as making the punishment indefinite. A general expression on a vague and undisclosed action is more important in changing behavior than almost any definitely expressed declaration can be.

The Overzealous Student

Another student we should discuss is the one who is too cooperative, the know-it-all, who is overzealous. He can quickly get himself in trouble with his associates by answering every question and being just too smart. He can be a nuisance in a class by monopolizing the time blurting out answers while others are trying to figure them out. In other ways he can distract the teacher's attention from students who do not know the answers. Actually, a teacher has a greater obligation to those who don't know and who seemingly don't seem to be able to find out for themselves than to the other type of student.

When I have taught such a student, I have called him aside, complimented him on his preparation, and given him a special assignment. "You will be my reserve," I have told him. "I'll call you in as the last resort. I'll give the other students an opportunity to respond to the questions. However, if we ever have a question that they can't answer, then I'm going to call on you. I will expect you to have the right answer."

This generally worked very well. Such students were proud of their quiet and unannounced role; it was something of an agreement between them and the teacher. They were helping me teach. They were anxious not to be embarrassed by giving an incorrect answer when called upon as the last resort. It did not seem to inhibit their enthusiasm for study. I called on them just often enough to give them the ego satisfaction of answering. That satisfaction was intensified because they were succeeding after others had failed. I would often look at them with a meaningful glance and occasionally say privately, "I just about had to call on you to get that answer today."

We will discuss elsewhere the use of humor in teaching, but a word about it with respect to discipline. Sometimes a tense situation can be relieved by a teacher who has a sense of humor. "John Jones, if you don't be quiet, I'm going to call your name out before this whole class." Everyone laughs, including John, but the effect is usually enough.

A teacher does better if the students refer to him in terms of respect. In the Church they call him "Brother" and not "Mister." He is aware that students do not need a friend—they have plenty of those. They need a teacher, a counselor, an adviser. They need to reach upward, not outward. This teaching distance that exists between the teacher and his students is always there, although it is crossed frequently from him to them. This teaching distance, this dignity, secures him—his office and his character and his kindness—from trespass by his students. We will speak more of this when we discuss the teacher as a visual aid.

Occasionally in a Sunday School class, a seminary class, or elsewhere, we'll find a youngster who just wants to bait the teacher, to disrupt the class. This is sometimes done by his asking an extraneous question. When this happens, he sometimes can be diverted if the teacher says, "We'll take that up next time if you'd like to bring it up again." Or the teacher might look at him without a smile and say in a serious manner, "I will take up that question with you personally later."

This kind of a problem brings us to a discussion of peer group influences, and that is worthy of a chapter by itself.

CHAPTER TWENTY-TWO

The Peer Group

A teacher should keep in mind the power found in peer group pressure. Young people particularly are conscious of the feelings and attitudes of their associates. They are more concerned about criticism from their associates than they are about being corrected by a teacher. This is a powerful tool and can be successfully handled by a teacher. It is one of the few things I have learned will work on young people who are out of order. If you can bring peer group pressure to bear to accomplish good things, you have a powerful influence. Let the class know you regard each individual so highly that you will not permit any one of them to disrupt the learning for any one or all of them.

If someone in class begins a disturbance and you stop talking, soon the other students will look at the offender and not infrequently will nudge him or tap him or comment to him to let him know that his conduct is unacceptable — not just to the teacher but also to the other members of the class.

Peer group pressure is a powerful thing in discipline and also in the transformation of young people who need help. This influence is used constantly for unworthy purposes.

" . . . In the Attitude of Mocking . . . "

One of the best illustrations in scripture of the serious effects of peer influence is in the eighth chapter of 1 Nephi in which Lehi recounts the dream that he had. It is worth reading carefully. In it Lehi traveled through a dark and dreary waste for the space of many hours and then, after fervent prayer, he came upon a spacious field and beheld a tree whose fruit was desirable to make one happy.

After having tasted the fruit, he "began to be desirous" that his family should partake of it also. He looked around for his family and saw a river, an iron rod extending along it, and a straight and narrow path that came along by the iron rod to the tree where he was standing. He saw a concourse of people pressing forward, and a mist of darkness arose, and many of them were lost. Others pressed forward and caught hold of the end of the iron rod and came forth and partook of the fruit of the tree.

This may well describe the condition of members of the Church. The dream is interpreted in 1 Nephi, 15, wherein Nephi defines the tree as a "representation of the tree of life." Notice in this vision what happened to those who had come along the straight and narrow way, holding the iron rod, having made their way through the mist of darkness, reached their goal, and partaken of the fruit of the tree.

"And after they had partaken of the fruit of the tree they did cast their eyes about as if they were ashamed.

"And I also cast my eyes round about, and beheld, on the other side of the river of water, a great and spacious building; and it stood as it were in the air, high above the earth.

"And it was filled with people, both old and young, both male and female; and their manner of dress was exceeding fine; and they were in the attitude of mocking and pointing their fingers towards those who had come at and were partaking of the fruit.

"And after they had tasted of the fruit they were ashamed, because of those that were scoffing at them; and they fell away into forbidden paths and were lost." (1 Nephi 8:25–28.)

This story illustrates how easily people will change their behavior to win the approval of those around them. Most people, particularly young people, quickly conform to what they feel the desires of the group to be. A wise parent and a wise teacher can often manage this tendency for righteous purposes. Much of the activity in the Church is designed to bring our youth into association with young people who will set high standards and who will expect conformity to principles of righteousness.

Many medicines are made of substances that otherwise are poisonous. Properly compounded and carefully administered, they can have a healing influence. The influence of peers upon young people is something like this. It can be used with healing and redeeming effects by wise parents and teachers.

A Miracle

There was a girl in one seminary class who seemed to be helpless and almost hopeless. I tried to encourage her and draw her out; I sensed that she wanted desperately to belong and to do something. But when she was asked to respond, give a prayer, or read a scripture, she would struggle for a while and then start to cry and return to her seat. There was some sympathy on the part of the class for her, but there were also some students who were often brutal in their comments.

She almost never combed her hair, she had very poor clothing, and she frequently wore mismatched socks, if she wore any at all. If she arrived for class a little early, the chairs on either side of her would almost invariably be empty. If she got to class late, she could sit by someone because that would be the only seat open.

I knew enough about her background to understand why she was the way she was. Her mother was a widow with almost no income.

In that class were the studentbody president of the high school and also a girl who had been elected the beauty queen. Besides being very handsome and intelligent students, they were talented otherwise and involved in many activities.

One day I called the two of them into my office and asked if they would like to perform a miracle. They were interested. I told them some miracles were a little slow in developing, but they were miracles nevertheless. We then talked a little about the girl, and I made assignments. The studentbody president was to smile and speak to her every time he saw her around school. That was all. He didn't have to take her on a date; he didn't have to stop and talk to her; he didn't have to associate beyond that or single her out—merely the happy, encouraging "I think you're great" or "Hello, how are you today?"

The beauty queen accepted the assignment of walking with the girl across the road from the high school to the seminary. That was all. She didn't have to include her in her circle of friends other than to walk to and from the seminary every day. She would simply hurry to catch up with her or slow down to wait for her when they were coming across the street and just talk about whatever she wanted to talk about.

The two of them went about their tasks quietly but enthusiastically, saying not a word to anyone else. The miracle was not long in coming. One day I knew there was something different about the girl. It took me most of the class period to figure out what it was. And then I saw what it was. She had combed her hair that day. That was an event!

Over the next month or two the transformation continued. Our beauty queen became friendly and chatty with her during that time. She could never walk with her alone because she had her own friends following her. And so other girls were included in the group, and soon the girl was surrounded for those few minutes each day with the most popular girls at school.

There are so many interesting details that could be related about the miracle. Our wallflower transformed herself, went to college, found good employment, married in the temple, and those who know her would never believe the ugly duckling of her youth.

All this detail is provided to make this point: What good would it have done for me to walk with her from school to seminary every day? What good would it have done if I had smiled and said "Hello" as I saw her around school? The answers are obvious. It took those of her peer group to set in motion the transformation. A wise teacher can bring this influence to bear to accomplish much good.

A young person does not begin to smoke cigarettes because he likes the taste of them. He begins to smoke because he wants to belong somewhere. This great desire to belong and fraternize can be used to promote righteousness among young people. A wise teacher has it at his disposal. A single sentence will ofttimes bring this influence to bear on a student who insists on getting attention by disturbing the class. He wants attention and approval from his associates — not necessarily from the teacher.

One time I had gone unsuccessfully through all of the usual things to try to settle down an "attention-getter" so we could proceed with the classwork. He enjoyed occasional approval of his associates for his sometimes humorous interruptions. One day during a moment of scriptural importance his comment destroyed the spirit of the occasion, and it was useless to proceed. In exasperation I turned to the class and said with some disappointment, "Do we have to put up with things like this?" I was surprised at the reaction. There was some low-key growling about him, and he found himself faced with the intense resentment of his peers, not their approval. That's all it took. There was a dramatic change in his behavior. Never again was there an outburst in the class, and before long an opportunity arose that gave him a chance to win their approval by well-prepared participation with special personal help.

A teacher should never overlook the power of peer group pressure. In the social structure of young people it can be destructive, but a wise teacher can put that power to positive use. It has to be managed subtly, but it is a remarkably powerful tool in encouraging good behavior.

The Fear of Man

The importance of carefully considering peer influence is attested by many scriptures, including the following:

"Thou shalt not follow a multitude to do evil; neither shalt thou speak in a cause to decline after many to wrest judgment." (Exodus 23:2.)

"And Saul said unto Samuel, I have sinned: for I have transgressed the commandment of the Lord, and thy words; because I feared the people, and obeyed their voice." (1 Samuel 15:24.)

"The fear of man bringeth a snare: but whoso putteth his trust in the Lord shall be safe." (Proverbs 29:25.)

"For do I now persuade men, or God? or do I seek to please men? for if I yet pleased men, I should not be the servant of Christ." (Galatians 1:10.)

"But as we were allowed of God to be put in trust with

the gospel, even so we speak; not as pleasing men, but God, which trieth our hearts." (1 Thessalonians 2:4.)

"For the time speedily shall come that all churches which are built up to get gain, and all those who are built up to get power over the flesh, and those who are built up to become popular in the eyes of the world, and those who seek the lusts of the flesh and the things of the world, and to do all manner of iniquity; yea, in fine, all those who belong to the kingdom of the devil are they who need fear, and tremble, and quake; they are those who must be brought low in the dust; they are those who must be consumed as stubble; and this is according to the words of the prophet." (1 Nephi 22:23.)

"But behold, it is to get gain, to be praised of men, yea, and that ye might get gold and silver. And ye have set your hearts upon the riches and the vain things of this world, for the which ye do murder, and plunder, and steal, and bear false witness against your neighbor, and do all manner of iniquity." (Helaman 7:21.)

"And behold, how oft you have transgressed the commandments and the laws of God, and have gone on in the persuasions of men." (D&C 3:6.)

"And now I command you, my servant Joseph, to repent and walk more uprightly before me, and to yield to the persuasions of men no more." (D&C 5:21.)

"Behold, I say unto you, David, that you have feared man and have not relied on me for strength as you ought." (D&C 30:1.)

"But with some I am not well pleased, for they will not open their mouths, but they hide the talent which I have given unto them, because of the fear of man. Wo unto such, for mine anger is kindled against them." (D&C 60:2.)

"Therefore, hold on thy way, and the priesthood shall remain with thee; for their bounds are set, they cannot pass. Thy days are known, and thy years shall not be numbered less; therefore, fear not what man can do, for God shall be with you forever and ever." (D&C 122:9.)

Peer group pressure *is* a powerful tool. It can be used destructively or constructively. The wise teacher will be alert for opportunities to use it in a positive way in his classroom and in helping change for the better the lives of his students.

CHAPTER TWENTY-THREE

Feed My Sheep

Surely you have noticed how a group of noisy, unsettled children of all ages will quickly settle down and be quiet and well-ordered once you start to feed them. Pandemonium stops on a half-note, and the only sound is a little clinking from the silverware.

The easiest way to have control over those whom you teach is to teach them something—to feed them. Be well prepared and have an abundance of subject matter organized and ready to serve. There is no substitute for this preparation. As long as you are feeding the students well, few discipline problems will occur.

Most people want to learn. There is no better evidence for the goodness of man than his desire to learn the principles of the gospel of Jesus Christ. He delights in being instructed from the scriptures; he delights in pure revelation flowing into his mind as they are unfolded to him. There is great nourishment in the scriptures. The pure gospel is the best influence in discipline that any teacher can use. The substance of the meal is critical.

If you are teaching a class of children or adults, they will not return with any enthusiasm unless they are being taught something. They must learn something to want to return. They will come willingly, even eagerly, to a class or a family home evening in which they are fed.

182

Grain in a Bucket

If you have a horse in a large pasture, it is tiresome if you must corner him in the field every time you want to ride. If he's not responsive, you'd better have a long lariat. There is, however, a much better way. It is ordinary procedure to take a bucket of grain each time you catch the horse and to gently coax him to the grain. Then, as he comes for the reward, you slip the bridle gently over his head.

Most horsemen have had the experience of wanting to catch a horse when there was no grain handy. An empty bucket will do, of course, or just put a little sand in the bucket and shake it. The horse will come running—that is, he will come once or perhaps twice. After that, even if there is grain in the bucket, it may be difficult to catch him.

It is essential that those you teach be fed, that they be taught something. Each time they come there should be at least one thought, one idea, one inspiration that is theirs for having been in the class. It can be a little thought, an ordinary one—in fact, the more fundamental it is, the more you have accomplished.

In the seminary program many teenagers attend seminary class before going to high school. These classes are held early, some of them at six o'clock in the morning. It is almost against human nature for a teenager to get out of bed on a dark and dismal winter day to go to a class to be taught religion. Yet they do it by the tens of thousands. Why? Because they hunger to learn about the gospel.

The Wrong Kind of Food

A teacher in Canada taught us a lesson about this. She was getting only part of the young people to attend seminary, and she wanted to attract the others. After a long period of planning she had a special breakfast one day at the early morning seminary class. The next morning she repeated with a different theme and a different menu and decorations. So it went through the week. To her surprise, at the end of the week she had not more students, but fewer. They would not get up early to be entertained. She gave up entertaining and returned to teaching.

Students will (and they did) come in increasing numbers when they are taught. After hearing about the teacher's experience, we had a saying: "If you want to close an early morning seminary class, have a party every morning!" Young people come to be taught the principles of the gospel, but they will not respond for entertainment.

"I" Trouble

One reason many teachers in the Church have such a hard time sharing the gospel is that they have acquired it for the wrong purpose and have stored it away in their own minds in the wrong kind of packages.

When we attend a sacrament meeting, for instance, and hear a gospel truth expounded, we may be touched by it and react in our minds something like this: "That is a wonderful truth. I am so glad I was here. That will do *me* a great deal of good. *I* will have to remember that and use it in *my* life. *My* life will be much better because *I* have been here. What a privilege it has been for *me* to come to this meeting. *I* will come back to sacrament meeting again. *I* will go to the other meetings because *I* need all of the gospel *I* can get. It is such a joy to learn things to make *me* better."

Do you notice the "I" trouble in that attitude? There is only one person involved; it is all first person singular.

How much easier it is to learn if we carry this spirit instead: "What an important gospel principle! How grateful I am to have heard it! I can help *so many people* with it. *My children* need to know it. I can teach it to my *Sunday School class*."

184

If we have others in mind, we store the knowledge away in our minds in a different way than if it is all *me* or *I*. We know we will use it and why. It is much more easily recalled. We can add to it much more easily. Then we are not left without resources when we have an opportunity to teach either our own children or others in the Church.

There is a lesson that few members of the Church ever seem to learn. The lesson is this: We are not merely receptacles for the gospel; we are also conveyers of it. This idea is so important.

It is difficult to give away something you have purchased for your own use. However, if you acquire it to give, you soon are able to do so, even to unwilling receivers.

This principle has application for students as well as for teachers.

Are you teaching in such a way that the students are gathering the information for themselves alone, or with the thought that they can serve?

One of the big problems in the mission field is that young missionaries arrive with basically a selfish motivation. "*I* will go on *my* mission. It will do *me* good. *I* will have great benefits from it. *I* will be able to travel. *I* will be able to get things that *I* want to get in *my* life."

An obligation of the teacher is to be unselfishly interested in others and to teach his students to be unselfish also. That is what was meant earlier by the instruction for every teacher to be a conveyer of the truths of the gospel, not just a receptacle for them.

Nothing is truly ours until we can give it away. That is true with property; unless we hold title to it, it is not our legal privilege to give it away. In a similar way the gospel is not ours until we first hold title to it—until we know it. Then we can give it away, and in return we have a more certain title to it. The process for giving it away is

ARE YOUR LESSONS...

TURNED IN?

WHAT WILL MY
PRIESTHOOD
DO FOR ME?

WHAT WILL I
GAIN THROUGH
ATTENDING
CHURCH MEETINGS?

HOW WILL
A MISSION
HELP ME?

HOW WILL I
BENEFIT BY
PAYING MY
TITHING?

WHAT BLESSINGS
WILL I RECEIVE
THROUGH BEING
HONEST?

WHAT HAPPINESS
WILL I RECEIVE
FROM A TEMPLE
MARRIAGE?

OR OUT?

HOW DOES MY PRIEST-
HOOD PERMIT ME TO
BUILD THE KINGDOM
OF GOD?

HOW WILL MY ATTEND-
ANCE AT CHURCH
MEETINGS BENEFIT
OTHERS SPIRITUALLY?

HOW WILL MY TEMPLE
MARRIAGE PROVIDE A
BETTER HOME FOR
MY CHILDREN?

HOW CAN I BUILD THE
KINGDOM THROUGH
TITHES & OFFERINGS?

HOW DO I BLESS
OTHERS THROUGH
BEING HONEST?

HOW CAN I BE OF DY-
NAMIC SERVICE TO
OTHERS ON A MISSION?

teaching. A teacher must know this; then he will structure his lessons so as to develop the same attitude in his students.

If we do not gather gospel facts with the thought of sharing them, we store them in our minds in a different way and they become less valuable to us. It is so much easier to gather them with a desire to give them away in simple terms so that all can understand them.

It is interesting to observe talented, able, well-endowed young men and women arrive in the mission field with sharp and alert minds, well-framed physical bodies, impressive appearance, enthusiasm, and determination to preach the gospel. But even with all these talents, they cannot succeed until they are humbled to the point where they will do it the Lord's way. They must learn to forget themselves and their own selfish concerns and determine that it is not *"my* mission"; it is *"His* mission." Let me cite some examples.

Boxes of Books

When I was a mission president, my assistants and I occasionally checked apartments. Missionaries sometimes have the tendency not to keep their apartments clean, and so every few months we would stop and make some inspections. (This procedure had an interesting side effect. Through the missionary "grapevine," word would be passed on, and though we personally inspected only one or two apartments, all were cleaned up!)

In St. Johnsbury, Vermont, I was surprised one morning at about ten o'clock to find that when we knocked at a door, expecting to make contact with the landlord, an elder answered. He and his companion should have been out tracting.

I said, "Where's your companion?"

"He's studying in the bedroom."

The companion was reading *The Rise and Fall of the Roman Empire*. I had read the book, so I commented on it to him, asking, "How will it help you in missionary work?"

He replied something to the effect that the more you know, the better you can teach. I asked how many other books he had read. He was sitting on an old, high, four-poster New England bed. He reached down, took hold of the bedspread, and lifted it up so I could see several boxes of books under the bed. He had read them all.

"Where did you get all these books?" I inquired. He indicated that he had a relative who was in the publishing business and that he automatically received all of the books that came off the press relating to the Church. After some conversation I instructed him to box up all the books and send them home. I also instructed him to write to his relative and tell him to send him no more books. For the rest of his mission he would need only the scriptures and one or two other books we prescribed.

He vigorously protested, insisting that he was learning the gospel and that the more he read, the more he'd be able to teach. I tried to reason with him and finally, with some impatience, I said, "Elder, if you keep on this course, I'll tell you what will happen to you. You will come to know about many things relating to the gospel and much of it will be useless to you. You will be the kind of individual who goes to a Sunday School class to disturb the class and irritate the teacher by demonstrating your 'much knowledge.'

"You will have more factual knowledge than most of the teachers you will meet in the Church. You will want to correct them in every class. If ever a mistake is made, whether it be by a Sunday School teacher, a bishop, a counselor, or a quorum officer, you will correct it. Many mistakes will be made, because in the Church we are all learning as we grow. You will not be called to positions because your arrogant, know-it-all attitude will disqualify you. You will go through life wondering why you were passed over, blaming the Church and those in it, and eventually shriveling up spiritually.

"Your problem is selfishness. You are more interested in what will happen to *you* on your mission than what you can do for others. You already know far more than you need to know to introduce investigators to the gospel and bring them to the point where conversion can take place. Remember, elder, this is not *your* mission. It is *His* mission. You will never gain the most important eternal things by the course you are following. You and your companion need to be out now knocking on doors, imparting the milk of the gospel. The meat can come later, and you can learn it later."

The elder recognized what he had been doing and sent the books home. There would be time for that kind of study later in life, and I assume that he is now somewhere in the Church possessing an ever-greater knowledge of the factual things concerning the Church and its doctrines, imparting in a gentle way the basic principles to lift many around him.

Feed the Flocks

An important Scripture for a teacher to consider is the following from the Old Testament:

> Thus saith the Lord God unto the shepherds; Woe be to the shepherds of Israel that do feed themselves! should not the shepherds feed the flocks?
> Ye eat the fat, and ye clothe you with the wool, ye kill them that are fed: but ye feed not the flock.
> . . . my flock became meat to every beast of the field, because there was no shepherd, neither did my shepherds search for my flock, but the shep-

herd *fed themselves,* and *fed not my flock.* (Ezekiel 34:2–3, 8. Italics added.)

If we learn in order to serve, to give to others, and to "feed" others, we will find the acquisition of subject matter much easier. We then are trying not to glorify ourselves, but to teach our own children or others in the Church. Then there will come to us the full meaning of this scripture: "He that findeth his life shall lose it: and he that loseth his life for my sake shall find it." (Matthew 10:39.)

We will also come to know the meaning of the scripture, "Treasure up in your minds continually the words of life, and it shall be given you in the very hour that portion that shall be meted unto every man." (D&C 84:85; see also D&C 100:6 and Matthew 10:19–20.)

Our obligation is to share the gospel in everyday life, as parents, as missionaries, as teachers in the Church organizations. If you keep this constantly in mind, you will learn in order to give. It will then be so much easier to learn how to feed His sheep.

CHAPTER TWENTY-FOUR

The Glory of God Is Intelligence

 W hile it is important that the teacher be competent in his subject, this, as in all things, must be in balance. Teachers, particularly those who are inexperienced or just beginning, often are looking for something new or exciting to teach. They go afield to find something startling to teach when a knowledge of the basic fundamentals applied and reapplied and applied yet again to life's situations could be most important to the students.

Wise parents are constantly reteaching simple things, going over very elementary lessons, rehearsing them over and over again. This is one reason they are effective teachers.

Correct Teaching in the Beginning

One of the reasons we have difficulty teaching some elementary things is that we don't take time in the beginning to teach them correctly. It is important to help the student organize his learning and see it through from the beginning to the end in proper sequence so he can put it all together. Sometimes we teach bits and pieces but never organize these pieces on a meaningful background so the student knows they fit.

For instance, a little boy comes home, throws open the

door, takes off his coat, throws it on the floor, takes off his cap, throws it on the floor, and goes to his bedroom. An exasperated parent will tell him to close the door, pick up his cap, and pick up his coat. After an unpleasant encounter, he does so. The next day he throws open the door, throws his cap on the floor, throws his coat on the floor, and goes to his room. The lesson is repeated. It may be repeated many times, and the youngster still will not change his procedure.

There is a better way. The parent could call the child from his room, have him put on his coat, button it up, put on his cap, and go outside—then go through the whole procedure properly. Under supervision, the youngster could be required to open the door, come in, close the door, take off his cap, hang it up, take off his coat, hang it up, and go to his room. Then the lesson is finished. It can be half-taught a dozen times and still be unlearned, or fully taught once or twice at the most and then it is accomplished.

A number of years ago the dean of education at a large university in California spoke at the inauguration of a new president for Brigham Young University on the subject "The Glory of God Is Intelligence." He recited the following interesting experience:

> While I was an undergraduate at Columbia University, there was a man in attendance already known as the perennial student. He had been left a modest but adequate bequest with the stipulation that it should continue as long as he was engaged in collegiate study; thereafter the income was to be given to charity. When I returned for graduate work twelve years later, he was still there and he remained a student until he died just a few years ago.
>
> It was said that he had been granted every degree offered by Columbia. He had taken practically every course. He was a man who was the epitome

of erudition. No field of knowledge was foreign to him. He was probably more widely read than the best of his professors. He was a cultured gentleman. But, he was not a truly intelligent man.

Certainly such intelligence as he possessed was not that which is the Glory of God. Inherently he was selfish. He never married. He was without ambition or influence. He was a joke to the students and a freak to the faculty. He knew a prodigious lot, but his real index of intelligence was low, no matter what his I.Q. (Address delivered by Dr. Edwin A. Lee at the inauguration of Howard S. McDonald as president of Brigham Young University, Provo, Utah, November 14, 1945.)

The Student Is Most Important

An example of the knowledge-centered teacher is well illustrated with a quotation from Elder John A. Widtsoe. Dr. Widtsoe was a great teacher and an Apostle whose book *In a Sunlit Land* is a great treatise on teaching. Many insights are to be found in it.

> Within the last few decades a vicious practice has grown up in academic circles. Every beginning student is looked upon as a possible candidate for an advanced academic degree. Consequently, the beginning courses of a subject are crowded with difficult, remote problems. For example, the first course in chemistry gives endless time to the mathematics of the laws of Boyle and Avogadro, until the freshman loses interest in the whole subject. Were the fascinating descriptive parts of the science taught first, with laboratory work, a successful return to the laws now heavily stressed might be made. If students are thought fit to enter a class, it should be so taught as to be within easy understanding of the students and taught in such a manner that the student will thoroughly enjoy learning the new facts presented. A professor who boasts of failing many of his students, should, were ed-

ucation held in right esteem, be quickly dismissed from service. By his own testimony he is a poor teacher, out of sympathy with human life and understanding. Learning new truths is an exhilarating experience and a good teacher awakens that joy. (*In a Sunlit Land,* 1953, p. 90.)

When Elder Widtsoe was president of Utah State University, he had something of a contest with the faculty, which he described in the following words:

It was equally difficult in many cases to make faculty members understand that educational institutes are founded and maintained for the benefit of the students. There are teachers who believe that they or their departments are of first consequence. As I have previously said, in many a science, the beginning courses are so taught as if the whole class were intending to become candidates for the Ph.D. degree in that subject. Students fall out in despair. Such teachers, if indeed that noble title may be applied to them, pride themselves on the number they fail. To such faculty members it was often necessary to speak very plainly. The high standard of education means many things. To the men who delighted in failing their students, thinking that thereby they were demonstrating their own high scholarship, it took some time to make them understand that a good teacher does such work as to enable his students to pass, with ordinarily diligence. He is a poor teacher who confuses his students or fails to make his subject interesting. (*In a Sunlit Land,* p. 150.)

It is easy for a teacher to develop an arrogant attitude that he is the most important person in the class. Always we must remember that the student is the most important. "He that is the greatest among you shall be your servant" (Matthew 23: 11) is what the Lord said. The purpose of all that relates to teaching is to benefit the student. Sometimes teachers and administrators lose track of that.

I am reminded of the day that I was to defend my master's thesis at Utah State University. I, of course, was anxious, even frightened, and felt very inadequate. The committee chairman opened those services with a treatise on how fortunate I was to be granted an audience. He explained that I was being especially accommodated and that it was a great privilege for me to attend school. I began to feel much out of place, like an interloper or intruder.

One of the other committee members, Dr. Wilford W. Richards, then director of the institute of religion there, sensed my anxiety. At the proper moment he agreed with the chairman of the committee and said, "Yes, Mr. Packer is very fortunate to be able to study here, and really, it is quite essential that we have him. You know, it would be a little difficult to operate a school without students, wouldn't it?" The chairman took the chastisement; the atmosphere changed; and we proceeded with the defense of my thesis, which incidentally was entitled "An Evaluation of the Teaching of Jesus in Terms of Selected Principles of Education."

A Notetaker

A teacher is, of course, always alert for new subject matter, and an alert teacher must be a good notetaker. Things seem to move in and out of our minds so quickly, and lesson ideas come in so many places. Once they are in your mind, be sure to jot them down. Then you've captured them and can have them as your resource for as long as you teach. Many illustrations and experiences have gone by the wayside because the teacher didn't take notes. Sometimes you can remember something of the incident, but not some names and places that would make it usable; therefore, make sure you keep notes.

There are a number of plans for underlining scriptures. They vary somewhat and should suit the individual. The important thing is to underline them and make marginal notes of some kind so you can find them again.

I almost never read a borrowed book. I don't like to read borrowed books because I don't want to read a book without underlining things I want to remember. Since one doesn't underline someone else's book, I feel that if a book is worth reading, it is worth owning. The exception, of course, is in the library, and there a longer process of taking notes is necessary.

So underline your books and make your notes while you're thinking about it. I don't know how many hours I've spent going back to try to locate something I could have found very quickly if I had regularly followed this procedure. I do much better now than I did before.

A good file drawer with some folders for your notes and pictures and other resource materials gathered over the years is invaluable. I frequently find myself going through files and pulling out materials that I haven't used for twenty years, which fill an immediate, pressing need. Meetinghouse libraries throughout the Church have a filing system for information that is useful, and it can be adapted on an individual basis for your own teaching resource material.

Stay on the Track

If you are called to teach a Sunday School class or a priesthood quorum, it is wise to stay close to the outlined lesson. Ordinarily sufficient material is given if properly illustrated, and the references studied and cited, to more than fill the class period allotted—particularly if points in the manual are illustrated with real-life situations of your own.

There is good reason for the Brethren over the years to have counseled the people to leave the mysteries alone. There are those who dig deeply to find things that in some

197

cases may be true but are not essential to the salvation of any mortal individual. How much better that we teach generously all who need to know the basic principles of the gospel.

I cite two leaders of the Church to sustain the idea that after all is said and done, when teaching in the Church, the scriptures themselves are the basic subject matter. President J. Reuben Clark, Jr., said:

> Spiritual truths are to be found and are governed and controlled by the revelations of our Heavenly Father as contained in the scriptures and in inspired utterances of the prophets. Spiritual truths are your field as teachers of the revealed word of God under the restored gospel, and as teachers you have none or little concern with temporal truths; although, as President Joseph F. Smith said, "There never was and never will be any conflict between truth as revealed by the Lord to his servants the prophets and truth revealed by him to the scientist who makes his discoveries through his research and studies." And Brother Brigham proclaimed the same doctrine.
>
> I trust I may not be considered either unjust or unkind if I suggest that probably few of us are sufficiently trained in the temporal truths to be able to teach them as gospel truths to the students who come before us. We should remember this. . . .
>
> You, as teachers, have the right to think and speculate regarding temporal truths and whether or not you believe or disbelieve thereon, but you may not teach them to your students as spiritual truths save only where the Lord has revealed the ultimate truth on the matters you are discussing. And I am sure you will wish to be very cautious when you undertake that position. We must always remember that we are not scientists but are teachers of scriptural, spiritual truths, and when we advance temporal truths and our view thereon, which should be seldom done, we should make it clear

that we are speaking merely our own opinion. As to spiritual truths, we should be almost equally careful because so often a given paragraph, particularly if wrenched from its text, may mean one thing to one man and another thing to another, and a third thing to still another. This will particularly be true as to all matters in which the Lord has revealed his knowledge definitely for our understandings. (Excerpts from talk given June 17, 1958, at Brigham Young University.)

President Joseph Fielding Smith said: "So far as the philosophy and wisdom of the world are concerned, they mean nothing unless they conform to the revealed word of God. Any doctrine, whether it comes in the name of religion, science, philosophy, or whatever it may be, if it is in conflict with the revealed word of the Lord, will fail. It may appear plausible. It may be put before you in language that appeals and which you may not be able to answer. It may appear to be established by evidence that you cannot controvert, but all you need to do is to abide your time. Time will level all things. You will find that every doctrine, every principle, no matter how universally believed, if not in accord with the divine word of the Lord to his servants, will perish. Nor is it necessary for us to stretch the word of the Lord, in a vain attempt to make it conform to these theories and teachings. The word of the Lord shall not pass away unfulfilled, but these false doctrines and theories will all fail. Truth, and only truth, will remain when all else has perished." (General Conference address, October 1952.)

In 1954 Elder Harold B. Lee was assigned by the First Presidency and the Council of the Twelve to teach the seminary teachers for a summer. The message he repeated over and over again during those remarkably stimulating class periods was simply, "Resolve toward that which is true." He explained that when we are a little in doubt, we

199

should resolve toward that which we feel *ought* to be true, always looking for that which is right.

Years ago two teachers on the faculty of one of the large institutes of religion were both talented in their classroom procedures, and both enjoyed a large registration of students. One teacher, however, was always embroiled in controversy. The complaint would be oft-coming, and not without some foundation, that his teachings were destructive in faith. He took the position (and there is much to recommend it) that he was teaching alert, inquiring college students, and there must be freedom to explore and analyze all problems. Often they spent the class periods contesting issues that were very touchy and open to much speculation. After careful study, we were firmly convinced that although he was popular, his teaching did not foster faith. Indeed, it raised doubts.

The other teacher, in the same building and likewise popular with the students, seemed to consistently stabilize them. Faith was the product of his effort.

I sat through classes of both of these teachers. The second teacher was no more restrictive than the first. He was willing to discuss any question an alert, inquiring university student wanted to bring up. He would discuss the main channel of the question or readily be diverted up any side canyons. He talked just as freely about the same issues as the first teacher. The result of his teaching, however, was faith, whereas the first teacher left his students unsettled and doubting. It took some careful analysis to determine the difference between them, and it was a very simple difference.

Building Faith

The second teacher concluded every class period with a testimony — not always a formal, sacrament meeting-type testimony, but there was always a message at the end of his lessons. Quite often, of course, the lesson would conclude in the middle of the discussion, and the students would be left to ponder on and wrestle with the effects of the discussion sometimes for several days or a week until the new class period convened. He would simply say, "Now, we haven't been able to complete this discussion, and before you leave I want you to keep one thing in mind. When we've found all we need to find about this subject, you will come to know as I know that God lives and that He directs this church and kingdom and that He sustains a prophet of God who is our leader."

Or he would say, "While you are thinking about this during the week, keep in mind the certain truth that God is our Heavenly Father, that He loves us, and that we can come to know that as perhaps the most important part of the knowledge we gain. I know that and I want you to come to know that even better than I know it, if possible."

Learn from Your Students

In preparing subject matter and preparing oneself as a teacher, one must always be learning. From whom should he learn? What is untoward about learning from his students? This applies particularly to parents. Parents learn infinitely more from their children than the children ever learn from their parents. That is the great privilege of parenthood. Let me recite a lesson I learned from one of our children.

Several years ago we had a cow ready to calve. I had not been home in daylight hours for several weeks. One day before catching a plane for a conference, I went out to see the cow. She was in trouble. I called the veterinarian, who came immediately and looked at her. He tested her and said, "She has swallowed a wire, and it has punctured her heart. She will be dead before the day is over."

The next day the calf was to come. The cow was important to our economy. I asked the veterinarian if he could do anything, and he said he could take some measures, "but it will likely be useless—money down the drain." After asking, "What will it cost me?" I told him to go ahead.

The next morning the calf was born, but the cow was lying down gasping. I called the vet again, thinking the calf might need some attention. He looked the cow over and said she would be dead within an hour or so. I went to the house, got the telephone directory, copied down the number of an animal by-products company, put it on the hook by the phone, and told my wife to call them to come and get the cow later in the day.

We had our family prayer before I left for the plane. Our little boy was praying, and in the middle of his prayer—after he said all that he usually said, such as, "Bless daddy that he won't get hurt in his travels, bless us at school," and so on—he started to pray with deep feeling. He said, "Heavenly Father, please bless Bossy so that she will get to be all right."

While I was in California I remembered that prayer, and when the subject of prayer came up in a meeting, I told of the incident, saying, "I am glad he prayed that way, because he will learn something. He will mature and he will learn that you do not get everything you pray for just by asking. There is a lesson to be learned."

And truly there was—but it was I who learned it, not my son, because when I got home Sunday night Bossy had "got to be all right." And it was the father who had learned the lesson about faith and prayer as much as, if not more than, the son.

CHAPTER TWENTY-FIVE

Parables

Ine of the few instances when the Lord answered a question directly is recorded as follows:

> And the disciples came, and said unto him, Why speakest thou unto them in parables?
>
> He answered and said unto them, Because it is given unto you to know the mysteries of the kingdom of heaven, but to them it is not given.
>
> For whosoever hath, to him shall be given, and he shall have more abundance: but whosoever hath not, from him shall be taken away even that he hath.
>
> Therefore speak I to them in parables: because they seeing see not: and hearing they hear not, neither do they understand.
>
> And in them is fulfilled the prophecy of Esaias, which saith, By hearing ye shall hear, and shall not understand; and seeing ye shall see, and shall not perceive:
>
> For this people's heart is waxed gross, and their ears are dull of hearing, and their eyes they have closed; lest at any time they should see with their eyes, and hear with their ears, and should understand with their heart, and should be converted, and I should heal them.

But blessed are your eyes, for they see; and your ears, for they hear.

For verily I say unto you, that many prophets and righteous men have desired to see those things which ye see, and have not seen them; and to hear those things which ye hear, and have not heard them. (Matthew 13:10–17.)

Representing a Real-Life Situation

In the four Gospels in the New Testament are recorded thirty-six parables that the Lord used. With a little resourcefulness, all of us as teachers can use this technique. It is simply the process of developing, creating, or inventing an imaginary situation that represents a real-life situation. For some reason, it is used very little. This is unfortunate, because it is an easy way to drive home an otherwise difficult lesson. When I say an easy way, that is comparatively speaking. It takes work and imagination and resourcefulness to create a parable, but great profit comes from the time expended when the results are considered.

The Savior related to the experiences of His listeners by suggesting they consider (meditate upon or observe) the lilies of the field (Matthew 6:28; Luke 12:27) and the ravens (Luke 12:24), or behold (think over a thing in their minds) the fowls of the air (Matthew 6:26). Then He proceeded to compare the Lord's concern for these with His concern for His children (application). Parables or illustrations might appropriately be introduced by using "consider" or "behold" as well as "suppose" or "imagine."

A teacher has to have a good "supposer" or a good imagination. Once this is developed, illustrations will be available on every hand.

Not infrequently the Lord concluded His parables with a question, which encouraged His listeners to ponder in their minds the meaning He intended for the parables.

The parables and stories of the Lord have great meaning, but the teacher who repeats them or the student who listens to them must remember to use the great power of the human mind and project himself above the literal. For instance, He said, "The kingdom of heaven is like unto a net." Well, if you want to be positively literal, it isn't. A net, as one of my students once said, is just a bunch of holes held together with string. And if you get too literal, you will find not much to compare a net and the kingdom of heaven. But it isn't the net that's important in the illustration. That's just a stepping-stone. It is just a reference; it is just a beginning place.

For All Ages

A student can draw from the teachings of the Lord in a measure equal to that which he brings to it. That is why any of the great illustrations He used are useful in teaching Primary and in illustrating to tiny minds principles that they will come to understand in a greater measure later in life. Likewise the same parable or the same story can be the subject of a lesson in the Gospel Doctrine class in Sunday School or in the high priests quorum, to be wrestled by venerable senior members of the Church, still drawing lessons and instructions and meaning by association with other things they have learned in life.

There is no ideal age at which each or any of the illustrations might be used. They are good for every age and any age. They never become outdated. They were meaningful in Palestine in the meridian of time; they were powerful in the Middle Ages; they were necessary at the turn of the century; they are vital to us now; and they will be useful as the century turns again and will be important to each of us wherever we are then, on this side of the veil or beyond it.

The Book of Mormon has numerous examples of the

use of symbolism. Particularly good examples of this are Lehi's dream of the tree of life (1 Nephi 8) and Nephi's vision of the same thing (1 Nephi 11 and 12).

Another good example of symbolism in the Book of Mormon is the comparison of the house of Israel unto an olive-tree. This symbolism is used extensively in Jacob, chapters 5 and 6. The following quotations indicate how the explanation of the symbol reinforces with the student the concept to be learned.

> Behold, I say unto you, that the house of Israel was compared unto an olive-tree, by the Spirit of the Lord which was in our fathers; and behold are we not broken off from the house of Israel, and are we not a branch of the house of Israel?
>
> And now, the thing which our father meaneth concerning the grafting in of the natural branches through the fulness of the Gentiles, is, that in the latter days, when our seed shall have dwindled in unbelief, yea, for the space of many years, and many generations after the Messiah shall be manifested in the body unto the children of men, then shall the fulness of the gospel of the Messiah come unto the Gentiles, and from the Gentiles unto the remnant of our seed—
>
> And at that day shall the remnant of our seed know that they are of the house of Israel, and that they are the covenant people of the Lord; and then shall they know and come to the knowledge of their forefathers, and also to the knowledge of the gospel of their Redeemer, which was ministered unto their fathers by him; wherefore, they shall come to the knowledge of their Redeemer and the very points of his doctrine, that they may know how to come unto him and be saved.
>
> And then at that day will they not rejoice and give praise unto their everlasting God, their rock and their salvation? Yea, at that day, will they not receive the strength and nourishment from the true

vine? Yea, will they not come unto the true fold of God? (1 Nephi 15:12–16.)

O then, my beloved brethren, come unto the Lord, the Holy One. Remember that his paths are righteous. Behold, the way for man is narrow, but it lieth in a straight course before him, and the keeper of the gate is the Holy One of Israel; and he employeth no servant there; and there is none other way save it be by the gate; for he cannot be deceived, for the Lord God is his name. (Jacob in 2 Nephi 9:41.)

Teachers who use the parables and imagery their students can understand find greater meaning is imparted. Gospel principles can come alive if they are related to the everyday experiences of the hearers.

CHAPTER TWENTY-SIX

The Destroyers

I have in my office a repro-
duction of the Nike, or Winged Victory of Samothrace. The
original sculpture is in the Louvre in Paris. I keep the
reproduction in my office to remind me of a lesson I learned
once.

A number of years ago I was appointed supervisor of
seminaries for the Church. I moved hesitantly and ner-
vously among the men, most of whom were senior to me
in years, in service, in academic achievement, and, I
thought, in almost every other way. It was my responsibility to supervise teaching. Someone reminded me that
supervision contemplated superior vision, and it was my
responsibility to provide it. This did not add measurably
to my assurance.

In the first few months in that assignment, I attended
a meeting of seminary and institute men who were holding
inservice training sessions. I was happy to sit with the
teachers as they were instructed by one of their number.

One teacher, in making his presentation, thought it
was necessary to play the role of the debunker. He vigorously criticized the history of the Church and some of
the traditions that have been established. He listed a number of things that he alleged, from his careful, scientific

inquiry, just weren't so. His words impugned the characters of some of the early leaders of the Church, and perhaps some of the present ones. He was presenting this material, he said, to make the teachers think! "We've got to wake up and be more critical and selective."

The spirit of his presentation did little to engender faith. As he closed his presentation, one wondered what to believe. It was then announced that I would give a few closing remarks. I felt like a green recruit among veterans of a great campaign and was praying earnestly for some inspiration to know what to say to make the meeting come out all right.

The Inspiration of the Sculptor

For some reason there came into my mind a picture of the Winged Victory statue. I remember as a boy in elementary school seeing a picture of it, probably in a history book. I remember looking at it and thinking how beautiful it was. Over the intervening years I did not remember paying much attention to it, though I am sure, because of its fame, I had seen many pictures of it.

Then the inspiration came. I told the teachers about the statue. I described it to them and told them I remembered seeing a picture of it when I was a boy.

"The statue has endured many things," I said. "The head is gone; both arms are gone; the wings are chipped; there are cracks and scrapes here and there; a foot is missing; yet it is regarded as probably the single most valuable piece of artwork existing today. Why?

"Among other things it is hard rock—adamant, undeniable, irrefutable proof that somewhere, sometime, someone with supreme artistic genius took some stone and with his tools fashioned this statue. With all that has been chipped away, with all of the flaws, that truth remains. There is enough to be a testimony of the inspiration of the sculptor.

"Regarding the Church," I said, "I suppose if we look we can find flaws and abrasions and a chip missing here and there. I suppose we can see an aberration or an imperfection in a leader of the past or perhaps the present. Nonetheless, there is still absolute, hard-rock, undeniable, irrefutable proof, because the Church is what it is and because that someone, sometime, with supreme inspired spiritual genius set to work obediently under inspiration and organized it, and so it came into being. It is best that we should enlarge ourselves to appreciate the beauty and genius of it, rather than debunk and look for the flaws.

"The story is told of two frivolous girls clattering through a great museum and then flippantly remarking as they left the building that it hadn't impressed them much. One of the door-keepers standing by commented to them, 'Young ladies, this museum is not on trial here today. Its quality cannot be contested. You are the ones who are on trial.'

"My fellow teachers, it isn't the Church or the gospel that is on trial. We are."

After that meeting several of the older brethren came forward and commented that they had felt uncomfortable with the first part of the meeting, and they were in harmony with what I said. "Some of us seem to want to draw attention to ourselves by criticizing this or that in order to show our own great learning," they said.

I was gratified with the response, and I think I was much more accepted in my administrative role thereafter.

I often look at the replica of the statue in my office and am reminded that at critical moments an inspiration can come as a prompting, and a very ordinary experience in the past can be recalled and can provide an important teaching moment.

Some years later I read the following statement by President Stephen L Richards, with which I am very much in agreement:

> I wish to say something about "debunking." I am sure you must know what this term, which has come into rather general usage in recent years, signifies. Literally it means to take away a man's bed or bunk, and that is what it means in modern parlance. If a man of history has secured over the years a high place in the esteem of his countrymen and fellow men and has become imbedded in their affections, it has seemingly become a pleasing pastime for researchers and scholars to delve into the past of such a man, discover, if may be, some of his weaknesses, and then write a book exposing hitherto unpublished alleged factual findings, all of which tends to rob the historic character of the idealistic esteem and veneration in which he may have been held through the years.
>
> This debunking, we are told, is in the interest

of realism, that the facts should be known. If an historic character has made a great contribution to country and society, and if his name and his deeds have been used over the generations to foster high ideals of character and service, what good is to be accomplished by digging out of the past and exploiting weaknesses, which perhaps a general contemporary public forgave and subdued?

Perhaps, with propriety, we might look into the lives and purposes of these debunkers themselves to make plain to the people their objectives in destroying this idealism for our heroes and great men of history. Perhaps some of these debunkers would tell you, if you asked them, that their investigation and writing are prompted by a desire to show that men can be human, with human frailties, and still be great. If they were to say that that was their purpose, I would be inclined to doubt them, and much more inclined to believe that their writings were prompted by a desire to make money out of sensational, unsavory disclosures.

I am sure you will readily see that I am against debunkers as a class, and I earnestly hope they will not be successful in breaking down the idealisms we entertain for great men and women in history. (*Where Is Wisdom?* Deseret Book, 1955, pp. 155–56.)

Teachers and leaders must be scrupulous to win the confidence of those whom they teach. I have never had much sympathy for playing tricks on a class, or deceiving them in any way, or testing them in any way that could be negative.

When I was in high school a friend of mine was working for a company. In the evenings he swept up the building. One night he found on the basement floor, in the dust behind the furnace, a five-dollar bill—an old bill, dusty and dirty. He picked it up and looked at it. After wrestling with his conscience during the night, he returned to work the next day and gave the five-dollar bill to his employer.

212

His employer said, "Well, thank you. I put it there yesterday. I was testing you." I recall that this young man thoroughly resented the action of his employer, and he commented to him, "I thought it was Satan who had the job of tempting."

There seem to arise from time to time teachers who have great influence and great ability to lead astray the members of the Church. Often they possess the talents of a good teacher and the qualities of a great leader, and yet they are spiritually counterfeit. They seem to gather around them a following of people who stoutly defend them, and there grows a formidable force to be reckoned with.

In the Church we have certain members who smart under the restrictions of rigid discipline. Their approach to the gospel is largely intellectual. They have not learned to tap into the great sources of intelligence available through spiritual inquiry.

A typical individual in this category is active in the Church. He responds to calls, accepts the doctrines "for the most part," but is disturbed by one or two things, generally among them the restriction the Lord has put on bestowing the priesthood. When called to teaching positions, he has a great deal of difficulty hiding his doubts. While basically he accepts the doctrines and tries to keep the standards, he frequently objects to "the way the Church is being run."

Moved Left of His Father

Let me relate an experience I had with one such brother. He was teaching at a large university in the East and was serving as a member of a stake high council, but in a contact or two I had with him he was always trying to reconcile some matters that he couldn't resolve. "Why doesn't the Church do this?" he would say, or "Why doesn't the Church do that?"

213

On one of my visits I spent considerable time with him and cautioned him, "You have a wonderful family. I hope that you will bring them up in faith."

"Oh, I'll do that," he said, "but I won't bring them up in blind obedience like my father tried to bring us up."

"I knew your father. He was a wonderful man," I said. We then talked about his father, a man of little formal training who had been a great spiritual influence in his community. The father had wanted his sons to get an education, and from his meager income he had sent them all to the university.

This brother said, "My father has been worried about me since I came east for advanced training. But he needn't worry. I've been active in the Church; I have a temple recommend; I've paid my tithing and been faithful. But I feel quite emancipated from many of the restrictive views held among the older members of the Church. My father," he added, "was very conservative."

I asked, "How would you classify yourself?"

He said, "Oh, as a faithful member, but I'm a good deal more liberal than my father. But then I've had a good deal more education than he had."

"You've moved left of your father?" I asked.

"Yes, quite a bit," he said.

"Has it ever occurred to you," I inquired, "that if your children move as far left of their father as you have from yours, they will grow up out of the Church? They will gravitate away from the safeguards of the Word of Wisdom and the standard of morality and will lose their spiritual inheritance."

He pondered for a few minutes and then turned pale. It had never occurred to him that the influence he was having on his children by his constant interquarreling with "the Church" would be accentuated in their lives. His approach was academic; it was intellectual; it was only casually spiritual. If he were willing to balance the spiritual influence in his life, a change would come, and he would become more like his father than like his present self.

None of us lives for himself alone. Others are following in our footsteps, watching carefully, and taking license from the things we say and the things we do. When we have doubts, it is wise to keep them to ourselves and to ponder on them and study and pray and inquire. One by one they are resolved. When we have questions that are unresolved, it is wise to take them on faith. Otherwise it may be that we will enjoy the fruits of the gospel and never stray "too" far, and yet those who come after us who depend upon us most may be robbed of their spiritual inheritance. They may forsake the standards and become ineligible for those redeeming ordinances that make life eternally happy.

"The Children's Teeth Are Set on Edge"

I know of a father "born of goodly parents" who was an illustrious figure in the academic world. Nominally active in the Church, he never quarreled openly with the doctrines of the Church. He sent his sons on missions, at least some of them. But there were some things about the doctrines of the Church that he felt were a bit beneath him.

His family has moved along in the world, several of them in prominent positions in their chosen fields. Now none of them is active in the Church. In the lives of his children and his children's children we see the fulfillment of the prophecy that "the fathers have eaten a sour grape and the children's teeth are set on edge." (Jeremiah 31:29.) They have been helped along that way by the folly of their father.

Responsibility rests likewise with teachers who could have reinforced their students with faith but who did just the opposite.

On one occasion in a council meeting, when such a subject was being discussed, President Harold B. Lee said, "If it comes to the point that we must take action against the membership of that individual, you will see, Brethren, that his influence fades immediately; he will be abandoned even by those who encourage him in his wickedness."

In my experience I have found this to be so. Those who have such motives are seeking to recommend themselves and are riding on a crest of selfishness or egotism or apostasy; and when action is taken, they quickly fade away into oblivion and are never heard from again.

On the other hand, there have been others I have known who have been deceived or led astray but who, when corrected, have hung tenaciously to the principle of obedience and have become tractable and repentant. They move forward and upward much the stronger and the wiser for their experience.

The Book of Mormon records that Nephi and Lehi taught the gospel to the Lamanites: "And it came to pass that they did preach with great power, insomuch that they did confound many of those dissenters who had gone over from the Nephites, insomuch that they came forth and did confess their sins and were baptized unto repentance, and immediately returned to the Nephites to endeavor to repair unto them the wrongs which they had done." (Helaman 5:17.)

It is invariably true that those who set their hand to disturb or thwart the work of the Lord, or destroy faith — those who challenge or ridicule or criticize His chosen servants, whether in the wards, the stakes, or the Church — fade into spiritual oblivion and lose what might have been theirs.

The Lord consoled the Prophet Joseph Smith while he was in Liberty Jail, saying:

Cursed are all those that shall lift up the heel

against mine anointed, saith the Lord, and cry they have sinned when they have not sinned before me, saith the Lord, but have done that which was meet in mine eyes, and which I commanded them.

But those who cry transgression do it because they are the servants of sin, and are the children of disobedience themselves.

And those who swear falsely against my servants, that they might bring them into bondage and death—

Wo unto them; because they have offended my little ones they shall be severed from the ordinances of mine house.

Their basket shall not be full, their houses and their barns shall perish, and they themselves shall be despised by those that flattered them.

They shall not have right to the priesthood, nor their posterity after them from generation to generation.

It had been better for them that a millstone had been hanged about their necks, and they drowned in the depth of the sea. (D&C 121:16–22.)

When people are given new responsibilities, they either grow and develop new abilities to meet their new challenges or else they swell to fit their new size. Some teachers have a tendency to become "puffed up" in their learning. They should exercise care not to do this, because students can quickly detect any signs of sham or hypocrisy. Wise men have written in the scriptures concerning this matter.

And they shall contend one with another; and their priests shall contend one with another, and they shall teach with their learning, and deny the Holy Ghost, which giveth utterance.

Because of pride, and because of false teachers, and false doctrine, their churches have become corrupted, and their churches are lifted up; because of pride they are puffed up. (2 Nephi 28:4,12.)

O that cunning plan of the evil one! O the vainness, and the frailties, and the foolishness of men! When they are learned they think they are wise, and they hearken not unto the counsel of God, for they set it aside, supposing they know of themselves, wherefore, their wisdom is foolishness and it profiteth them not. And they shall perish.

But to be learned is good if they hearken unto the counsels of God. (2 Nephi 9:28–29.)

But it came to pass in the twenty and ninth year there began to be some disputings among the people; and some were lifted up unto pride and boastings because of their exceeding great riches, yea, even unto great persecutions;

For there were many merchants in the land, and also many lawyers, and many officers.

And the people began to be distinguished by ranks, according to their riches and their chances for learning, yea, some were ignorant because of their poverty, and others did receive great learning because of their riches. (3 Nephi 6:10–12.)

And he had gone about among the people, preaching to them that which he termed to be the word of God, bearing down against the church; declaring unto the people that every priest and teacher ought to become popular; and they ought not to labor with their hands, but that they ought to be supported by the people. (Alma 1:3.)

As we are called to teach, and in our dealings with our own families, may we scrupulously avoid misleading or leading astray those for whom we are responsible.

CHAPTER TWENTY-SEVEN

What Students Should Know about Destroyers of Faith

There are some teachers who deliberately destroy faith. It is worthwhile to warn all students against them and to describe them so their students may not drift and become like them and so that each of us as teachers and as parents may guard against becoming one of them. This chapter, prepared for another purpose, expresses my feelings on this subject, which is vital to teachers and students.

Graduation time at a school is a time for assessment and appreciation for things gained at school. At the dormitory and in the apartment, students sort through things that they have accumulated during their school days. Some, such as old workbooks and test papers, will be discarded. Others will be saved.

In a review of what a student has gained at school or in a class, he should give attention to things he may have lost. If he knew the value of some things he may have discarded, he would dig frantically through the wastebasket and trash can to rescue them before they are hauled away permanently.

He came to school basically to learn an occupation, and likely he has. But as always, there was a price to pay, and occasionally students pay an exorbitant price. Not infrequently students will jettison things essential to life and end up well-occupied but unhappy.

These questions are appropriate. Did they as freshmen come with idealism, and put it aside? Did they come with faith, and carry away in its place skepticism? Did they come with patriotism, and replace it with cynicism? Did they come free from any binding habits, and now leave with an addiction? Did they arrive aspiring for marriage, a home, and a family, and now have abandoned those aspirations? And critically important, did they come with virtue and moral purity, and now must admit to themselves that while they were here they have lost it?

How did this happen? Was that an essential price to pay for an occupation or for broadened cultural horizons? The intangibles they carry away may not equal in value the intangibles they may be leaving behind.

If they are gone now, do they know how it happened? Did they give them up willingly? Did they set them aside, or were they taken from them? Many students in schools today have fallen victim to an academic confidence game.

The large body of university professors represent the finest standard of our civilization. However, some few professors delight in relieving the student of his basic spiritual values. Many faculty members look forward to the coming of a new crop of green freshmen with a compulsive desire to "educate" them.

The Trusting Victims

During my term as mission president, I was responsible for the Joseph Smith Memorial in Vermont. The visitors center with its lawns and gardens is surrounded by woods. A doe took up residence there and each spring brought twin fawns onto the lawn. They were tame enough that the caretaker, on occasion, could pick them up.

One fall a bow hunter came into the grounds and killed

a half-grown fawn with an arrow. The unsuspecting animal stood watching a few feet away, interested in whatever it was he was doing. There is no way that that man could be classed as a sportsman or even a hunter. "Like shooting fish in a barrel" is the expression. No doubt both the trophy and the hunt became exaggerated in the conversation of the man, but there is no way his contemptible deed could give him any sense of achievement.

Each year many trusting students fall victim in the colleges and universities. There, as captive audiences, their faith, their patriotism, and their morality are lined up against a wall and riddled by words shot from the mouth of irreverent professors.

Study the Professor

While they are taking courses students should find enough time after the study of their subjects to study the professors. One may well learn more from studying the professor than by studying the subject.

Most professors influence their students' lives for good. But there are others, those few, who delight in destroying faith. I have found it generally true that a professor who ridicules faith and religious beliefs and downgrades patriotism, who continually presses for the loosening of standards of campus discipline for both faculty and students, is a very interesting subject for study. Students would do well to look him over. May I predict what they will find.

Be assured that one who strives to widen the breadth of accepted moral conduct does so to condone what he is doing. Not infrequently you will find him unworthy. If he derides spiritual development, it can generally be concluded that he failed in the subject. He defends himself by declaring it an unnecessary discipline. He is the one who ridicules faith and humility, who would smile in contempt when anyone mentions virtue, or reverence, or dedication, or morality.

There is something very interesting about a person who is anxious to forsake the standards of his church, particularly if he leaves them and encourages others to do likewise.

Have you ever wondered what it means when a person can leave the church but he cannot leave it alone? Normal behavior would have him cancel his affiliation in the church and let that be that. Not so with this individual. He can leave it, but he cannot leave it alone. He becomes consumed and obsessed with it. That says something about him.

And one might ask, Is he talking to students, or is he really talking to himself? You might also ask, and he might ask himself, Is he happy, really happy?

Let me alert you to one other thing. The professor who is "up-tight" about the subject of religion, the one who just positively cannot seem to conduct a class without tossing a barb or two at the Church, belittling the bishop or the stake president and the standards they teach, is not the major source of concern. His bald-faced brand of prejudice is obvious even to the unwary student. Even the freshman fawn will move aside when this person strings his bow.

Deceit by a Gesture, an Inflection

But there is another that I would like to describe to you. I can best make the point by referring to Shakespeare's *Othello.*

Othello claimed the two desires of his life. He became the general—he had arrived at the top—and he won the hand of the lovely Desdemona. Two other characters in the play complete the main cast: Cassio, Othello's trusted lieutenant, and Iago, conspiring and jealous.

222

Iago wanted most in life to be general. Motivated by malignant jealousy, he set out to destroy Othello, never openly, always careful and clever. In the play he does not tell an open, bald-faced lie. He works by innuendo and suggestion.

"Where is Desdemona tonight?" he might ask.

"Oh, she has gone to Relief Society," Othello might answer.

"Oh, *has* she?" Iago might question.

It is not the words. On paper they are a harmless inquiry, but the inflection makes them contagious with suspicion.

On one occasion Cassio comes to Othello's home with a message. After a conversation with Desdemona, he leaves to attend to other matters. As he is leaving the home, Othello and Iago approach.

Iago perverts an innocent situation with his comment, "I cannot think it that he would steal away so guilty-like, seeing you coming."

And so it unfolds. Nothing to incriminate Iago, so innocent is he. Just a sly reference, a gesture, an inflection, the emphasis on the word or the sentence.

Othello is finally convinced that Desdemona is unfaithful, and he determines to destroy her. The tragedy concludes with Othello threatening his innocent wife. She pleads for a week, for a day. Her final plea: "But while I say one prayer." However, he denies her that. How terrible the tragedy of her death when he then finds proof of her innocence.

Students may well meet an Iago one day as they move through life. Through innuendo and sly remarks, through an inflection or a question, in mock innocence, he might persuade them to kill their faith, to throttle their patriotism, to tamper with drugs, to kill their agency, to abandon morality and chastity and virtue. If they do so, they have an awakening as terribly tragic as that of Othello.

This is the man who ridicules belief in a hereafter and says there is no such thing as God. He'd better hope he is right, for if, as some of us know, the opposite is true, the final scene will be his, for justice more than poetic and penalties adequate in every way will be exacted from him. Ultimately we are punished quite as much by our sins as we are for them.

At a university, theory has it that learning may be pursued in an atmosphere of academic freedom. Freedom, one might ask, for whom? Some interesting changes have occurred in the past generation.

The Religion of Atheism

Some years ago in the United States a plaintiff prospered in her grievance concerning the saying of prayers in public schools. The practice was declared unconstitutional by the Supreme Court. That decision was partial to one ideology, for the effect, regardless of the intent, was to offer great encouragement to those who would erase from our society every trace of reference to the Almighty.

There is a crying need for the identification of atheism for what it is, and that is, a religion albeit a negative one. Atheism is a religious expression; it is one extreme end of religious philosophy.

Those who are spiritually sensitive recognize God, a living being who rules in the affairs of man. The so-called atheist declares that God is not. Not just that He isn't the cause of things, but that He indeed is not.

We put sunshine and rain under the heading of weather. It would be a little ridiculous to talk about clear weather or cloudy weather and claim that the two are not related and could not be considered as part of the same discipline.

It is equally ridiculous to separate theism from atheism and claim that they are two separate matters, particularly when we condone, and in some instances encourage, the atheist to preach his doctrine in the school classroom and then at once move with great vigor to eliminate any positive reference to God. The atheist is protected, as they say, by the principle of academic freedom.

The school administrator who intends to maintain academic freedom had better see to it that he administers impartially. Otherwise he offends the very principle he claims to sustain. When standards of discipline are dominated by the influence of the atheist, then the administrator is partial.

Atheism, like theism, is divided into many sects: communism, agnosticism, skepticism, humanism, pragmatism, and others.

The atheist proclaims his own dishonesty in accepting pay to teach psychology, sociology, history, or English, while he is indeed preaching his atheistic religious philosophy to his students.

If the atheist wants to teach his doctrine at a public school, let him purchase property off campus and build himself a building and offer classes. Let him label the classes for what they are.

A student in a public school should have the right to register for a course in English and be taught the subject of English or to register for a course in history and be taught the subject of history, and not be exposed, like a fish in a barrel or a tame fawn before a bow hunter, to the atheistic philosophies of an unhappy teacher.

The patrons of a school, the citizens who finance it, have the right to send their sons and daughters to school without the anxiety that they will be taught sectarian religion, including that of the atheist. They have the right to expect that the standards of campus discipline and dor-

225

mitory living are not dictated by a few ultraliberals who are confined by no moral standards whatsoever.

We are very particular to forbid anyone from preaching Catholicism, or Protestantism, or Mormonism, or Judaism in a public school classroom, but for some reason we are very patient with those who teach the negative expression of religion.

Where separation of church and state is proclaimed, we ought to demand more protection from the agnostic, from the atheist, from the communist, from the skeptic, from the humanist and the pragmatist, than we have yet been given.

I have had university administrators tell me that they would like to correct this situation in this school or that one, but they cannot act. The offending teacher is protected in what he does. He hides behind tenure and draws support from professional societies.

I claim that the atheist has no more right to teach the fundamentals of his sect in the public school than does the theist. Any system in the schools or in society that protects the destruction of faith, and forbids, in turn, the defense of it, must ultimately destroy the moral fiber of society.

That lesson is abundantly clear in our present society. Evil has unclothed herself and walks the streets in brazen, impudent defiance. When students leave school and go on in life, Iago will still be there—perhaps not under the title of teacher, but he will be clamoring for their attention, subtly urging them to destroy their faith.

There are some rights and wrongs. We must come to understand that there are basic truths and basic principles, basic conformities, necessary to achieve happiness. There are some things that are false, that are wrong. For instance, we cannot be happy and at the same time be wicked — never, regardless of how generally accepted that course may be.

If it were printed in every book, run on every news press, set forth in every magazine; if it were broadcast on every frequency, televised from every station, declared from every pulpit, taught in every classroom, advocated in every conversation — still wrong would be wrong. Wickedness never was happiness, neither indeed can it be, neither indeed will it ever be.

Speak for Justice

I declare in favor of full academic freedom. If prayer is to leave the public schools, let the ridicule of prayer leave also. I speak for humility, for faith, for reverence, for brotherhood, for charity, for patriotism. I speak for temperance, and I likewise speak for justice.

I yearn for the day when the rank and file of public school teachers will assert themselves, when the moral fiber in them will set itself against the decay in our schools.

I pay tribute to the great body of men and women who teach with integrity. I pay tribute to those men and women of complete integrity who command a discipline and are able to teach it. They are the ones most worth studying. That is something every student should know. These teachers reflect a balance in development of the whole man. These are the men and women to be trusted, to be emulated.

God grant that teachers may soon look up from their books, set aside their papers, turn from their studies, and stand to be counted with those administrators who struggle to keep the moral foundation of our schools in place. These men and women wield heavy influence and plant in the hearts and minds of students a fundamental respect for truth and integrity.

As students leave school satisfied with the things they have gained, they would do well to go through their pockets, look through their luggage, and see if something may have been lost—spiritual things—essential if there is to be happiness in their future.

And as they leave, they should take with them their faith, their patriotism, their virtue. If they are battered a bit, they can be repaired. Even virtue, if tarnished, can be polished again. Students should carry these things away with them. They can be renewed. They will come to know in the years ahead that life has precious little to offer without them.

Students are taught in the course of their school experience to seek information from that teacher who has inquired and studied a field—English, mathematics, sociology, the humanities, or other subjects. Students also can make inquiry into spiritual things. I have come to know that God lives, that ultimately He will rule in the affairs of men. I know that many of the treasures that students may have set aside will prove to be those that were of most worth to them.

CHAPTER TWENTY-EIGHT

Counseling

In recent years, counseling has become a profession. Nevertheless, parents and teachers and leaders often must act as counselors. Counseling is, of course, one type of teaching—usually a person-to-person kind. In the chapter on "How to Teach the Moral Standard" are some comments that relate to counseling. I shall not repeat them here, but urge you to add them to the suggestions listed in this chapter. Particularly do I call attention to the warning on the dangers of digging too deeply into the lives of others. Although the suggestions in this chapter will be aimed more directly at the classroom teacher, the principles apply as well to parents in the home and to leaders in the Church.

If you are a classroom teacher, it is good advice to keep the deep personal problems of students in the proper channels. Remember, if you are a teacher, it does not make you the parent of the student, nor his bishop. Just because counseling needs to be done—and it may very desperately need to be done—it does not mean you are the one who should give the counsel.

Proper Channels

The Lord has set up some precise channels in the Church, and He invariably extends inspiration through these channels. However, we are often guilty of an "end run" to someone in higher authority than those who are immediately available. While we do not always follow the proper channels of authority and while we sometimes preempt responsibility that belongs to the parent or to a bishop, the Lord invariably stays in channel. He will not yield revelation and inspiration to us when we are out of those channels.

A teacher must be wise in distributing love to his students, and common-sense maturity is essential. In almost every Sunday School, Primary, or seminary class is someone so starved for love that any gesture will make him a complete disciple of the teacher. I have known a student to hang around a teacher like a starved puppy waiting for any morsel of attention or affection that may be thrown to him. At times it takes restraint to keep the relationship formal enough that it does not injure the youngster. A wise teacher will use that devotion and hand out love in such a way that he leads the student to the proper channels and proper relationship so that the dependence does not become damaging.

Though it is important for the teacher to keep those channels always in mind, it is not always easy to get them properly established. Sometimes there are parents who do not know how to adequately respond. A good teacher, of course, will have the confidence and love of his students and they will be willing to confide in him. That is why parents must be good teachers.

It is not unusual for someone to come to a seminary teacher or a Sunday School teacher visibly disturbed, and want to delve deeply into a problem. Perhaps it is a young person who says, "I've got something I've got to talk to you about. A week ago I was on a date. We stayed out very late and while we were in the car . . . " About that time the wise teacher will say, "I have a feeling that this is a serious problem that others can help you with better than I can. Do you have a good relationship with your parents? Do you think you can talk this matter over with them?"

I've known that channel to parents to be opened up many times. But the tendency, unfortunately, is for a teacher to become interested or intrigued and think, "Well, I've got to know just a little bit more about this in order to help," or "I can help him more than anyone else," or "He trusts me," and therefore get too deeply involved.

Helping the Student Get in the Right Channel

On many occasions I've seen the solution to problems such as this, and many others surrounding it, open up as soon as the young person was in proper channels and counseling with his parents. Sometimes, if this isn't advisable or possible, the youth can be referred to the bishop. Not infrequently a youngster will say, "I couldn't go to the bishop, I'd be too embarrassed," or "He wouldn't understand," or—well, you know all the other diversions. It is time then for the teacher to say, "I know the bishop well. Have you ever made an appointment with him? Let me tell you how to do that." In some cases he may even have to say, "Would you like me to make the appointment and then go with you?"

In that situation, when the appointment is arranged, you arrive at the bishop's office, and the usual pleasantries are over, be alert to the first opportunity to leave the two of them alone. About the time the bishop says, "Sit down, please," the wise teacher will suddenly remember he left the water running in the bathtub, or the house is on fire, or some equally urgent matter will call him away, and he will leave the young person with the bishop.

Were there space in this chapter I could recount many experiences in which teachers who were able and well-intentioned have been drawn into counseling situations in which they have little or no right to inspiration, and who have found themselves in compromising or morally fatal situations. The desire to help someone is not justification for a teacher to want to follow every counseling opportunity to its conclusion. A teacher in the Church is a very wise teacher if he will have clearly in mind the kinds of problems that ought to be solved in channels other than the teacher-student relationship. Even at the risk of feeling unattentive or unsympathetic, he should make it a rigid rule to see that the problems are diverted to where revelation can be delivered.

Counseling Is Like . . . the Church Welfare Program

In the chapter on the ego we used the educational principle known as transfer. I should like to use it again in talking about a familiar program in the Church — the welfare program — and then transfer the fundamental principles of it to the teacher and the counseling opportunities that come to him. Church welfare, however, is not the subject of this discussion. I only use it to illustrate a point.

The Church was two years old when the Lord revealed that "the idler shall not have place in the church, except he repent and mend his ways." (D&C 75:29.) President Marion G. Romney explained this principle with his characteristic simple directness: "The obligation to sustain one's self was divinely imposed upon the human race at its beginning. 'In the sweat of thy face shalt thou eat bread, till thou return unto the ground.' (Genesis 3:19.)"

The welfare handbooks have always taught that we must earnestly teach and urge members to be self-sustaining to the fullest extent of their power, and that no Latter-day Saint will voluntarily shift from himself the burden of his own support. So long as he can, under the inspiration of the Almighty and with his own labors, he will supply himself with the necessities of life.

We have succeeded fairly well in establishing in the minds of Latter-day Saints that they should take care of their own material needs and then contribute to the welfare of those who cannot provide the necessities of life. If a member is unable to sustain himself, he is to call upon his own family and then upon the Church, in that order, and not upon the government at all.

We have counseled bishops and stake presidents to be very careful to avoid abuses in the welfare program. When people are *able* but are *unwilling* to take care of themselves, we are responsible to employ the dictum of the Lord, that the idler shall not eat the bread of the laborer. The simple rule has been, to the fullest extent possible, to take care of one's self.

It's not an unkind or an unfeeling bishop who requires a member of the Church to work to the fullest extent he can for what he receives from Church welfare. It is not a quick handout system merely for the asking. It requires a careful inventory of personal resources, all of which must be committed before anything is added from the outside. There should not be the slightest embarrassment on the part of any member of the Church to be assisted by the Church welfare program — provided, that is, that he has contributed all that he can contribute. Every personal resource of his own must be called upon first.

When the Church welfare program was first announced in 1936, the First Presidency made this statement:

> Our primary purpose was to set up, insofar as possible, a system under which the curse of idleness would be done away with, the evils of the dole abolished, and independence, industry, thrift, and self-respect be once more established amongst our people. *The aim of the Church is to help people help*

233

themselves. Work is to be re-enthroned as a ruling principle in the lives of our Church membership. (*Conference Report,* October 1936, p. 3.)

President Romney has emphasized, "To care for people on any other basis is to do them more harm than good. The purpose of Church welfare is *not* to relieve a Church member from taking care of himself." (Welfare services meeting, October 5, 1974.)

The Principle of Self-Reliance

The basic principles of the welfare program are inspired principles. Teachers should understand that, as well as that the principle of self-reliance is fundamental to a happy life. That same principle has application in emotional and in spiritual things.

If we provide an overabundance of counsel without at once emphasizing the principle of self-reliance as it is understood in the welfare program, we can cause people to be so totally dependent emotionally and spiritually upon others that they subsist on some kind of emotional welfare. They can become unwilling to sustain themselves and become so dependent that they endlessly need to be shored up, lifted up, encouraged, and taught to contribute little of their own. A teacher should not unwittingly allow someone to get in this position; that is not responsible teaching.

It is possible to do to ourselves emotionally (and therefore spiritually) what we have been working so hard for generations to avoid materially. If we lose our emotional and spiritual self-reliance, we can be weakened quite as much as, and perhaps even more than, when we become dependent materially. On the one hand, we counsel bishops to avoid abuses in the Church welfare program. On the other hand, we dole out counsel and advice without the slightest thought that the member should solve the problem himself or turn to his family, and that only when

234

those resources are inadequate should he turn to the Church.

We ought to be very careful, therefore, not to dole out counsel indiscriminately, or try to totally sustain our members in every emotional need. If we are not careful, we can lose the power of individual revelation. The Lord said to Oliver Cowdery (and this has meaning for all of us):

> Behold, you have not understood; you have supposed that I would give it unto you, when you took no thought save it was to ask me.
>
> But, behold, I say unto you, that you must study it out in your mind; then you must ask me if it be right, and if it is right I will cause that your bosom shall burn within you; therefore, you shall feel that it is right.
>
> But if it be not right you shall have no such feelings, but you shall have a stupor of thought that shall cause you to forget the thing that is wrong. . . . (D&C 9:7–9.)

A student came to my office one day with a difficult problem. He was trying to decide whether he should or should not marry. I asked him, "You've come for counsel?" "Yes, indeed," he said. "Are you going to follow it when I give it to you?" I asked. That was a surprise to him. Finally he agreed, "Yes."

I happened to know his father, a leader in the Church and a wonderful man. I said, "This is my counsel: Go home this weekend and talk to your father. Meet with him in some private place, tell him your dilemma, ask him for his counsel, and do what he tells you to do. That is my counsel."

I think an emotional dole system can be as dangerous as a material dole system, and we can become so dependent that we stand around waiting for the Church to do everything for us.

He Would Not Act for Himself

A few years ago I received a telephone call from a bishop whose son had been inducted into the military service and was at an army basic training center. The father said, "He's been there for three weeks and he hasn't been to church yet." Then he described his son as being an active Latter-day Saint, always faithful in his duties. "He's never missed a church meeting before," his father said. "Isn't there something you can do to help?" The son had telephoned and said that no one had come yet to invite him to go to church.

I made an investigation of the circumstances. Can you picture the following: In the barracks, just a few feet from the serviceman's bunk, was a bulletin board. On it was a picture of the Salt Lake Temple and a list of the meeting times at the base chapel. The young man had attended an orientation for all new inductees, conducted by one of the base chaplains. While in this case it was not a Latter-day Saint chaplain, there was a Latter-day Saint chaplain at that installation, which fact had been noted in the lecture. He had been told that if he wanted to know about church services, he could talk to the sergeant on duty or he could contact any chaplain's office, and that information would readily be given him.

The serviceman, however, had been told before he left home that the Church had a wonderful program to help young men in the military service, and that we would find them and look after them and bring the full Church program to them. He had, therefore, lain back on his bunk, propped up his feet, and waited for the Church to do everything for him. He waited three weeks and was disappointed enough that he called his father, the bishop, to say that the Church had failed him.

Now this was not malicious. It was just that he had been brought up with the idea that the whole effort and

236

duty of the Church was to look after him; he had missed the very point that the whole effort of the Church is to give him the opportunity to serve someone else. Surely, since he was away from home and in a strange place and needing attention more than he had ever needed it in his life, all of that help, he was certain, would be forthcoming immediately without any effort on his part. He had been weakened by a dole system and was now in spiritual jeopardy because he would not act for himself.

First the Individual, Then the Family, Then the Church

That experience had a great effect on me, and when we reorganized the military relations program, we changed the emphasis from what it had been before. For example, the old program urged the ward or the quorum to subscribe to the general Church magazine for every man entering the military service. It was the duty of the bishop to see that the subscription was renewed during the time of the serviceman's enlistment.

Now we have changed all of that. We now counsel the young man to subscribe to the magazine himself and to pay for it himself. He ordinarily has money to spend on less useful things, and he should learn to take care of himself from the very beginning. If for one reason or another he cannot do so, then his family should supply the subscription. If they cannot, or if they will not, then and only then would it be the responsibility of the ward or the quorum to step in and see that this important Church publication is sent to him.

We found that many of our men would not bother to file change-of-address cards for the magazines if the subscriptions had been doled out to them. They had done nothing to earn the publications and they didn't appreciate them. It is interesting to see what has happened in that military relations program. We have put the shoe on the other foot. Our young men are now more self-reliant.

"Counselitis"

If you have a calling or assignment that requires you to counsel others, there are some things to keep in mind. In virtually every ward or branch and in some classes there are chronic cases of individuals who endlessly seek counsel but never follow the counsel that is given. That, some may assume, is not serious. I think it is very serious! Like the common cold, it drains more strength out of humanity than does any other disease. We can develop an epidemic of "counselitis" that will drain spiritual strength from the Church. Spiritual self-reliance is the sustaining power of the Church. If we rob our students of that, how can they get the revelation that there is a prophet of God? How can they get answers to prayer? How can they *know?* If we move so quickly to answer all questions and provide so many ways to solve all problems, we may end up weakening those whom we counsel or teach, not strengthening them.

Some who have been trained in counseling are apt to say, "My counseling does not rob one of his self-reliance, because I use the nondirective counseling approach. I am scrupulously careful not to take a position. I merely reflect back comments and feelings of the individual so that he will make the decision totally himself. I do my counseling by nondirection and never make a value judgment."

While I have respect for this procedure of counseling as a method, I think that if nondirective counseling is all one does, often that's precisely what we get from the counseling—no direction. When a counselor schedules an interminably long session to say as little as possible and allows the student to struggle with whether or not something is right or wrong, which the counselor already

238

knows, that is a waste of time. So is fussing around trying to determine whether it is right for the student under the circumstances, or wrong for him under the circumstances. When anyone with any moral sense knows that a course is wrong, then it is wrong for *anybody* and it is wrong for *everybody*.

Directive Counseling

In the Church, the directive pattern of counseling is at least as respectable, decent, desirable, and needed as is the nondirective approach to counseling. Unfortunately, however, we see little of it anymore. How sweet and refreshing for a teacher or a leader to declare to a student, "This course is right and that course is wrong. Now, you go make the decision." The student ought to know what is right and what is wrong by the quickest method possible, and that may be very directive. There is a crying need for counselors who will say pointedly and plainly, "This course is wrong. It's evil. It's bad. It will bring you unhappiness. This other course is right. It is good. It is desirable. It will bring you happiness." Then free agency comes into play when the individual determines for himself whether or not he will follow the right course.

In the world a preoccupation with counseling has led to a number of experiments from which we are not entirely free in the Church. There are those counselors who want to delve deeper into the lives of subjects than is emotionally or spiritually healthy. There are those who want to draw out and analyze and take apart and dissect. While a certain amount of catharsis is healthy and essential, too much of it can be degenerating. It is seldom as easy to put something back together as it is to take it apart.

Group Therapy

Several procedures have been developed for group therapy. They are promoted under a number of titles. Some function under such names as value clarification, character education, and so on. Such things come and go, and as soon as one has run its course and is out of vogue, another, a little different from the rest, comes onto the scene. Although they differ in some respects, one or more of the following elements is apparent in many of them: They recognize no ultimate source for truth. All values are those that are established by the individuals or the group. There is no reference to God. Free and full expression before the group is encouraged—often a confession—of every intimate and personal feeling and experience. An openness, a touching and a closeness may be encouraged among the members as they attempt to resolve problems simply by finding a comfortable interaction. Above all, they try to avoid any feelings of guilt.

There are major emotional and spiritual dangers involved in such procedures, and members of the Church would do well to be very cautious. It is difficult at times to determine whether or not the sessions are for the good of the counselee or for the curiosity and amusement of the counselor.

I remember seeing a little sign years ago in a photographer's shop on the island of Kauai that said, "If there is beauty, we will take it. If there is none, we will make it." I fear that some of us, in our counseling in the Church, seem to be saying, "If there are problems, we'll abate them. If there are none, we'll create them."

There are times when deep-seated emotional problems will respond to the procedures we have been talking about. Such procedures can have therapeutic value. There is, however, no justification to employ them in the absence of deep-seated emotional problems. There is no more justification for doing that than there is justification for a medical doctor to perform unnecessary surgery. When someone is just experimenting or riding the crest of the wave of a new counseling theory, I would not encourage anyone to submit to such counseling procedure.

Don't Cause What You Want to Prevent

I emphasize that it is very easy, when dealing with things of the mind and spirit, to cause the very thing you're trying so desperately to prevent. Consider the bean in the nose illustration in the chapter titled "How to Teach the Moral Standard." When someone comes to receive counsel, make sure you are in a position to receive inspiration to help him. This is always true with parents in counseling their children. Parents can receive inspiration and they ought to. It is often true with teachers, but they must be careful. If students are just trusting in their mortal wisdom, they should keep in mind this statement from the Book of Mormon: "Cursed is he that putteth trust in man, or maketh flesh his arm, or shall hearken unto the precepts of men, save their precepts shall be given by the power of the Holy Ghost." (2 Nephi 28:31.)

The Lord also gave this warning:

> . . . O the vainness, and the frailties, and the foolishness of men! When they are learned they think they are wise, and they hearken not unto the counsel of God, for they set it aside, supposing they know of themselves, wherefore, their wisdom is foolishness and it profiteth them not. And they shall perish.
>
> But to be learned is good if they hearken unto the counsels of God. (2 Nephi 9:28–29.)

The basic principles underlying the Church welfare program have application in our emotional and spiritual lives: specifically that independence, industry, thrift, self-reliance, and self-respect should be developed; that work should be enthroned as a ruling principle in our lives; that the evils of an emotional or spiritual dole should be avoided; and that the aim of the Church is to help the members help themselves.

We mentioned earlier that there should not be the slightest embarrassment for any member of the Church to receive welfare assistance, provided he has first exhausted his own personal resources and those available in his family. Likewise, there should not be the slightest embarrassment on the part of any member of the Church who needs counsel to receive that counsel. At times it may be crucial that he seek and that he accept counsel.

When someone is discouraged and feels that he cannot solve a problem on his own, he may be right, but at least he is obligated to try. Every personal resource available to him should be committed before he takes another step, and he does have powerful resources. The Book of Mormon declares this one, which is often overlooked: ". . . for the Spirit is the same, yesterday, today, and forever. And the way is prepared from the fall of man, and salvation is free. *And men are instructed sufficiently that they know good from evil . . .* " (2 Nephi 2:4–5. Italics added.)

Decide to Do Right

It is critically important that a person understand that he already knows right from wrong, that he is innately, inherently, and intuitively good. When someone says, "I can't! I can't solve my problems!"—I want to thunder out, "Don't you realize who you are? Haven't you learned yet that you are a son or a daughter of Almighty God? Do you not know that there are powerful resources inherited from Him that you can call upon to give you steadiness and courage and great power?"

Most of us have been taught the gospel all our lives. We know the difference between good and evil, between right and wrong. Isn't it time then that we decide that we are going to do right? In so doing we are making a choice—

242

not just *a* choice but *the* choice. Once we have decided that, with no fingers crossed, no counterfeiting, no reservations or hesitancy, the rest will fall into place.

Most people who come to stake presidents, bishops, branch presidents, General Authorities, and teachers for counsel don't come because they are confused and unable to see the difference between right and wrong. They come because they're tempted to do something that deep down they know is wrong, and they want that decision ratified.

When someone has a problem, he should work it out in his own mind first. He should ponder on it, analyze it, meditate on it, and pray about it. I've come to learn that major decisions can't be forced. We must look ahead and have vision. As the prophet said in the Old Testament, "Where there is no vision, the people perish." (Proverbs 29:18.)

We should ponder on things a little each day and not always be in the crisis of making major decisions on the spur of the moment. If a person is looking ahead in life, he can see major problems coming down the road toward him from some considerable distance. By the time they meet one another, he is able, at the very beginning, to take charge of the situation. Once in a while a major decision will jump out at him from the side of the road and startle the wits out of him, but not very often. If he has already decided that he is going to do what is right and let all of the consequences follow, even those encounters won't hurt him.

Early Morning Meditation

I have learned that the best time to wrestle with major problems is early in the morning. Our minds are then fresh and alert. The blackboards of our minds have been erased by a good night's sleep. The accumulated distractions of the day are not in our way. Our bodies have been rested also. That is the time to think something through carefully and to receive personal revelation. For me, it is the best time to prepare lessons for a class I am to teach.

I heard President Harold B. Lee begin many a statement about matters involving revelation with an expression something like this: "In the early hours of the morning, while I was pondering upon that subject . . . " He made it a practice to work in the fresh, alert hours of the early morning on the problems that required revelation.

The Lord knew something when He directed in the Doctrine and Covenants, "Cease to sleep longer than is needful; retire to thy bed early, that ye may not be weary; arise early, that your bodies and your minds may be invigorated." (D&C 88:124.)

I have a friend who bought a business. A short time later he suffered catastrophic reverses, and there just didn't seem to be any way out for him. Finally it got so bad that he couldn't sleep, so for a period of time he followed the practice of getting up about three o'clock in the morning and going to the office. There, with a paper and a pen, he would ponder and pray and write down every idea that came to him as a possible solution or contribution to the solution of his problem.

It wasn't long before he had several possible directions in which he could go, and it wasn't much longer than that until he had chosen the best of them. But he had earned an extra bonus. His notes showed, after he went over them, that he had discovered many hidden resources he had never noticed before. He came away more independent and successful than he would ever have been if he hadn't suffered those reverses.

There's a lesson in this experience. A year or two later he was called to preside over a mission overseas. His business was so independent and well set up that when he came back he didn't return to it. He now has someone else managing it, and he is able to give virtually all his time to the blessing of others.

I counsel our children to do their critical studying in the early hours of the morning when they're fresh and alert, rather than to fight physical weariness and mental exhaustion at night. I've learned the power of the dictum, "Early to bed, early to rise." When I'm under pressure, you won't find me burning the midnight oil. I'd much rather be in bed early and getting up in the wee hours of the morning, when I can be close to Him who guides this work.

Revelation

We have all been taught that revelation is available to each of us individually. The question I'm most often asked about revelation is, "How do I know when I have received it? I've prayed about it and fasted over this problem and I still don't quite know what to do. How can I really tell whether I'm being inspired so I won't make a mistake?"

First, do we go to the Lord with a problem and ask Him to make our decision for us? Or do we work and meditate and pray and then make a decision ourselves? We should measure the problem against what we know to be right and wrong, make the decision, and then ask Him if the decision is right or if it is wrong. We should remember what He said to Oliver Cowdery about working a problem out in our minds. (See D&C 9.)

If we foolishly ask our bishop or branch president or the Lord to make a decision for us, we have used precious little self-reliance. Think what it costs every time we have somebody else make a decision for us.

May I mention one other thing — and I hope this won't be misunderstood. We often find young people who will pray with great exertion over matters that they are free to decide for themselves. Suppose a couple has money available to build a house and they have prayed endlessly over whether the architecture should be Early American, ranch, modern, or perhaps Mediterranean style. It has never occurred to them that perhaps the Lord just plain doesn't care. Let them build what they want to build. It is their choice. In many things we can do just what we want.

Now there *are* some things He cares about very much. If they are going to build that house, then they should be honest and pay for the material that goes into it and do a decent job of building it. And when they move into it, they should live righteously in it. Those are the things that count.

On occasions I've had to counsel people for whom the Lord would probably quite willingly approve the thing they intend and want to do. It's strange that they would come and almost feel guilty about doing something because they want to, even when it's righteous. The Lord is very generous with the freedom He gives us. The more we learn to follow the right, the more we are spiritually self-reliant, the more our freedom and our independence are affirmed. "If ye continue in my word," he said, "then are ye my disciples indeed; And ye shall know the truth, and the truth shall make you free." (John 8:31–32.)

Laman and Lemuel complained to Nephi, "Behold, we cannot understand the words which our father hath spoken." "Have ye inquired of the Lord?" Nephi asked them. Now think of this answer. They said to him, "We have not; for the Lord maketh no such thing known to us."

"How is it," Nephi answered, "that ye do not keep the commandments of the Lord? How is it that ye will perish, because of the hardness of your hearts? Do ye not remember the things which the Lord said?—If ye will not harden your hearts, and ask me in faith, believing that ye shall receive, with diligence in keeping my commandments, surely these things shall be made known unto you." (1 Nephi 15:7–11.)

If we lose the spirit and power of individual revelation, we have lost much in this church. We have great and powerful resources. Through prayer we can solve our problems without endlessly going to those who are trying so hard to help others.

If we become so independent and insecure that prayer and the answer to prayer are such that we are hesitant to rely on them, then we are weak. If we follow a course where on one hand we would carefully scrutinize an order for welfare products and yet, on the other hand, we would dole out counsel and advice without sending a person to his own storehouse of knowledge and inspiration, then we have done him a disservice.

This church relies on individual testimony. Each must earn his own testimony. It is then that each can stand and say, "I know that God lives, that He is our Father, that we have a child-parent relationship with Him. I know that He is close, that we can go to Him and appeal, and then, if we will be obedient and will listen and use every resource, we will have an answer to our prayers."

Counsel to Counselors

One's parent is the first in line as the counselor to each member of the Church. The bishop comes next. He is the common judge in Israel. The quorum president is responsible to "teach his members according to the covenants."

Teachers are to teach. Among the most important things a teacher can teach is where members of the Church should go for counsel. He should be alert that it is his privilege to help them solve problems themselves by taking them through those channels where revelation and inspiration will be available to those who counsel as well as to those desiring to solve problems.

I was surprised on one occasion to hear a lovely lady with whom I am well acquainted tell this incident from her early childhood. She described herself as having been a willful, selfish child. As I recall, she had been raised with a family of brothers and was, by her own description, spoiled.

She came home from her first Valentine's Day at school as a tearful first-grader and sobbed to her mother that she had not received one valentine from a classmate. She received more than sympathy from a wise mother who said, "Ruth, my dear, a valentine is an expression of love. If you are to receive the love of those around you in the world, you must be the kind of person who earns and deserves their love." The wise mother gently told her that she had not received their love because she had not deserved it. She told her other things also, and concluded by giving her a beautiful valentine.

I said I was surprised to hear her relate this incident from her childhood, because one could not imagine her being willful or selfish in any way. She grew to be a teacher, a leader of women in her ward and stake, the wife of a bishop and a stake leader, then at the side of her husband as he presided over a mission in one of the far places of the world. Anyone who knows her could not help but love her.

I cannot think of that wise mother counseling her little girl and expressing love to her, yet not indulging her, without suggesting to you as a teacher: Go thou and do likewise.

CHAPTER TWENTY-NINE

Humor in the Classroom

I have always thought it significant and sad that textbooks in the field of education might be characterized as scholarly and erudite and dull. Isn't it interesting that colleges of education expose prospective teachers to a couple of dozen textbooks or more in the course of their specialized training and they do not have a bit of humor in any of them. It's as though we expected students to suspend whatever natural spirit they might have to qualify them as teachers while they are in the process of training to be teachers. That has always impressed me as being a mistake. It seems to me that textbooks on the subject of teaching people to teach ought to be the most interesting of all books.

To have a sense of humor is not merely to collect and tell jokes. It is to sense those things which are humorous and add a little humor, a little sparkle, to a lesson. Someone has said that a sense of humor is oil for the machinery of life. A good sense of humor is a characteristic of a well-balanced person.

It has always been apparent that the prophets were men with very alert and pleasing senses of humor. Despite the fact that they are dealing with the most serious and sometimes the most tragic and difficult things in life, the Brethren can always smile.

Someone confronted with a very difficult situation once said, "Well, you either have to laugh or cry, and laughing is easier."

A sense of humor is a powerfully important attribute of a good teacher. The gospel is a happy and a pleasant gospel. There are times when we may be solemn almost to tears, but a good teacher will develop a sense of humor. Always there will be students in the class with sharp wits, and they can be depended upon to break the tension.

Following are a few illustrations of humor that can be used in a classroom. Some are experiences I have had that have tended to keep my sense of humor active and alert. A sense of humor has been valuable to me as a leader in the Church, a teacher in a class, and the father of a family.

Perhaps the most humorous thing that happened to me as a teacher occurred when I was teaching seminary. One of the most popular entertainers of that day was Edgar Bergen, the ventriloquist, with his dummies Charlie McCarthy and Mortimer Snerd. Charlie McCarthy, dressed in a black tuxedo, was a suave and polished city boy. Mortimer Snerd, on the other hand, was a caricature of the stupid country bumpkin. When asked a question such as, "Who is buried in Grant's Tomb?" he would struggle for awhile, give several incorrect answers, and finally give up.

A boy in one of the seminary classes was not entirely unlike Mortimer Snerd, and of course he soon had the nickname. It was good-natured on the part of the other students, and yet it was a cruel thing to call him "Mortimer" or "Snerd" all the time.

One day an announcement came over the intercom asking him to report to the principal's office. He left amid the teasing taunts of his classmates. As soon as the door was closed, I lowered the boom. In anger I lectured the class on their inexcusable cruelty. "Do you realize what you are doing to him? There is not the slightest justification for calling him Mortimer as a nickname," I said.

Suddenly the door opened. He'd made a very quick trip to the office and had returned too soon. I was so surprised to see him enter in the middle of my lecture that I mistakenly blurted out, "Good heavens, Mortimer! What are you doing back here so soon?"

On one occasion I began a seminary class by solemnly announcing, "We shall now call the roll." An obedient student began, as though calling a dog, "Here Roll! Here Roll!" The class, of course, responded with great laughter. When I joined in, we were off to a good start. It was the beginning of a pleasant association.

A Lesson a Teacher Must Learn

To have a sense of humor is a lesson a teacher must learn. I have known teachers who did not learn it.

When I was attending college, I enrolled in a physiology class. One day during a lecture the professor asked me to sit up on the high table at the front of the room so he could demonstrate the principle of reflexes. He took a little mallet, similar to the one a medical doctor would use, and proceeded to tap me on the knee, expecting my leg to jerk noticeably in typical reflex action. However, I held my leg very rigid and flipped my arm in the air when he tapped my knee.

The class roared with delight. The professor was not amused. We did not thereafter appreciate one another. I was branded as an impudent upstart, and at the end of the semester my grade reflected that categorization.

Humorous stories can often be told to illustrate points in a lesson. If I were giving a lesson on resourcefulness, I think I could use this one. It was told to me by the president of a stake a great distance from Church headquarters. It seems that two members of the stake, both endowed, were critically ill and neither was expected to live. The person in charge of burial clothes telephoned the stake president one night, exercised over the possibility of two funerals and only one set of burial clothes. "What shall I do?" he asked the president.

The president, seeing no solution, said he would just have to work it out himself, for there would not be time to send to Church headquarters for the clothing. Then he forgot the incident. He was reminded of it when he saw that person at a meeting some weeks later. "How did you come out with your problem?" he inquired.

"All right," said the man, "no trouble."

"What did you do?" the president inquired.

"Oh," he answered, "I went out and administered to one of them."

On one occasion I was teaching summer school at Brigham Young University. It was an early morning class beginning at seven o'clock. President Ernest Anderson of the La Grande Stake in Oregon, who is a personal friend, was traveling with his family, and we invited them to stay overnight with us. Brother and Sister Anderson were given our bedroom for the night. Since we were late getting settled down, I hurriedly got my clothes from the closet so I could be off at an early hour to teach the class.

When I got dressed in the morning, to my surprise, I had taken one black shoe and one brown one from the closet. I debated as to whether I should disturb our guests' sleep in order to get a mate for either shoe. Since they had gone to bed so late, I thought it would be unkind to disturb them. I reasoned that if I were a good enough teacher, I could hold the attention of the students so well that none of them would notice. I tried to be very impressive that day. Either no one noticed my mistake, as I would hope, or they *did* notice it and merely thought it typical of the absent-minded professor.

A fellow seminary teacher had a good rebuttal to a student who said he didn't like school and wished it were out. "You should feel bad. I have to stay here till I'm sixty-five!"

I once heard of a teacher who disliked Friday. He said it was too close to Monday.

Sometimes teachers are misunderstood, like the girl who complained that her Sunday School teacher had called her a "dirty elephant." Her irate parents got the bishop and the Sunday School teacher together, and when they finally had resolved the problem, they found that the teacher had told the daughter she was a "disturbing element" in the class.

In the minds of little youngsters, teaching can be interesting in its interpretation. When we lived in Lindon, Utah, one of the neighbor families moved over to Orem, a distance of three miles. One of the youngsters in the family was thereafter reluctant to go to church, causing some concern to her parents. She wanted to go back to Lindon for church. They thought it was the appeal of her friends until she finally explained. She had been told in Lindon that she belonged to the only true church, and so she didn't want to go to the ward in Orem. She wanted to go back to the true one.

And then there's the story of the youngster who was too sick to go to school, complaining that it hurt too much. "Just where does it hurt?" asked the father. "In school," was the answer.

I suppose every teacher has been misquoted and perhaps misrepresented and misunderstood in a lesson, and you have to learn to take that without complaint and be philosophical about it. It's like the account of the man who said to his wife, "Did you hear the story of the window that needed cleaning?" The wife said, "No, tell it to me." "Well, I guess I won't; you couldn't see through it anyway," was his reply. The woman, thinking that was a clever joke, told her neighbor, "Have you heard the joke about the window you couldn't see through?" "No," was the reply. "Well, it's too dirty to tell."

> I don't like the teacher;
> The subject is too deep.
> I'd quit this class
> But I need the sleep.

Our little brown-eyed boy came home one day from kindergarten chuckling to himself. I asked him what was so amusing.

"Nuffin," he replied, still chuckling.

"What is so funny?" I persisted.

"Nuffin."

When he chuckled even more, I pressed him and said, "Well, what *is* so funny?"

And then he said, "Oh, dey's a tid over in tindadarten dat tain't tok plain."

I suggest that our grownup judgments of one another, and maybe our judgments of ourselves, are just about that mature.

Whenever I say the word *Africa,* I remember one of those unforgettable characters we've all met. I met one in Africa where we were to attend a branch conference. In South Africa one's accent is either very English or very Dutch or very Afrikaans. We arrived at the chapel a little early, and the first person I met was a little boy about seven, small for his age and "veddy English."

I made several diplomatic blunders in my encounter with this unforgettable character. The first one was to say, "Well, hello, young man. How are you?" He looked up and said, "Well, I'm 'aving a tuff tame of it, really."

My second blunder was to say, "Well, what seems to be the trouble?" He proceeded to tell me something about

254

being in school and not being able to sing. He failed in music and had to rearrange all his classes, etc., etc., etc.

Finally I thought maybe I'd better be greeting some of the other people, but the little boy wasn't finished yet. As I began shaking hands with others, he was still talking to me. Then he became excluded from the circle, as can happen with someone that little, and I thought to myself, "Well, I've survived that." But later, as we went up to the stand to start the meeting, I felt someone tug at my coat. I looked down and there he was again. He said, "Besides, a've 'ad a totch a' the flu."

Here is another lesson, drawn from a little girl who reported to her mother that her brother was setting traps for birds. She didn't like that at all. "He won't catch any birds in his traps, will he, Mother?" she asked.

The mother said, "Perhaps he will—you cannot be sure he will not."

"I have prayed about it and asked Heavenly Father to protect the birds," the girl said. Then, becoming more positive, she said, "I *know* he won't catch any because I have prayed about it."

The mother asked, "How can you be so positive?"

Then came the meaningful reply: "He won't catch any birds because after I said my prayers, I went out and kicked those old traps all to pieces."

Practice looking for the humorous side in teaching situations—at home and in the classroom. You might be surprised at the change it can make in the attitudes of those whom you teach, the ice it can help break, the warm feelings of joy it can generate.

CHAPTER THIRTY

Teachers, the Treasurers of Time

Time, the basic commodity of life, is the medium from which all activities of life are created. Time is inexorable and relentless in its progress. "A few minutes ago" vanishes to join a column of yester-days that follow last year into the country called the past. Time has never been successfully stockpiled. Illusive of all storage procedures, it must—absolutely must—be consumed in one fashion or another as it is produced.

So commonplace is time that it is frequently wasted. Around us we constantly see those who are throwing large amounts of time to waste with such abandon as to suggest that they have a great surplus, even unlimited wealth of the commodity. Almost never in this life does one see a balance sheet showing a total of just how much remains. Such a statement of account would surely compel us to use our time prudently.

Often we awaken to the realization that we have been duped—swindled of part of our priceless legacy by one of many agencies clamoring for the attention of mankind. No protective agency can redeem it. It cannot be insured; it will never be recovered and returned. No public statutes compel the wise use of time, perhaps unfortunately so, else many a speaker and many a teacher could be charged with embezzlement.

Teachers are treasurers of time. They act as brokers assisting large groups of students to invest time wisely. They are charged with the responsibility of providing each student with dividends worthy of his investment.

In acting as the broker for someone else's time, consider the following:

A careful audit of the use of time is always appropriate. Consciously determine what you expect to accomplish with the time. In other words, have an objective.

Carefully judge what ideas or concepts the students will receive as dividends for time spent. Students usually retain concepts and principles; they seldom retain facts.

Select from the many facts available sufficient to illuminate your ideas. Choose only enough facts to convey the ideas, but not so many as to cover them up.

Begin efficiently in Church classes. A short, impressive devotional is time wisely spent to gain a mind-set for the student. It must be followed immediately with some productive action.

Determine what will be gained if you monopolize all of the time. Is it possible that the wisest teacher is one who allots to the students a large portion of the time and assists them in spending it wisely?

Be conscious of time *during* the lesson presentation. Make regular, systematic progress through the lesson, the unit, and the course. There is a moral in the story of the tortoise and the hare.

Double dividends come to the alert, efficient classroom manager in the form of impressed, well-disciplined students. Remember that students, like anyone else, are reluctant to follow a disorganized rambler, a waster of time.

Punctuality is an essential trait of the teacher. It is a foundation, not an embellishment.

One of the most effective techniques we can use in classroom control is to convey to the student the impression that we consider his time to be valuable. Five minutes per class period spent in calling the roll can total fourteen hours and ten minutes for the average school year. The efficient teacher can easily reduce this time to an hour and thirty minutes, substantially less, if he calls a student assistant. Roll calling, passing out papers, late beginnings, needless clerical maneuvers — all probably rob the average class of fully twenty percent of its instructional time, more hours indeed than the full time scheduled for many college courses. A Sunday School teacher may spend something over four hours each year in calling the roll.

You need not be a fidgety clock watcher. The teacher who is serene but definite, leisurely but persistent, always has a balance of time on hand for the timely question, the extra activity, the valuable interview. The wise teacher is always on course and on schedule. The nonproficient teacher who denies his students twenty percent of their instructional time may well rob any number of individuals of that extra impressive moment of learning that may result in a lasting testimony.

Arranging a Meeting or Program

Determine the limits of the available time. Remember, a congregation or audience never gives a blank check to you, and few will tolerate it if you raise the amount of the check, even when expending only time. If the normal time is used wisely, going overtime is at best not necessary.

As you assign participants, be wise enough to know human nature. Five five-minute talks will almost never take only twenty-five minutes.

If you assign students to appear on programs, be helpful enough to review their contributions in order that the time of the audience will be most wisely served and the student in turn experiences success in the effort.

Be sure to explain to each speaker or participant the

whole program, noting how many other speakers will appear, what time has been allotted for each, and the total time for all.

When in doubt, underschedule the time. Was anyone ever offended by a program that was completed a few minutes early?

Be specific in assignments. Never assign "a short talk" but rather specify a five-, seven-, or ten-minute talk. Be helpful to the speaker. "Take what time you need" is not always fair to him; at least give some suggestion as to the length of the meeting or normal closing time. Acquaint each performer with the entire agenda, giving helpful suggestions on subject matter and theme.

As you plan graduation programs, student conventions, or other special meetings, and you are to have a special address or sermon, allow ample time to justify the speaker's preparation and travel. Never impose on him by introducing him near the time the meeting should be closing. This is discourteous.

When You Are Called to Speak

If the subject assigned is too broad for the allotted time, give a concise, outlined overview.

Do not waste time apologizing for lack of preparation or qualifications. Remember that a short talk requires more intensive preparation than a longer one. You will be most impressive if you do not waste words. Avoid verbiage of the "lead, guide, and direct" type. Speak directly to a point.

Remember, if you are asked to inspire and teach, do not merely entertain. Pay quite as much attention to your audience as you do to your notes. If you are note-bound or book-bound, you may miss the little signs of unrest and lack of interest, not the least of which is the glancing at clocks or watches.

Above all, the most important preparation is of yourself. Prepare so as to have the influence of the Holy Ghost.

Lesson Preparation

The lessons of the gospel are essentially lessons of attitude and behavior. Facts are merely tools or equipment necessary to establish meanings.

To manage the time of many individuals in a classroom with proficiency requires much preparation time for the teacher. The facts of the lesson constitute the mechanical framework and are learned through common study.

A finer preparation, the "finish" preparation, may always be done on time by your doing double duty. While doing manual work, while traveling, during those all-too-often wasted moments of waiting, the resourceful teacher is preparing not only tomorrow's lesson, but also making general preparations for many future lessons through observation of nature and of life and through prayer.

Remember, the Savior frequently prayed and relied upon meditation and observation, as indicated in his parables and other teachings.

Great teachers constantly employ their time wisely. An inspiring teacher confessed, when complimented on the marvelous knowledge of literature that embellished his lessons, that he had memorized most of it while guiding a plow. Another who seemed to have an endless repertory of illustrations and stories admitted that almost all of them had been gained during the time he was doing double duty.

The scriptural injunction to "treasure up in your minds continually the words of life, and it shall be given you in the very hour that portion that shall be meted unto every man" (D&C 84:85) has much significance for teachers of the gospel of Jesus Christ. Let your mind find constant employment in observation, in meditation, in prayer; then let your hand always be near a pencil and paper to record the essentials of such preparation before they vanish as quickly and completely as time itself.

When our brothers and sisters allot you part of their time as a speaker, as a program director, and most of all, as a teacher, they place at your disposal a portion of their lives. See that you respect the gift. Use it wisely; consider it a treasure. Know too that you as a teacher, giving of your time in the classroom and out, are giving of your life. That you may give it little by little does not diminish your qualification for the reward that comes to those who willingly give their lives in the service of others.

CHAPTER THIRTY-ONE

Visual Aids

 $\mathbf{M}$ any years ago I heard President Oscar Kirkham tell this experience. He had been at a conference somewhere in southern Utah. In those days much of the week was spent by the Brethren traveling to and from the conferences. On Tuesday afternoon on his way back to Salt Lake City he came to a place where the road had been washed out by a flash flood and there was a large puddle of mud and silt. Every car that tried to cross it was stuck.

An enterprising farmer stood by with a team of horses. For a fee he would hitch his team and pull the cars across the puddle. The farmer recognized President Kirkham and introduced himself as the bishop of the local ward. "I'll pull you through for nothing," he said, "provided you'll stay over and speak to our young people in MIA tonight."

President Kirkham, who was anxious to be on his way home, said he'd rather just pay the fee. "In that case," said the bishop, "you can stay where you are." President Kirkham decided that under the circumstances, he would lose no more time if he stayed overnight and got an early start, so it was agreed upon.

On the way to the meeting the bishop explained they'd been having trouble with the teenage boys in the ward.

He said they couldn't hold a good MIA because of the disturbance. He said that he wouldn't feel so bad if the boys would just not come, but they always showed up to disturb whatever was going on in the chapel.

The chapel was a little frame building with steps from both sides to a landing outside the front door. Word had been sent out that one of the General Authorities was to speak and so the young people had gathered, including the rowdy boys. However, they did not come in the building but, as was their custom, assembled on the steps where they could effectively disturb all that was going on.

President Kirkham knew that he had but one chance to take charge of the situation, and he seized upon an experience of the previous weekend. He didn't begin his talk on the Word of Wisdom or reverence or obedience. He began by saying that down in the community where he had been at the conference, somebody had brought a monstrous bear out of the mountains. Everyone in town had assembled to look at it.

"I have never seen such a big animal," he said. "Why, the claws on that bear were this long," he said, gesturing with his two hands to show the length of the claws.

The boys on the steps outside could hear what he was saying, but could not see what he was doing. Soon a face or two appeared at the door.

"The teeth on the animal were this big," he said, gesturing. The faces appeared again.

He went on to describe with some words, but mostly in gestures, the monstrous bear. And, he later told us, by the time he was finished, the boys had all crept in from the porch and were seated on the back row. He moved on from his bear story to teach the gospel to them without further interruption.

That dead bear in a community many miles away

brought the boys to meeting and became a very effective visual aid.

Use Sparingly

In education, as in other fields, there comes along every now and then some new development, some so-called discovery or innovation or invention that is said to be the final answer to all of the problems in teaching. Such things sweep the world, are enthusiastically adopted by teachers, professionally and in other organizations, then either fade away or adjust themselves into the small niche that they will fill thereafter.

I remember a few years ago when teaching machines were proclaimed as the final answer. There was much to recommend them. They could be adapted to the fast learner or to the slow student. They were excellent for individual study. Any subject matter could be programmed to fit them, and there were any number of other virtues. But somehow they were not the final answer, and so it goes.

Teachers would do well not to be extremists on anything and to be cautious and wise in adopting new techniques or procedures.

Audio and visual aids in a class can be a blessing or a curse, depending upon how they are used. They might be compared to spices and flavorings that go with a meal. They should be used sparingly to accent or make a lesson interesting, but the basic instruction, when all is said and done, will for the most part be lecture, question and answer, and recitation.

A lot of verbal references are found in the New Testament which indicate that the Lord used visual aids to emphasize a lesson. When He said, "Consider the lilies of the field . . . they toil not, neither do they spin" (Matthew 6:28), it is possible, even probable, that lilies were in view at the time.

When He asked for a coin and asked whose superscription was upon it, a coin was there for all of them to see.

There was also the fig tree, and on many occasions there were people—the lepers, those sick with palsy, the blind, the lame, the deaf. All visual aids.

In the chapter on apperception, we talked about the ability of man, by using the alphabet, to reproduce in symbolic form the world in which he lives. In recent generations we have acquired the ability to produce images of the world around us to near perfection. With printing and photography, both still and motion pictures, developed to the degree that they are, we have the whole world at our disposal in the form of visual aids.

If you have been to Jerusalem (and I have not), you can show me the slides you took. If neither of us has been there, we can go to the library and get pictures or motion pictures. Incidents in the life of the Savior and the lives of the prophets can be reproduced in dramatic form and filmed so that we can relive them.

Be careful to use visual aids sparingly. The best of them are really the simplest and are often those that are readily available. On balance I think that no teaching aid surpasses, and few equal, the chalkboard: first, because it is simple to use, and next, because it is universally available — everywhere in the world you can get a chalkboard. You can use it to focus the eyes of your students while the main lesson is presented audibly. As you talk, you can put just enough on the board to focus their attention and give them the idea, but never so much that the visual aid itself distracts them and becomes more interesting than your lesson.

Perhaps the most common mistake in employing written words as visual aids is in not synchronizing sight and sound. The mistake is made so frequently that only occasionally do you see it done correctly. If you have words to write on the chalkboard, or if they are on a chart, or if they are put on a flannelboard, or if they are thrown on a screen from a projector, the students should see with their eyes and hear with their ears at the same time.

Suppose you flash a list of five objectives on a screen and then describe them in words other than those the students can see on the screen. You have the eye and the ear out of synchronization. Some of the students are concentrating on reading, and their minds are forming those words. Others are listening only to you, and most of them are trying to do both at once and are doing neither very well. When you flash a list on the screen, it should be read so that the eye is directed and the ear is focused on the same word at the same time. Otherwise the chances of permanent learning taking place are greatly reduced.

Unfortunately this is rarely done. To fail to do it is to make very poor use of the powerful tools available in visual aids. Many of them are right in front of us all the time but are ignored.

I have always thought that films, filmstrips, and tapes that are not complete — that is, that are open-ended — can be very helpful in sponsoring meaningful discussion. Too often we want to tell the whole story.

In using visual aids, be sure they have a purpose. Don't use them merely as decoration. Bring them out when you are ready to refer to them, so they don't distract class members and draw their attention away from the lesson. And don't use visual aids that are merely decoration for the classroom.

A picture may be worth a thousand words, but only if it is used judiciously to enhance the lesson and make a point.

CHAPTER THIRTY-TWO

Object Lessons

 A mong a number of types of visual aids is the type used in the object lesson, in which the teacher uses an object to focus attention or make a particular point. A tangible object that is small enough to bring to class can be helpful in anchoring a lesson. At times a subject that is difficult to teach can be taught with the aid of this technique.

When I was president of the New England Mission, we were not doing well in convert baptisms. The missionaries contacted many people who were willing to receive the first discussion and the second, but then almost all of them faded away. It was reasonable to assume that if we had them for the first and second discussions, if we taught them well enough, they would show sufficient interest to continue.

We determined that we should do something to improve the teaching of the missionaries. We were using the six discussions with the flannelboard characters to go along with them, so we analyzed each of the discussions and the teaching techniques that would apply and began to have the missionaries meet to improve their presentations.

There was not much enthusiasm for the project. It took

hours in district meetings, with zone and district leaders appraising each pair of missionaries and criticizing their presentation. What they needed was to be motivated.

I remembered that a number of years before, Elder A. Theodore Tuttle had made a presentation to a special meeting of priesthood leaders at general conference. The priesthood course of study for that year was on the apostasy. It was a scholarly work, in many ways more fitted for a symposium of intellectuals and scholars, and the priesthood quorum teachers in the Church were having much difficulty with it. In October those instructors attending general conference were invited to attend a special meeting. Brother Tuttle and I and one or two others were invited to show them ways to make their lessons more interesting and to help them prepare more easily.

For my part I presented a brief lesson on the Apostasy on a flannelboard, a teaching aid that had not been used much in the Church theretofore. After my presentation, Elder Adam S. Bennion opened the meeting for questions and answers. He stood by me at the microphone as the questions came in. After one or two questions, one older gentleman stood up and, in a very negative way, referring to the flannelboard, said, "Don't you think it's rather childish to use something like that in a priesthood quorum?" I was nervous anyway, and was taken aback by his question. I looked at Elder Bennion and he simply said, "Go ahead."

To this day I am certain I was prompted by inspiration. "Yes, I agree," I replied. "I think it is perhaps very childish, but we should all remember that 'except ye become as a little child, ye shall in nowise enter the kingdom of heaven.' " A chuckle of approval went through the audience, and there was no more negative comment in the meeting.

Brother Tuttle gave his instruction on the importance of having well-prepared lessons and concluded with an object-lesson demonstration. That was the one that served my needs so well in the mission field. I will explain how we used it with the missionaries.

A Piece of Cake

We scheduled zone conferences. For each one, Sister Packer baked a three-tiered cake, which she and Sister Bateman decorated beautifully—thick, colorful layers of frosting, trimmed beautifully, and with "The Gospel" inscribed across the top. When the missionaries were assembled, with some ceremony we brought the cake in. It was something to behold!

As we pointed out that the cake represented the gospel, we asked, "Who would like to have some?" There was always a hungry elder who eagerly volunteered. We called him forward and said, "We will serve you first." I then sank my fingers into the top of the cake and tore out a large piece. I was careful to clench my fist after tearing it out so that the frosting would ooze through my fingers, and then as the elders sat in total disbelief, I threw the piece of cake to the elder, splattering some frosting down the front of his suit. "Would anyone else like some cake?" I inquired. For some reason, there were no takers.

Then we produced a crystal dish, a silver fork, a linen napkin, and a beautiful silver serving knife. With great dignity I carefully cut a slice of the cake from the other side, gently set it on the crystal dish, and asked, "Would anyone like a piece of cake?"

The lesson was obvious. It was the same cake in both cases, the same flavor, the same nourishment. The manner of serving either made it inviting, even enticing, or uninviting, even revolting. The cake, we reminded the missionaries, represented the gospel. How were they serving it?

After the demonstration we had no difficulty—in fact,

some considerable enthusiasm—for the effort to improve the teaching of the discussions. A few months later I thought the missionaries might well be reminded of the lesson, so I sent out a bulletin with a sketch of the cake.

When I met the missionaries again, I said, "You received a bulletin recently, didn't you?"

"Yes indeed."

"And what did it say?"

Invariably the missionaries said, "It reminded us to sharpen up on presenting our lessons and to do more studying, to learn the lessons carefully, and then to help one another in our procedure for having them taught."

"You got all that out of a picture?"

"Yes, that's one lesson we won't soon forget!"

I should, of course, add that I was very happy where necessary to pay the bill to clean the elder's suit!

Object lessons, I have found, can also get you into trouble. A number of years ago I was chairman of a building committee for the Brigham City (Utah) Seventh Ward chapel. We did all the usual things to raise money, including a bake sale one Saturday evening. Most of the sisters had contributed baked goods, and the sale was successful. Bishop White asked me to make a report to the ward in sacrament meeting the following night.

It was at this time that we were to purchase the bricks for the building. So, after we had tabulated all of the money, I divided it by the number of items we had sold, giving an average income per item of baking. In making my report, I wanted to demonstrate how many bricks each item would purchase for the new chapel. I took several bricks to the pulpit and clumsily began my report by saying, "Brothers and sisters, these bricks represent the baking of the sisters of our ward." I was in serious trouble!

If you plan to use an object lesson approach, therefore, be forewarned. Be certain you plan well how you will use the object and know what you are going to say. It can make a deep impression on your audience if you don't allow it to backfire on you!

CHAPTER THIRTY-THREE

Like unto a Glove

In an earlier chapter we noted that the principle of apperception, as employed by Jesus in His teaching, opens the world of visual aids for our use. An otherwise difficult subject can be taught by using a simple, well-known object as a visual aid and then relating it to the untaught, intangible principle.

On one occasion I wanted to explain the Resurrection and was having considerable difficulty in doing so. I pondered on it for a time, and then one day as I was putting on a glove, it occurred to me that the glove would make a good visual aid. I used it a few times in talking to young people and finally felt confident enough to employ it in a general conference sermon.

After some practicing, I prepared the talk, in which I likened the physical body to a glove and the hand to a spirit. It was my intention to talk to the five-year-olds and the six-year-olds and the seven-year-olds, knowing full well that if I was successful in teaching them, I would not lose any member of the audience in the older age groups.

The results of the preparation are as follows:

* * *

There is something very important that I want to say to you children. Something I hope you'll always remember.

Something you should learn when you are children and things are easy to remember.

Did you know that you lived before you were born on earth? Before you were born to your father and mother you lived in the spirit world.

That is a very important thing to know. It explains many things that otherwise are very difficult to understand. Many people in the world do not know that, but it is the truth.

When you were born into this life you were not created then. Only your physical body was created. You came from somewhere. You left the presence of your Heavenly Father, for it was your time to live upon the earth.

There were two reasons you were to come into this life. First, to receive a physical body. This is a great blessing. Our Heavenly Father arranged things so that through a very sacred expression of love between your father and mother your body was conceived and began to grow. Then at some time, I don't know just when, your spirit entered into your body and you became a living person. But it did not all begin with your birth as a little baby.

Your body becomes an instrument of your mind and the foundation of your character. Through life in a physical body you can learn to control matter and that will be very important to you through all eternity.

The Spirit and the Body

Pretend, my little friends, that my hand represents your spirit. It is alive. It can move by itself. Suppose that this glove represents your physical body. It cannot move. When the spirit enters into your physical body, then it can move and act and live. Now you are a person—a spirit with a physical body, living on earth.

It was not intended that we stay here forever. Just for a lifetime. Your grandparents and great-grandparents are

274

nearly finished with theirs. It wasn't long ago that they were little fellows and little girls just like you are now. But one day they will leave this mortal existence, and so will you.

Someday, because of old age, or perhaps a disease or an accident, the spirit and the physical body will be separated. We then say a person has died. Death is a separation. All of this was according to a plan.

Remember, my hand represented your spirit and the

glove represented your physical body. While you are alive, the spirit inside the physical body can cause it to work and to act and to live.

When I separate them, the glove, which represents your physical body, is taken away from your spirit; it cannot move any more. It just falls down and is dead. But your spirit is still alive. "A spirit born of God is an immortal thing. When the body dies, the spirit does not die." (First Presidency, *Improvement Era,* March 1912, p. 463.)

It is important that you get in your mind what death is. Death is a separation.

The part of you that looks out through your eyes and allows you to think and smile and act and know and be, that is your spirit and that is eternal. It cannot die.

Do you remember when someone, perhaps a grand-mother, died? Remember your parents explained to you that it was just her body lying in the casket, that grand-mother had gone to live with Heavenly Father, and that she would be waiting there. You remember hearing them say that, don't you?

Death is a separation and is according to the plan. If the plan ended there, it would be too bad, because we came to obtain a physical body, and it would be lost.

We Can Return to Heavenly Father

When He made it possible for us to come into this world, our Heavenly Father also made it possible for us to return to Him, because He is our Father and He loves us. Do not think that because we are living on this earth away from Him and because we can't see Him, He has forgotten us.

Didn't you notice, when your older brother was away on his mission, or your sister was away at school, how your parents did not stop loving them? Sometimes it seemed to you they loved them more than they did you.

At least they would talk about them and sometimes worry about them. They sent help and messages to encourage them. Distance can make love grow stronger.

Little children, our Heavenly Father knew that we would need help. So, in the plan He provided for someone to come into the world and help us.

This person was Jesus Christ, the Son of God. He is a spirit child as all of us are; but also, Jesus was God's Only Begotten Son on the earth. I speak very reverently of Him. And He it was, my little friends, who made it possible for us to overcome death and get things put back the way they should be.

You are learning about Him in Sunday School, in Primary, and in family home evening. It is very important that you remember Him and learn all you can about what He did.

He overcame the mortal death for us. Through the Atonement, He made it possible for our spirit and our physical bodies to be one again. Because of Him we will be resurrected. He made it possible for us to be resurrected, for the spirit and the body to be put back together. That is what the Resurrection is. That is a gift from Him. All men will receive it. That is why He is called our Savior, our Redeemer.

The second reason you came here was to be tested. This is something like going away to school to learn good from evil. It is very important for us to be able to know the right from the wrong.

It is important for you to know that there is an evil one who will tempt you to do wrong. Because of this, there is another separation you should know about. Even when you are very young you should know about it. There is another separation that you need to think about—not the separation of the physical body from the spirit; rather, a separation from our Heavenly Father.

If we remain separated from Him and can't get back to His presence, then it would be as though we were spiritually dead. And that would not be good. This separation is like a second death—a spiritual death.

You are now learning to read, and you can begin to read the scriptures—the Bible, especially the Book of Mormon, the Doctrine and Covenants, and the Pearl of Great Price. From them we know that little children can learn spiritual truths. For the prophet said:

"He imparteth his word by angels unto men, yea, not only men but women also. Now this is not all; little children do have words given unto them many times which confound the wise and the learned." (Alma 32:23.)

In the scriptures we learn that our spirits must be clean and free from evil in order to return to the presence of our Heavenly Father. "There cannot any unclean thing enter into the kingdom of God." (1 Nephi 15:34.)

Two important things must happen to us, then. First, somehow we must get our physical bodies back after we die—that is, we want to be resurrected; and second, we must find a way to keep ourselves clean, spiritually clean, so that we will not be separated from our Heavenly Father and may return to where He is when we leave this earth life.

We Must Repent and Be Baptized

We are sure you will overcome mortal death. You will be resurrected because of what Christ did for us. Whether or not you overcome the spiritual death—that separation from the presence of our Heavenly Father—will depend a great deal on you.

When Jesus Christ was living on the earth He taught His gospel and organized His church. If we live the gospel, we will remain spiritually clean. Even when we make mistakes, there is a way to become clean again. That is what repentance is.

To enter His church, we must have faith in the Lord Jesus Christ. We must repent, and we must be baptized.

Baptism is like being buried in the water. When we come out of the water it is like being born again — and we are clean. We receive a remission of our sins. The sins are taken away. We can retain this remission of our sins if we will.

We are then confirmed as members of His church, The Church of Jesus Christ of Latter-day Saints. We may have the gift of the Holy Ghost to guide us. That is like receiving messages from our heavenly home, to show us the way to go.

The Lord called prophets and apostles to lead His church. He has always revealed His will through His prophets.

Although I sit now in the Council of the Twelve, I have never lost that reverent feeling about these men. Often when we meet in the council, I look around the circle and know again that these are the apostles of the Lord Jesus Christ upon the earth. They are special witnesses of Him.

You Will Be Tested

Little ones, you will be tested, perhaps more than any generation that ever lived here. You will meet many people who do not believe in Christ. Some will be agents for the evil one and will teach wickedness. Sometimes this will be very tempting.

There will be times when you have made mistakes (and all of us make mistakes). There will be times when you will wonder if you can live the way He taught we should live. When you are tested, when you are disappointed, or ashamed, or when you are sad, remember Him and pray to your Heavenly Father in His name.

279

Some men will say that He did not come to earth. But He did. Some will say that He is not the Son of God. But He is. Some will say that He has no servants upon the face of the earth. But He has. For He lives. I know that He lives. In His church there are many thousands who can bear witness of Him, and I bear witness of Him, and tell you again the things you should remember, things you should learn when you are yet a little one.

Remember that each of you is a child of our Heavenly Father. That is why we call Him our Father.

You lived before you came to this earth. You came to receive a physical body and to be tested.

When your life is over, your spirit and physical body will be separated. We call that death.

Our Heavenly Father sent His Son, Jesus Christ, to redeem us. Because of what He has done, we will be resurrected.

There is another kind of death you should think of. That is the separation from the presence of our Heavenly Father. If we will be baptized and live His gospel, we may be redeemed from this second death.

Our Heavenly Father loves us, and we have a Lord and Savior.

I thank God for a church where you, our little children, are precious above all things. I thank God for our Savior, who suffered the little children to come unto Him.

You have sung these words:

> I think when I read that sweet story of old,
> When Jesus was here among men,
> How He called little children like lambs to His fold,
> I should like to have been with Him then.

> I wish that His hands had been placed on my head,
> That His arms had been thrown around me,
> That I might have seen His kind look when He said,
> "Let the little ones come unto me."

My little brothers and sisters, my little children, I know that God lives. I know something of how it feels to have His hand put upon you to call you to His service. I bear witness and share with you the witness that has been given me, that special witness. He is the Christ! He loves us! I pray for you, our little ones, and plead with Him to behold our little ones and to bless them, in the name of Jesus Christ. Amen.

* * *

Even so simple an object as a glove can be used to provide a powerful object lesson. Remember that the Savior Himself used the simplest objects in His teaching. Need we do more?

CHAPTER THIRTY-FOUR

The Teacher Is a Visual Aid

It should be comforting to know that a teacher can be unimpressive in appearance and yet be a powerful influence among the students if one or two principles are observed.

A teacher, of all people, should be carefully groomed. This has little to do with basic, physical features or age or proportion, but it has to do with neatness, with being presentable and clean. When you are going to teach a Sunday School class, give a priesthood lesson, make a presentation in Relief Society, or conduct a meeting, it is a good idea to have your husband or wife or some other member of the family give you a quick once-over just as you leave the house. Then you will feel confident that you look your best.

In the home or the classroom, the parent or teacher is under constant scrutiny. There is an inconsistency in a parent who is always complaining, wanting the youngsters to pick something up or to clean up their room and keep things neat and orderly, when the parent is shabby and unkempt.

I have admired greatly a lesson my wife has taught all of us in our family. She gets up early in the morning to begin her day's activities. She does not lounge around in pajamas or a housecoat with her hair in curlers. She is a lesson in complete "casualness." She quickly brushes her hair, slips on something neat, and is about her work. I have come to know that this attitude contributes greatly to the orderliness, the peace, and the tranquillity of a home. A visual aid—not much preaching, but a lot of example.

They Want to Reach Up—Not Over

I have always urged teachers to be just a little on the formal side. I recall visiting a teacher in Arizona who was having a good deal of trouble maintaining his position as a teacher. "I just can't seem to get the class's attention and keep it," he said.

He was dressed in a pair of slacks, and the cuffs of his shirt were turned back, his collar was open, and he wore no tie. "It's a little difficult," I said, "when one walks into the class, to pick out exactly who is the teacher. I think you'd get along much better if you signaled this information to the students every time they looked at you. Why don't you wear a suit coat," I suggested, "or at least button your cuffs and your collar and put on a tie? Just stay that much more formal than the students."

It made the difference in his success with discipline.

Regardless of what students say when you discuss this matter, the buddy system of teaching is not a classroom system. If you have groups to deal with, you'll soon find that students want to reach *up* to a teacher, not *over* to him. When they have real problems, they want to go beyond what they can get from a buddy. They want to reach up. And there are some little elements of formality in dress and in grooming that help immeasurably in teaching classes.

Some teachers have the feeling that they must have complete fraternity with their students, and that to be otherwise is stilted or stuffy. It's worth giving that a second thought. There are some tangible ways in which a teacher can be "set apart" for his calling.

No Different from the Crowd

On one occasion I went to a stake conference in a large city. When I arrived at the airport I glanced around the large semicircle of people waiting for the passengers to disembark and did not see the stake presidency. I had not met them previously, but it is usually easy to recognize our Church leaders in a crowd. Seeing no one there to meet me, I headed for the lobby. A moment or two later someone was calling my name and running to catch up with me. It was a counselor in the stake presidency. He explained that the stake president had been unavoidably delayed and would meet us at the stake center for the meetings.

The following day, after stake conference, the stake president took me to the airport. As we rode along, the conversation went something like this.

"Brother Packer, you haven't said very much during our conference. Please feel free in giving me some counsel on how we might improve the work."

He then explained that they were holding all of the meetings, and I had observed that they were trying with real dedication to reach the young people. "But we just can't seem to influence them," he said. "Our reports show we are failing, and yet we don't know why. Certainly we are doing enough work. We have enough activities and we try hard enough. Why is it that we're not doing better? Can you tell me?"

"I think I can tell you," I said, "if you will understand what I mean by this illustration. When I got off the airplane yesterday and your counselor was there to meet me, I didn't recognize him in the crowd. That, I think, is what is wrong with your stake. I have observed that your leaders are trying to reach the young people by joining them in their dress and grooming standards. It is important for leaders to know that when young people really want help, they want to reach up and not over. Do you understand what I mean?"

He was quick to understand and explained that they had deliberately determined that they would dress like the young people and groom like the young people and try to be in the young people's world as much as possible in order to be buddies with them, and in that way they would lead them into the Church activities.

"I have observed that you're putting in the time," I said. "You are working hard, but you're not getting a fair return on your effort. I think that if you will analyze this matter of dressing like the young people, you will find that you are saying things and doing things in a different way than you would if you maintained the image of stake and ward leaders. I have an idea that if you were to change your image, the young people would respond to you more quickly and more spiritual power would come through."

On other occasions I have observed leaders of young people trying so hard to be like them. They have not realized that such actions demonstrate visually that they want to join them, not lead them.

The teacher is the most important visual aid in the classroom. When I have seen a stake presidency, a high council, or a bishopric dressed and groomed like teenagers, all of my teaching experience seems to confirm the probability that they are not as strong an influence among the youth as they would be if they were to maintain the dignity and image of their leadership callings.

There are times, on picnics and other informal occasions, when they can mingle with and dress like the young people, but that would be an exception.

I repeat, when young people want help—when they *really* want help—they reach up, not over.

CHAPTER THIRTY-FIVE

Tell Us a Story

Stories can be used effectively to interest a class and teach them. I suppose there are stories that might occasionally be used merely to entertain them. That would be true perhaps only of little children. Everyone has so many experiences that might be useful in teaching if they were alert to them and recorded them.

As useful as stories are, I have always been scrupulously careful in telling stories not to give the impression that a fictitious story is true or that I participated in an incident when I did not. I know there are those who will want to make the stories appear to be part of their own experience. Personally, I feel that is dishonest. I would not do it, nor would I recommend it to anyone else. If I ever tell a story in my teaching and indicate that it is from my own experience, it did happen to me or I would never identify it that way. Nor should you feel it necessary to embellish or extend or decorate a story. If it won't stand on its own to illustrate the point, then don't use it. If you tell a fictitious story as though it were an experience of your own and then it ends up to be humorous and a joke and a put-on, the students will not know when to believe what you say.

There are enough simple true experiences in everyday life and there are many ways to construct lifelike stories such as in the parables of Jesus that a person doesn't need to fabricate an experience.

"Here Comes Heavenly Father"

When we were first married, we lived across the street from a chapel. One day our oldest son, who was then four years old, was leaning on the window sill looking out across at the chapel. He calmly observed, "Here comes Heavenly Father." My wife and I were quite interested in that expression and went to the window. We could see Brother Hawkes coming across the street with a bucket in each hand. It was Saturday, and Brother Hawkes, the custodian of the chapel, would come over each Saturday morning and get two buckets of hot water to use in his cleaning.

"Oh, that's just Brother Hawkes," my wife said to our son. The child protested and said, "Well, you said that's Heavenly Father's house, and he's the one who always stays there and takes care of it." When Brother Hawkes arrived, we told him what an example he would now be expected to maintain, which, of course, is not too much to ask, because we all should aspire to that.

This illustration is an example of a story that merely recounts an incident that has happened in life. If you are alert, there will be many experiences that will have application quite as good as this one. Occasionally you may want to create a story in order to teach a principle. This, of course, is merely constructing a parable. It is a perfectly useful and respectable teaching procedure. As you study the teaching procedures of Jesus, you will find that He employed it many many times.

When you do this, it is important that you make it clear to the students that it is a lifelike story prepared to illustrate the point. You may introduce it by saying, "Suppose," or

287

"Imagine." The fact that you have invented the story does not in the least detract from the teaching power it has if it is carefully presented. Following is an example of that kind of a story.

At the Picnic

Suppose that our ward is having a picnic. We have arranged for a picnic area to be reserved for that day, and much careful preparation has been accomplished under the direction of the bishop. The Relief Society has been assigned to prepare the meal.

It is in the summertime, when so many wonderful foods are available. We will have all of the mouth-watering, delicious foods that seldom come together in one meal. This is to be a great event.

Our Relief Society president will always say, "Food must not only be nourishing and well-prepared — it must also be beautifully displayed. The table should be pleasantly arranged. Colors in the arrangement must all be complementary." And so it is with the table. One long table with all of us there. Never have we seen anything quite so beautiful, and never have we smelled anything quite so appealing as the food.

At last the time has arrived for the meal. The preparation of many weeks now has culminated; in a moment we are to begin this one unsurpassed meal. Our patriarch is invited to give the prayer. The little children, having a hard time restraining themselves, think, "I hope he doesn't pray all day."

Just as he prepares to give the blessing on the food, there is an interruption. A car rattles off the road into the picnic ground and comes to a halt not far from our table. It is a very noisy car and it is sputtering. We are all disturbed at the intrusion and complain to one another. "Why are they stopping here? Didn't they see the sign that this picnic ground is reserved?"

A man gets out of the car and with worried expression raises the hood and opens the radiator. There is a loud noise, and a column of steam shoots out. One of the ward members, a mechanic, observes, "That car isn't going anywhere without a great deal of help." Then the car doors fly open and seven or eight little children climb out, and the father and the mother have a worried conversation about the car.

The children, as children do, immediately become interested in what we're doing and come wandering around to see what's going on at the picnic ground. The parents, distracted by the condition of the car, do not call them back. One little boy thrusts his head between you and me at the table, looks for a moment, runs away, and soon returns with his little sister. They are not very clean. She has cried a lot that day; you can see, because the tears have washed clean that part of her face where they have run down her cheeks. Her brother points at the food on the table and says, "Mmm! Doesn't that look good! I wonder what it tastes like."

All of this time our patriarch is patiently waiting for things to settle down so he can give the blessing. We, of course, are not so patient, grumbling over this interruption. "Our food will get cold." Some comment is made to the parents to draw their attention, and they quickly gather their children and take them to a table not too far from ours.

It is mealtime, of course. The mother gets their lunch box from their car. It is a very meager offering. A little of this and that, a can that had been opened for an earlier meal and not all eaten. She looks at her children and at what is on the table, and then tries to move the food back and forth to make it look like there is more than there is.

Now, this is just a parable. But should it happen? If you were there and if I were there, what would we do? Let me suggest some choices:

1. We can insist that they behave while we have our meal. We rented the ground; we paid for it; it is our right; it is only just and fair that we have it without intrusion and without interruption. We can demand our rights.

2. We can be generous. We're Christians, aren't we? We have a little too much of this and too much of that; we could keep them from bothering us any more by sharing just a little. They can eat at that table over there. After all, their manners would obviously be poor, and they are not cleaned up and ready for an occasion such as we have prepared. They just don't fit in; and with a few crumbs as a cost, we can keep things pretty well to ourselves. Should we do that?

3. Of course, we know what might happen. I could move this way a little, and you could move that way a little, and we could set the little boy between us. His little sister could be across the table between Brother and Sister Jones. The mother and father could be down near the head of the table, and the patriarch could say the prayer. Wouldn't it be delightful to see how much we could make the youngsters eat? And as soon as we have had the meal, Brother Johnson, the mechanic, could go to work on the car. Brother Martin could run down to the nearest service station to pick up the parts that are needed. The Relief Society sisters, as they clear the table, could assemble a lunch box for the family to take, and Brother Bingham could be careful not to be observed when he slips the father a little extra to have on hand for the long journey they yet have ahead of them. That, of course, we like to think would be what would happen.

Well, yes, that would be what would happen. The first

two alternatives are unthinkable. The last is precisely what we would do all of the time — or is it?

We have been supposing, talking about feeding someone who is physically hungry. What about those around us who are spiritually hungry all the time? We have the fulness of the gospel, all that is worthwhile spiritually. Will we consume it without sharing it? Will we let those on either hand starve to death spiritually before we will share with them? Or will we count them unfit or unworthy to receive the gospel?

The Convertible

Another example of a parable is the following story about a convertible. This idea came from a comment by a teenager in class who had seen a beautiful sports convertible driven by a man in his early thirties. "What a shame to waste that car on an old fellow like him!" was the boy's comment.

It occurred to me that since teenagers are very interested in automobiles, I could appeal to that interest. I wanted to talk to teenagers in the Church about being obedient to their parents, and that could be a dull subject to them, even repulsive, if it were not handled carefully. So one day I stopped at an automobile dealership and looked at the new automobiles.

One in particular caught my eye — a convertible, sports model, with all the fancy equipment imaginable. It had push-button everything, and more horsepower than a division of cavalry. How I would have enjoyed a car like that when I was in high school!

From this experience the following story developed.

Imagine with me that I am your benefactor and I have decided to present to a typical teenager a car such as this, and you are the one who has been chosen. On the evening of the presentation, I see that you are not quite financially able to run such a car, so I generously include free gas, oil, maintenance, tires, anything your car would use; all of this, and the bills will come to me.

How you will enjoy that car! Think of driving it to school tomorrow. Think of all the new friends you will suddenly acquire. Now your parents may be hesitant to let you use this car freely, so I will visit with them. I am sure they will be reluctant, but because of my position as one of the leaders of the Church, they will consent.

Let us imagine, then, that you have your car, everything to run it, freedom to use it.

Suppose that one evening you are invited to attend a church social. "There are just enough of you to ride in my station wagon," your teacher says. "You may leave your car home."

When the group arrives to take you to the party, you suddenly remember your new convertible parked at the curb with the top down. You hastily go back into the house and give the keys to your father, asking that he put it in the garage, for it looks as though it may rain. Your father, of course, obediently agrees. (It is interesting how obedient parents have become these days.)

Later you come home and notice your car is not at the curb. "Dear old dad," you muse, "always willing to help out." But as the station wagon pulls into the driveway and the lights flash into the garage, you see that it is empty. You rush into the house, find father, and ask that very urgent question.

"Oh, I loaned it to someone," he responds.

Then imagine, seriously imagine, a conversation such as this:

"Well, who was it?"

"Oh, that boy who comes by here regularly."

"What boy?"

292

"Oh, that boy . . . well, I have seen him pass here several times on his bicycle."

"What is his name?"

"I'm afraid I didn't find out."

"Well, where did he take the car?"

"I really don't know."

"When will he bring it back?"

"There wasn't an agreement on that."

Then suppose your father says to you, with some impatience, "Now, you calm down. He rushed in here. He needed a car. You weren't using it. He seemed to be in a frantic hurry about something, and he looked like an honest boy, so I gave him the keys. Now relax and go to bed."

I suppose under the circumstances you would look at your father with a puzzled expression and wonder if some important connection had slipped loose in his thinking mechanism. It would take a foolish father to loan such an expensive piece of equipment on an arrangement such as that—particularly one that belonged to you.

I am sure that you have anticipated the moral of this little illustration. You are of high school age. It is in these years that dating begins. You're familiar with this custom of two sets of parents loaning their teenagers to one another for the necessary and important purpose of their finding their way into maturity, and eventually into marriage. Perhaps for the first time you notice, and begin to resent, the interest of your parents in, and their supervision of, your activities. Dating leads to marriage. Marriage is a sacred religious covenant and in its most exalted expression may be an eternal covenant. Whatever preparation relates to marriage, whether it be personal or social, concerns us as members of the Church.

Now I speak very plainly to you, my young friends. If you are old enough to date, you are old enough to know that your parents have not only the right but the sacred obligation to concern themselves with your dating habits, and in doing this they are under counsel from the leaders of the Church.

If you are mature enough to date, you're mature enough to accept without childish, juvenile argument their authority as parents to set rules of conduct for you.

No sensible father would loan your new convertible to anybody, to go anyplace, to do anything, to come back anytime. If you are old enough to date, you are old enough to see the foolishness of parents who would loan their *children* on any such an arrangement. Don't ask your parents to permit you, their most precious possession, to go out on such flimsy agreements.

Actually, the loan of the car would not be so serious as you suppose, for should it be destroyed, it could be replaced. However, there are some problems and some hazards with dating for which there is no such fortunate solution.

When you are old enough, you ought to start dating. It is good for young men and young women to learn to know and to appreciate one another. It is good for you to go to games and dances and picnics, to do all of the proper things young people do. We encourage our young people to date. We encourage you to set high standards of dating.

When are you old enough? Maturity may vary from individual to individual, but we are rather of the conviction that dating should not even begin until you are well into your teens. And then, ideal dating is on a group basis. None of this steady dancing, steady dating routine. Steady dating is courtship, and surely the beginning of courtship ought to be delayed until you are almost out of your teens.

Dating should not be premature. You should appreciate your parents if they see to that. Dating should not be without supervision, and you should appreciate parents who see to that.

Young people sometimes get the mistaken notion that a religious attitude and spirituality interfere with youthful growth. They assume that the requirements of the Church are interferences and aggravations that thwart the full expression of young manhood and young womanhood.

How foolish is the youth who feels that the Church is a fence around love to keep him out! O youth, if you could know! The requirements of the Church are the highway to love and to happiness, with guardrails securely in place, with guideposts plainly marked, and with help along the way. How unfortunate to resent counsel and restraint. How fortunate are you who follow the standards of the Church, even if just from sheer obedience or habit. You will find a rapture and a joy fulfilled.

Now, be patient with your parents. They love you so deeply. They are emotionally involved with you, and they may become too vigorous as they set their guidelines for you to follow. But be patient. Remember, they are involved in a big do-it-yourself child-raising project, and this is their first time through. They have never raised a child just like you before.

Give them the right to misunderstand and to make a mistake or two. They have accorded you that right. Recognize their authority. Be grateful for their discipline. Such discipline may set you on the path to greatness.

The Japanese Boy

In your teaching, some stories will come from your own life's experiences. For example, I had an experience on a train in Japan many years ago that I have never forgotten. I can remember it as clearly today as if it had happened yesterday.

The railroad station, what there was left of it, had been cold and forbidding. Starving children were sleeping in corners, the fortunate ones with a newspaper or a few old rags to fend off the cold. I slept restlessly on that train. The berths were too short anyway.

In the bleak, chilly hours of the dawn the train stopped somewhere along the way. I heard a tapping on the window and raised the blind to see where we were. There, reaching from the platform, tapping on the window with a tin can, stood a little boy. He was an orphan and a beggar. He might have been six or seven years old. His little body was thin with starvation. He had on a ragged shirt that looked like a kimono, nothing else. His head was shingled with scabs and scales. His left jaw was grotesquely swollen — an abscessed tooth perhaps. Around it he had tied a filthy rag with a knot on top of his head, a pathetic gesture of treatment.

When the boy saw that I was awake, he waved his can. He was begging. In pity I thought, "How can I help him?" Then I knew. I had money, Japanese money. I quickly groped for my clothing and found some yen notes in my pocket. When I tried to open the window it would not open. I slipped on my trousers and hurried to the end of the car. As I pushed at the resistant door, where he stood expectantly waiting, the train pulled away from the station. Through the dirty windows I could still see him holding the rusty can and with the rag around his swollen jaw.

There I stood, an officer from a conquering army, heading home to all of the material blessings, the warmth of family association, opportunity. There I stood half-dressed, clutching a handful of Japanese yen which he had seen but which I could not get to him.

I was impressed — perhaps scarred — by the experience. Sometimes I wish I could forget that sight. Perhaps I need, greatly need, to remember. I wanted to help him but couldn't. The only comfort I draw is that I did *want* to help him.

A great source of stories and accounts from the lives

of those who have gone before us can be searched out in history. I have always enjoyed reading history and have been touched by the many human interest illustrations that have powerful lessons to teach.

I read the following in the book *Handcarts to Zion* by LeRoy Hafen, and I present it as I have retold it on occasion.

The Lost Boy

In the late 1850s many converts from Europe were struggling to reach the Valley of the Great Salt Lake. Many were too poor to afford a covered wagon, so they had to walk, pushing handcarts with their meager belongings. Some of the most touching and tragic moments in the history of the Church accompanied the handcart pioneers.

One such company was commanded by a Brother McArthur. Archer Walters, an English convert who was with the company, recorded in his diary under July 2, 1858, this sentence: "Brother Parker's little boy, age six, was lost. The father went back to hunt him."

The boy, Arthur, was the next to youngest of four children of Robert and Ann Parker. Three days earlier the company had hurriedly made camp in the face of a sudden thunderstorm. It was then that the boy was missed. His parents had thought he was playing along the way with the other children.

Someone remembered that earlier in the day when they had stopped, the little boy had settled down to rest in the shade of some brush. You know how quickly a tired little six-year-old can fall asleep on a sultry summer day, and even the noise of the camp moving on might not awaken him.

For two days the company remained while all the men searched for him. Then on July 2, with no alternative, the company was ordered to head west.

Robert Parker, as the diary records, went back alone

to seek once again for his little son. As he was leaving camp, his wife, Ann, pinned a bright shawl around his shoulders with words such as these: "If you find him dead, wrap him in the shawl to bury him. If you find him alive, the shawl can be a flag to signal us."

Then, with the other little children, she took the cart and struggled on with the company. Out on the trail Ann and her children kept watch. At sundown on July 5, as they were watching, they saw a figure approaching from the east. Then, in the rays of the setting sun, Ann saw the glimmer of a bright red shawl.

One of the diaries recorded: "Ann Parker sank in a pitiful heap upon the sand. That night, for the first time in six nights, she slept."

In his diary on July 5, Brother Walters recorded: "Brother Parker came into camp with his little boy that had been lost. Great joy through the camp. The mother's joy I cannot describe."

We do not know all the details. A nameless woodsman had found the boy. He was described as being ill with sickness and with terror, but the woodsman had cared for him until his father found him.

Here a story, commonplace in its day, ends—except for a question. How would you, in Ann Parker's place, feel toward the nameless woodsman had he saved your little son? Would there be an end to your gratitude?

To sense this is to feel something of the gratitude our Father must feel toward any of us who saves one of His children. Such gratitude is a prize dearly to be won, for the Lord has said, "If it so be that you should labor all your days in crying repentance unto this people, and bring, save it be one soul unto me, how great shall be your joy with him in the kingdom of my Father!" (D&C 18:15.)

A Very Short Story

There is a brief illustration from the life of Karl G. Maeser, who was taking a group of missionaries across the Alps. Gesturing back down the trail to some poles set in the snow to mark the way across the glacier, he said, "Brethren, there stands the Priesthood. They are just common sticks like the rest of us . . . but the position they hold makes them what they are to us. If we step aside from the path they mark, we are lost." (Alma P. Burton, *Karl G. Maeser, Mormon Educator,* Deseret Book, 1953, p. 22.)

Although it is merely a paragraph, it is valuable for a teacher to have incidents like this recorded away to use in his lesson material.

Newspapers and magazines carry illustrations, and one by way of example is introduced by a bulletin I read in the newspaper on one occasion.

Undernourished

"Attending physicians at the LDS Hospital said the girl's blood condition is so improved she likely will need no more transfusions. . . . Doctors said her diet has been increased to include potatoes, eggs and puddings. She no longer requires intravenous feedings." (*Deseret News,* July 10, 1956.)

An eighteen-year-old girl had been brought to the hospital six days earlier, having survived nine days pinned under a car in Parley's Canyon east of Salt Lake City. The injuries she had sustained in the accident were not of themselves serious. It was the lack of food and moisture that had reduced her to such condition. It was many days before the doctors gave much hope for her recovery.

It isn't easy to administer to one so starved. It was not a matter of just putting food before her. The food had to be carefully administered, for delicate balances might be upsetting, and her life was at stake. Doctors were ever so careful, for their very treatment might prove fatal. Her recovery was regarded as something of a miracle.

So it is with those around us who are spiritually undernourished or starved. We refer to them as the lost sheep. We are called to minister to them. They are of all descriptions. Some have deficiencies of one kind or another that merely rob them of spiritual vigor. Others have starved themselves so far of spiritual things that we can scarcely hope to save them.

In our teaching, stories such as this can help make powerful points. As we feed those for whom we are responsible, at home or in the classroom, may we search out stories that are relevant and unforgettable, and help our youth relate saving gospel truths to their everyday lives.

CHAPTER THIRTY-SIX

How to Teach the Moral Standard

Perhaps no moral value is more challenging to teach than chastity. It is so easy to teach it negatively or to over-teach it. There is more danger of "over-kill" in teaching this subject than in teaching any other.

In chapter one we declared teaching to be the finest of the fine arts and no doubt the most difficult, for the students, including our own children, cannot be set aside like an oil painting or a musical composition and left untampered with until another teaching session is scheduled. They are being taught—perhaps a better word would be bombarded—on the subject of chastity constantly and continually. Most of such teaching is negative and destructive; much of it is visually taught.

It is our responsibility to teach the subject in such a way that the principles of truth will overcome the misconceptions and misleading falsehoods that are taught so widely. We must teach so powerfully and so permanently that the truth cannot be overcome by the temptation to immorality, no matter how enticing.

In 1958 seminary and institute teachers were assembled at Brigham Young University for a summer school. I was assigned by President William E. Berrett to talk on the subject "Problems in Teaching the Moral Standard." In preparation for that assignment, I made a more than usual investment in prayer and fasting, in research and inquiry, including interviews with some of the General Authorities.

In the process of that preparation I came to some conclusions that I have not since that time abandoned — indeed, they have become reinforced through all that I have since learned on the subject. I am convinced that two of the major mistakes are to teach too much about the subject and to teach it at the wrong time. I am firmly convinced of the following principles.

The notion that our young people need to be taught in great detail all of the facts relating to the physical processes involved in reproduction at an early age is nonsense. The overteaching of it is not a protection. Such things as they should know about the subject should be taught in a framework of reverence and modesty.

The Responsibility Is with Parents

The responsibility and the right to teach these sacred processes rest with the parents in the home. I do not believe that it is the responsibility of the public schools, nor is it the responsibility of the organizations of the Church. The contribution of the Church in this respect is to teach parents the standards of morality that the Lord has revealed and to assist them in their responsibility of teaching these sacred subjects to their children.

Because many parents do not accept this responsibility, some consideration of it is given by the Church. When this is justified, if it is justified, the subject ought always to be treated in the framework of reverence.

In treating this subject, I do not personally see the necessity of using clinical terminology. I do not see the necessity of using explicit names of the organs of the body, nor for those processes by which bodies are conceived as a tabernacle for the spirit.

The one place in the Church where some frank discussions may be appropriate is during an interview for priesthood advancement, for a call to a position, for a temple recommend, or in an interview in which a member is confessing transgression in order to get it resolved.

Occasionally, deep inquiry may be necessary. This teaching process, and that's what interviewing can be, ought likewise to be shrouded in modesty and the subject ought to be treated with reverence, wisdom, and restraint.

I know of more than one instance in which a young person has been led to experiment in gross and perverted immorality because of a suggestion that originated with his bishop in an interview.

Those who teach, and I refer to leaders, to teachers, and to parents, should keep in mind this message. Picture a father and mother leaving home for a period of time. Just as they go out the door they say to their little children who are to be left untended during their absence, "Now children, be good. Whatever you do while we are gone, do not take the footstool into the pantry, and do not climb to the fourth shelf and move the cracker box and reach back and get the sack of beans and take a bean and put it up your nose, will you?"

Some of us are just that foolish. The humor of the illustration is wry humor when you think of the first thing that happens after the parents are gone. Surely we can be wiser than that. Young people should know from the very beginning that chastity is a sacred subject.

At the summer school mentioned, I put together some thoughts on how I would like my children to be taught this subject by others outside our home. Then over a period of nearly fifteen years, I worked on this subject until I was confident enough to deliver it as a sermon in general conference under the title "Why Stay Morally Clean."

You may not immediately be aware as you read it that you will not find a certain three-letter word that is usually included in the title of this kind of education.

The favorable response from young people has been considerable, and I am continually grateful. Their responses frequently express gratitude for the declaration that the power of creation is sacred and that it is good. They seem to appreciate a positive indication of when and how and for what purpose that power is to be employed by them in mortality.

To me assuring evidence favoring such an approach has been the aforementioned response from young people literally all over the world, since "Why Stay Morally Clean" has been translated into many languages.

If you are a teacher and if you are a parent, I would urge that you approach the teaching of this subject with reverence, with humility, and with modesty and moderation. May the Lord bless you as you do so.

Why Stay Morally Clean

Surely all of us have been conscious of the fact that there has been a very powerful spirit with us in this session this morning. Few times, I suppose, have I desired so much for the sustaining power of the Spirit as I discuss a very delicate and difficult subject.

There are many young people in our audience today. It is to them, particularly to the teenagers, that I speak. The subject should be of great interest to you—why stay morally clean.

I approach the subject with deepest reverence. This may surprise some, for this subject is the most talked about, sung about, and joked about of any subject. Almost always it is talked about immodestly.

I intend to sustain modesty, not to offend it, as I venture to speak on this most delicate subject.

Young people, my message is of very deep importance to you. It concerns your future happiness. Some things that I say may be new to you who have not read the scriptures.

In the beginning, prior to your mortal birth, you lived with our Heavenly Father. He is real. He actually lives. There are those living upon the earth who bear witness of His existence. We have heard His servants do so in this session. He lives, and I bear testimony of it.

Going Away to School

He knew you there. Because He loved you He was anxious for your happiness and for your eternal growth. He wanted you to be able to choose freely and to grow through the power of correct choice, so that you may become much as He is. To achieve this, it was necessary for us to leave His presence. Something like going away to school. A plan was presented and each agreed to leave the presence of our Heavenly Father to experience life in mortality.

Two great things were in store for us as we came into this world. One, we would receive a physical body, created in the image of God. Through it, by proper control, we might achieve eternal life and happiness. Two, we would be tried and tested in such a way that we could grow in strength and in spiritual power.

Now this first purpose is wonderfully important, for this body given us will be resurrected and will serve us through the eternities.

Under the accepted plan, Adam and Eve were sent to the earth as our first parents. They could prepare physical bodies for the first spirits to be introduced into this life.

305

A Sacred Power

There was provided in our physical bodies, and this is sacred, a power of creation. A light, so to speak, that has the power to kindle other lights. This gift is to be used only within the sacred bonds of marriage. Through the exercise of this power of creation, a mortal body may be conceived, a spirit enter into it, and a new soul born into this life.

This power is good. It can create and sustain family life, and it is in family life that we find the fountains of happiness. It is given to virtually every individual who is born into mortality. It is a sacred and significant power, and I repeat, my young friends, that this power is good.

You who are teenagers, like every other son and daughter of Adam and Eve, have this power within you.

The power of creation, or may we say procreation, is not just an incidental part of the plan — it is essential to it. Without it the plan could not proceed. The misuse of it may disrupt the plan.

Much of the happiness that may come to you in this life will depend on how you use this sacred power of creation. The fact that you young men can become fathers and that you young women can become mothers is of utmost importance to you.

As this power develops within you, it will prompt you in the search for a companion and empower you to love and to hold him.

I repeat, this power to act in the creation of life is sacred. You can someday have a family of your own. Through the exercise of this power you can invite children to live with you — little boys and little girls who will be your very own, created in a way in your own image. You can establish a home, a dominion of power and influence and opportunity. This carries with it great responsibility.

This creative power carries with it strong desires and

306

urges. You have felt them already in the changing of your attitudes and your interests.

As you move into your teens, almost of a sudden a boy or a girl becomes something new and intensely interesting. You will notice the changing of form and feature in your own body and in others. You will experience the early whispering of physical desire.

It was necessary that this power of creation have at least two dimensions: One, it must be strong, and two, it must be more or less constant.

This power must be strong, for most men by nature seek adventure. Except for the compelling persuasion of these feelings, men would be reluctant to accept the responsibility of sustaining a home and a family. This power must be constant too, for it becomes a binding tie in family life.

You are old enough, I think, to look around you in the animal kingdom. You soon realize that where this power of creation is a fleeting thing, where it expresses itself only in season, there is no family life.

It is through this power that life continues. A world full of trials and fears and disappointments can be changed into a kingdom of hope and joy and happiness. Each time a child is born, the world somehow is renewed in innocence.

A Gift from God

Again I want to tell you, young people, that this power within you is good. It is a gift from God our Father. In the righteous exercise of it, as in nothing else, we may come close to Him.

We can have, in a small way, much that our Father in heaven has as He governs us, His children. No greater school or testing place can be imagined.

Is it any wonder, then, that in the Church marriage is

so sacred and so important? Can you understand why your marriage, which releases these powers of creation for your use, should be the most carefully planned, the most solemnly considered step in your life? Ought we to consider it unusual that the Lord directed that temples be constructed for the purpose of performing marriage ceremonies?

The Destroyer

Now there are other things that I will tell you as a warning. In the beginning there was one among us who rebelled at the plan of our Heavenly Father. He vowed to destroy and to disrupt the plan.

He was prevented from having a mortal body and was cast out, limited forever from establishing a kingdom of his own. He became satanically jealous. He knows that this power of creation is not just an incident to the plan, but a key to it.

He knows that if he can entice you to use this power prematurely, to use it too soon, or to misuse it in any way, you may well lose your opportunities for eternal progression.

He is an actual being from the unseen world. He has great power. He will use it to persuade you to transgress those laws set up to protect the sacred powers of creation.

In former times he was too cunning to confront one with an open invitation to be immoral. But rather, sneakingly and quietly he would tempt young and old alike to think loosely of these sacred powers of creation. He would bring down to a vulgar or to a common level that which is sacred and beautiful.

His tactics have changed now. He describes it as only an appetite to be satisfied. He teaches that there are no attendant responsibilities to the use of this power. Pleasure, he will tell you, is its sole purpose.

His devilish invitations appear on billboards. They are coined into jokes and written into the lyrics of songs. They are acted out on television and at theaters. They will stare at you now from most magazines. There are magazines — you know the word, pornography. Open, wicked persuasions to pervert and misuse this sacred power.

You are growing up in a society where before you is the constant invitation to tamper with these sacred powers.

I want to counsel you and I want you to remember these words.

Do not let anyone at all touch or handle your body, not anyone! Those who tell you otherwise proselyte you to share their guilt. We teach you to maintain your innocence.

Turn away from any who would persuade you to experiment with these life-giving powers.

That such indulgence is widely accepted in society today is not enough!

For both parties to willingly consent to such indulgence is not enough!

To imagine that it is a normal expression of affection is not enough to make it right.

The only righteous use of this sacred power is within the covenant of marriage.

Never misuse these sacred powers.

Wickedness Never Was Happiness

And now, my young friends, I must tell you soberly and seriously that God has declared in unmistakable language that misery and sorrow will follow the violation of the laws of chastity. "Wickedness never was happiness." (Alma 41:10.)

These laws were set up to guide all of His children in the use of this gift. He does not have to be spiteful or vengeful in order that punishment will come from the

309

breaking of the moral code. The laws are established of themselves.

Crowning glory awaits you if you live worthily. The loss of the crown may well be punishment enough. Often, very often, we are punished as much by our sins as we are for them.

Become Clean

I am sure that within the sound of my voice there is more than one young person who already has fallen into transgression. Some of you young people, I am sure, almost innocent of any intent but persuaded by the enticements and the temptations, already have misused this power.

Know then, my young friends, that there is a great cleansing power. And know that you can be clean.

If you are outside the Church, the covenant of baptism itself represents, among other things, a washing and a cleansing.

For those of you inside the Church there is a way, not entirely painless but certainly possible. You can stand clean and spotless before Him. Guilt will be gone and you can be at peace. Go to your bishop. He holds the key to this cleansing power.

Then one day you can know the full and righteous expression of these powers and the attendant happiness and joy in righteous family life. In due time, within the bonds of the marriage covenant, you can yield yourselves to those sacred expressions of love which have as their fulfillment the generation of life itself.

Someday you will hold a little boy or a little girl in your arms and know that two of you have acted in partnership with our Heavenly Father in the creation of life. Because the youngster belongs to you, you may then come to love someone more than you love yourself.

310

This experience can come, insofar as I know, only through having children of your own or perhaps through fostering children born of another and yet drawn close into family covenants.

Some of you may not experience the blessings of marriage. Protect nonetheless these sacred powers of creation, for there is a great power of compensation that may well apply to you.

Through this loving one more than you love yourself, you become truly Christian. Then you know, as few others know, what the word *Father* means when it is spoken of in the scriptures. You may then feel something of the love and concern that He has for us.

It should have great meaning that of all the titles of respect and honor and admiration that could be given Him, God Himself, He who is the highest of all, chose to be addressed simply as Father.

Protect and guard your gift. Your actual happiness is at stake. Eternal family life, now only in your anticipations and dreams, can be achieved because our Heavenly Father has bestowed this choicest gift of all upon you — this power of creation. It is the very key to happiness. Hold this gift as sacred and pure. Use it only as the Lord has directed.

My young friends, there is much happiness and joy to be found in this life. I can testify of that.

I picture you with a companion whom you love and who loves you. I picture you at the marriage altar, entering into covenants which are sacred. I picture you in a home where love has its fulfillment, and I picture you with little children about you and see your love growing with them.

I cannot frame this picture. I would not if I could, for it has no bounds. Your happiness will have no ends if you obey His laws.

I pray God's blessings upon you, our youth. May our Heavenly Father watch over you and sustain you that in the expression of this sacred gift you may draw close to Him. He lives. He is our Father. (General Conference address, April 9, 1972.)

CHAPTER THIRTY-SEVEN

Poetry in Teaching

Poetry is important in teaching, particularly in teaching moral and spiritual values, because of the insights and ideas that can be crystallized in just a verse or two. The ability of the poet to touch the emotional and the spiritual is very important as a tool in teaching.

Poetry is important because of the imagery. Images are created that convey not only facts, but also feelings.

I enjoy reading poetry and often use it in speaking and in teaching. Poets have insight, some of them very profound spiritual insights, and just as it is true that "everybody loves a story," so everybody loves a poem. Often you will not use the full poem, but just a verse or two to illustrate a point or to forcefully reteach it. A poem in a lesson is something like a touch of accent or color; it brightens things up.

A few lines of verse that have been very important in our family life are some that belong to the generation just past. My wife's mother, now gone, would open the door to the upstairs when my wife was growing up and call brightly in the morning these words:

Here has come dawning another new day;
Think, wilt thou let it slip useless away?
— Thomas Carlyle

A favorite that my wife has used over the years in Primary is "Plastic Little Children."

Plastic little children,
Made of Heaven's clay,
Oh Father, give us vision
To mold them right this day.

Potential gods in miniature,
We must have help from Thee,
For how they're fashioned here today,
Will endure through all eternity.
— Author unknown

Since we are writing about teaching, this chapter features some poems on that subject. It's good to build your own file. I usually file them in two ways: under the subject of the poem and also in a file called, simply, "Poetry." A favorite place for powerful messages in verse is the Church hymnbook. The lyrics of some of our hymns are powerful, some of them even more powerful as poetry than they are when sung, and they teach great messages. An example of that is "If You Could Hie to Kolob in the Twinkling of an Eye."

An example of a poem that can be used to teach an important point is "The Blind Men and the Elephant" by John Godfrey Saxe. It is often used in seminary classes to illustrate how people of other churches can be very sincere in their beliefs and at the same time be very wrong, when compared to the complete and true church. It emphasizes the declaration of the Prophet Joseph Smith that the Book of Mormon contains the fulness of the gospel and not just the gospel. The poem, while perhaps not great literature, is nevertheless useful in helping the teacher teach that point to children of all ages.

The Blind Men and the Elephant

It was six men of Indostan
　To learning much inclined,
Who went to see the elephant
　(Though all of them were blind),
That each by observation
　Might satisfy his mind.

The First approached the elephant,
　And, happening to fall
Against his broad and sturdy side,
　At once began to bawl:
"God bless me! but the elephant
　Is nothing but a wall!"

The Second, feeling of the tusk,
　Cried: "Ho! what have we here
So very round and smooth and sharp?
　To me 'tis very clear
This wonder of an elephant
　Is very like a spear!"

The Third approached the animal,
　And, happening to take
The squirming trunk within his hands,
　Thus boldly up and spake:
"I see," quoth he, "the elephant
　Is very like a snake!"

The Fourth reached out his eager hand,
　And felt about the knee:
"What most this wondrous beast is like
　Is very plain," quoth he;
" 'Tis clear enough the elephant
　Is very like a tree."

The Fifth, who chanced to touch the ear,
　Said: "E'en the blindest man
Can tell what this resembles most;
　Deny the fact who can,
This marvel of an elephant
　Is very like a fan!"

315

The Sixth no sooner had begun
　About the beast to grope,
Than, seizing on the swinging tail
　That fell within his scope,
"I see," quoth he, "the elephant
　Is very like a rope!"
　　　　　　　—John Godfrey Saxe

The following poems are about students or teachers or teaching—just a few to illustrate the kinds of verses that can be helpful in lesson preparation.

Building a Temple

A builder builded a temple,
　He wrought it with grace and skill;
Pillars and groins and arches
　All fashioned to work his will,
Men said as they saw its beauty,
　"It shall never know decay.
Great is thy skill, O builder:
　Thy fame shall endure for aye."

A teacher builded a temple
　With loving and infinite care,
Planning each arch with patience,
　Laying each stone with prayer.
None praised her unceasing efforts,
　None knew of her wondrous plan,
For the temple the teacher builded
　Was unseen by the eyes of man.

Gone is the builder's temple,
　Crumpled into the dust;
Low lies each stately pillar,
　Food for consuming rust.
But the temple the teacher builded
　Will last while the ages roll,
For that beautiful unseen temple
　Is a child's immortal soul.
　　　　　　　—Hattie Vose Hall
　　　　　　　The Instructor, July 1946

316

Tribute to a Sunday School Teacher

Perhaps she taught me more than books,
Perhaps because she smiled, I heard;
Perhaps her sweet sincerity
Convinced me that it was His word.
Perhaps it was her humbleness
That wak'd my soul and made me see;
Perhaps I felt a kindly touch
Of one who loves humanity.

Perhaps it was the power of truth
That through her words could reach my heart.
Perhaps the spirit of her work
Inspired me to do my part.

Perhaps? I really do not know
Just what it was about the class
That lives so vivid in my mind
Though many years have come and passed.

But this I know, because of her
A testimony, once so small,
Has grown in heart and soul and mind
Until it is my life, my all.

      —Mabel Jones Gabbott

To Those Who Teach Children

You are called to be true under-shepherds,
 To keep watch o'er the lambs of the fold;
And to point out the way to green pastures.
 Of more value than silver or gold.

Unto you is entrusted the children,
 Priceless treasures from heaven above.
You're to teach them the truth of the Gospel—
 Let them bask in the warmth of your love.

Do you ask for the help of our Father,
 In teaching His children so dear?
Do you put forth a true, honest effort?
 Is your message impressive and clear?

TEACH YE DILIGENTLY

Are you living a worthy example?
  Is your character what it should be?
When the children have gathered around you,
  Can you say, "Come, follow me"?

Earnest effort is always rewarded:
  Righteous lives are inspiring to all.
You can render your thanks to our Savior,
  By making the most of your call.
—Jayne Bradford Terry
The Instructor, November 1956

The Teacher

It is wonderful for men to build
With hammer, drill and forge,
A bridge to span the cataract
That rushes through the gorge.
It is wonderful to write a book,
To paint an azure sky,
And give to the world those breathless things
That never fade or die.
More wonderful to build the women and men
That man the cities, build the bridges
And wield the brush and pen.
Still more wonderful to build a soul,
To take the teacher's part
In building hopes and dreams
That stir the adolescent heart.
And when they have won
Through stress and strain,
More wonderful yet to be
A faithful teacher who can say,
"They learned life's game from me."
—Author Unknown

* * *

Today a professor, in garden relaxing
Like Plato of old in the Academe shade,
Spoke out in a manner I never had heard him
And this is one of the things that he said:

Suppose that we state as a tenet of wisdom
That knowledge is not for delight of the mind.
Nor an end in itself, but a packet of treasure
To hold and employ for the good of mankind.

A torch or a candle is barren of meaning
Except it give light to men as they climb.
And theses and tomes are but impotent jumble
Unless they are tools in the building of time.

We scholars toil on with the zeal of a miner
For nuggets and nuggets and one nugget more
But scholars are needed to study the uses
Of all the great mass of data and lore.

And truly our tireless and endless researches
Need yoking with man's daily problems and strife
For truth and beauty and virtue have value
Confirmed by their uses in practical life.
                                        —Author Unknown

CHAPTER THIRTY-EIGHT

Teaching with the Spirit

We have been instructed in the revelations that "if ye receive not the Spirit ye shall not teach." (D&C 42:14.) If there is one essential ingredient for the teaching of moral and spiritual values, for the teaching of the gospel, it is to have the Spirit of the Lord with us as we teach. Happily, the promise is given to us that this can be true. Across the world, members of the Church in their families and in their assignments enjoy the Spirit of the Lord as they prepare for it and are worthy of it.

President J. Reuben Clark, Jr., said:

"You teachers have a great mission. As teachers you stand upon the highest peak in education, for what teaching can compare in priceless value and in far-reaching effect with that which deals with man as he was in the eternity of yesterday, as he is in the mortality of today, and as he will be in the forever of tomorrow. Not only time but eternity is your field. Salvation of yourself not only, but of those who come within the purlieus of your temple, is the blessing you seek, and which, doing your duty, you will gain. How brilliant will be your crown of glory, with each soul saved an encrusted jewel thereon.

"But to get this blessing and to be so crowned, you must, I say once more, you must teach the gospel." ("The Charted Course of the Church in Education," p. 9.)

320

It should be the source of great comfort to any member of the Church who is called to a teaching position to know and understand that there are spiritual blessings to sustain the teacher. Each of us must begin where we are as teachers. Most of us come without experience and have little more to offer to begin with than the desire. It is humbling and comforting to know that there are spiritual powers to sustain such a teacher. We refer to the spiritual gifts talked about elsewhere.

"And again, I exhort you, my brethren, that ye deny not the gifts of God, for they are many; and they come from the same God. And there are different ways that these gifts are administered; but it is the same God who worketh all in all; and they are given by the manifestations of the spirit of God unto men, to profit them.

"For behold, to one is given by the spirit of God, that he may teach the word of wisdom;

"And to another, that he may teach the word of knowledge by the same spirit." (Moroni 10:8–10.)

An important message is found in the account of Jacob, a Book of Mormon prophet who called the people together at the temple. He had some instructions to give them, and in the course of it he said this:

"Wherefore I, Jacob, gave unto them these words as I taught them in the temple [and then this wonderful phrase], *having first obtained mine errand from the Lord.*

"For I, Jacob, and my brother Joseph had been consecrated priests and teachers of this people, by the hand of Nephi.

"And we did magnify our office unto the Lord, taking upon us the responsibility, answering the sins of the people upon our own heads if we did not teach them the word of God with all diligence; wherefore, by laboring with our might their blood might not come upon our garments; otherwise their blood would come upon our garments, and we would not be found spotless at the last day." (Jacob 1:17–19. Italics added.)

This matter of obtaining one's errand from the Lord is basic preparation for one who teaches. Who would want to go before a class to teach righteousness without first having importuned the Lord for his Spirit to attend the occasion? We have prayer meetings in our priesthood and auxiliary organizations to invite the inspiration of the Lord so that our teaching may be under the guidance of the Spirit. When that is present, permanent teaching can take place. Let me tell you about something I learned as a boy.

When I was about six or seven years old, my brother and I walked to the stake conference together. I can still go in that building in Brigham City and go back just under the balcony and say, "I was sitting about there when it happened."

President George Albert Smith

What was it that happened? There was a man speaking

at the pulpit—Elder George Albert Smith. He was a member of the Council of the Twelve at that time. I do not remember what he said, whether he was talking about the Word of Wisdom or repentance or baptism. But somehow while he was speaking it was impressed upon my little-boy mind that there stood a servant of the Lord. I have never lost that testimony or that feeling. In my mind I came to know that he was an apostle of the Lord Jesus Christ.

Pure Testimony

There is great responsibility in bearing pure testimony. Sometimes I think too little of it is done in the Church. I had an experience in the mission field that taught me much about testimony. In spite of the fact that all seemed to be under control, we were not progressing as we should. It was not something we were doing that we ought not to do so much, I felt, as something we were not doing that we ought to be doing.

We held a series of zone conferences to improve the spirituality in the mission. Rather than schedule instruction on the mechanics of missionary work, we determined to have a testimony meeting. In the last conference, in the testimony of one of the humble elders, I found the answer to the problem. There was something different about the brief testimony of this frightened new elder. He stood for less than a minute, yet I learned from his expression what it was that was missing.

The testimonies we'd heard from all the other missionaries went something like this: "I'm grateful to be in the mission field. I've learned a lot from it. I have a fine companion. I've learned a lot from him. I'm grateful for my parents. We had an interesting experience last week. We were out knocking on doors and. . . . " Then the missionary would relate an experience. His conclusion would be something like this: "I'm grateful to be in the mission field. I have a testimony of the gospel." And he would conclude "in the name of Jesus Christ. Amen."

This young elder was different somehow. Anxious not to spend an extra second on his feet, he said simply, in hurried, frightened words, "I know that God lives. I know that Jesus is the Christ. I know that we have a prophet of God leading the Church. In the name of Jesus Christ. Amen."

This was a testimony. It was not just an experience nor an expression of gratitude. It was a declaration, a witness!

Most of the elders had said "I have a testimony," but they had not declared it. This young elder had, in a very few words, delivered his testimony—direct, basic, and, as it turned out, powerful.

I then knew what was wrong in the mission. We were telling stories, expressing gratitude, admitting that we had testimonies, but we were not bearing them.

Teachers need to keep in mind the powerful force of the declarative bearing of testimony. It is appropriate in each class period for the teacher to bear testimony, not always in the "stand-up testimony meeting fashion," but a simple expression to the effect that you know that the things you are teaching in your lesson are indeed true.

For instance, a teacher who is giving a lesson on the Word of Wisdom might simply say, "I want the members of this class to know that the Word of Wisdom is a revelation from God. I have a testimony of this fact. I know that if we will live this principle, we will receive the blessings relating to it." A simple, affirmative declaration is a witness. Just to observe, "I *have* a testimony of the gospel" is not nearly as powerful as expressing it.

The Gift to Teach

On a number of occasions I heard William E. Berrett, one of the greatest teachers I have known, pay tribute to a teacher he had as a boy when he lived in the south end of the Salt Lake Valley in a rural ward. He told of an experience in which an older gentleman was appointed to teach a class of boys. The new teacher was a convert from Europe who spoke with a heavy accent and had to struggle with the language. President Berrett would say, "He was an unlettered man, deprived of a formal education, who had a hard time speaking English. But I will ever be grateful to him. What he lacked in expression he made up in spirit. We could have warmed our hands by the fire of his faith." I know of no greater tribute to a teacher in the Church than that.

The gift to teach with the Spirit is a gift worth praying for. A teacher can be inept, inadequate, perhaps even clumsy, but if the Spirit is powerful, messages of eternal importance can be taught.

We can become teachers, very good ones, but we cannot teach moral and spiritual values with only an intellectual or academic approach. There must be spirit in it.

When we teach spirituality, there are many faith-promoting incidents in the lives of others and in our own lives that might be recalled by way of illustration or testimony. There are accounts of miraculous events in the lives of members of the Church past and present.

The seventh Article of Faith states: "We believe in the gift of tongues, prophecy, revelations, visions, healings, interpretation of tongues, etc." There are many inspiring and inspired accounts of these gifts among the Latter-day Saints.

The teacher must, however, be very judicious in the use of experiences of this type. First of all, he must *know* that they are true. There are many things that are passed about that are not true. From time to time there seems to be a rash of accounts of visitations, of experiences that are fallacious.

Too Sacred to Repeat

A teacher must be wise also in the use of his own spiritual experiences. I have come to believe that deep spiritual experiences are given to individuals for the most part for their own instruction and edification, and they are not ordinarily to be talked about. I heard one member of the First Presidency say once, "I do not tell all I know. I have not told my wife all I know. I have found that if I tell everything I know and explain every experience that I have had, the Lord will not trust me."

There is also a scripture that says: "Give not that which is holy unto the dogs, neither cast ye your pearls before swine, lest they trample them under their feet, and turn again and rend you." (Matthew 7:6.) Sacred personal experiences are to be related only on rare occasions.

I made a rule for myself a number of years ago with reference to this subject. When someone relates a spiritual experience to me, personally or in a small, intimate group, I make it a rigid rule not to talk about it thereafter. I assume that it was told to me in a moment of trust and confidence, and therefore I never talk about it. If, however, on some future occasion I hear that individual talk about it in public in a large gathering, or where a number of people are present, then I know that it has been stated publicly and I can feel free under the right circumstances to relate it. But I know many, many sacred and important things that have been related to me by others that I will not discuss unless I am privileged to do so under the rule stated above. I know that others of the Brethren have the same feeling.

On one occasion, on a trip to South America, I had a special spiritual experience. When I returned I related it to President Kimball. Sometime later when I was presiding over the New England Mission I received a letter from him asking if he might include that experience in a conference address because it illustrated so well a point that he wanted

326

to make. He sent in that letter a copy of the account as he had recorded it in his journal. I was amazed at the accuracy of his record of the incident. He had recorded it in his journal perhaps that night or even a day or two later precisely as I had given it to him.

Inasmuch as he did use it in General Conference, I will include it here just as he gave it as an illustration of the type of account that we are discussing. The point to remember is that he would not quote it without permission, because it was a spiritual experience. That shows both wisdom and courtesy.

> May I conclude with this experience of my friend and brother, Boyd K. Packer, as he returned from Peru. It was in a branch sacrament meeting. The chapel was filled, the opening exercises finished, and the sacrament in preparation. A little Lamanite ragamuffin entered from the street. His two shirts would scarcely make one, so ragged they were and torn and worn. It was unlikely that those shirts had ever been off that little body since they were donned. Calloused and chapped were the little feet which brought him in the open door, up the aisle, and to the sacrament table. There was dark and dirty testimony of deprivation, want, unsatisfied hungers—spiritual as well as physical. Almost unobserved he shyly came to the sacrament table and, with a seeming spiritual hunger, leaned against the table and lovingly rubbed his unwashed face against the cool, smooth, white linen.
>
> A woman on the front seat, seemingly outraged by the intrusion, caught his eye and with motion and frown sent the little ragamuffin scampering down the aisle out into his world, the street.
>
> A little later, seemingly compelled by some inner urge, he overcame his timidity and came stealthily, cautiously down the aisle again, fearful, ready to escape if necessary, but impelled as though directed by inaudible voices with "a familiar spirit"

and as though memories long faded were reviving, as though some intangible force were crowding him on to seek something for which he yearned but could not identify.

From his seat on the stand, Elder Packer caught his eye, beckoned to him, and stretched out big, welcoming arms. A moment's hesitation and the little ragamuffin was nestled comfortably on his lap, in his arms, the tousled head against a great warm heart—a heart sympathetic to waifs, and especially to little Lamanite ones. It seemed the little one had found a safe harbor from a stormy sea, so contented he was. The cruel, bewildering, frustrating world was outside. Peace, security, acceptance enveloped him.

Later Elder Packer sat in my office and, in tender terms and with a subdued voice, rehearsed this incident to me. As he sat forward on his chair, his eyes glistening, a noticeable emotion in his voice, he said, "As this little one relaxed in my arms, it seemed it was not a single little Lamanite I held. It was a nation, indeed a multitude of nations of deprived, hungering souls, wanting something deep and warm they could not explain—a humble people yearning to revive memories all but faded—of ancestors standing wide-eyed, openmouthed, expectant and excited, looking up and seeing a holy, glorified Being descend from celestial areas, and hearing a voice say: 'Behold, I am Jesus Christ, the Son of God. I created the heavens and the earth, and all things that in them are . . . and in me hath the Father glorified his name. . . . I am the light and the life of the world. I am Alpha and Omega, the beginning and the end.' (3 Nephi 9:15, 18.)" (Spencer W. Kimball, General Conference address, October 2, 1965.)

I cannot read those words even after several years without being touched emotionally by that experience.

On several occasions President Kimball has told me

that that was an important experience. The last time we talked about it was when we were on a plane trip together. He brought up the subject again and told me that it was a very significant experience.

Declare the Truth

One thing professional teachers need to guard against is the tendency to be turned into skeptics or to be over-cautious when declaring the truth. Several influences in modern education have contributed to uncertainty and un-steadiness and ultimately to weakness in teaching. When I was working on my master's thesis, one of my committee members took some pains to coach me on the way I should put it together.

"Now, don't be positive about anything," he said. "It would be very arrogant for you to suppose that you have discovered anything that isn't already known. Therefore, make sure that your findings are set forth in loose terms. Use such expressions as 'It seems to be' or 'One is led to believe that' or 'One might reasonably draw the conclusion that' or 'It is possible to assume that.' "

Then he assured me, "When you are defending your thesis and someone questions one of your conclusions, you can protect yourself as well as your thesis by saying, 'Well, it seemed to *me* to be thus' or '*I* assumed it to be thus and so.' Then you will be safe."

Much of education is heavily influenced by the phi-losophy of pragmatism, which decries the existence of any ultimate truth and suspends the student and teacher alike in indecisiveness. What a refreshing thing to have a teacher who has the courage of his convictions and who can tell right from wrong and is willing to say so! To me one of the great and powerful characteristics of the Book of Mor-mon is the very definite and positive declaration of it.

Joseph Smith did not misunderstand his calling nor was he hesitant to declare it.

The Prophet declared himself to be competent to teach the truth. On one occasion Josiah Quincy, who had visited with him and had spent enough time with him to gain some appraisal of what he was about, said to him, "General, it seems to me that you have too much power to be safely trusted to one man." And Joseph's answer was, "In your hands or the hands of any other person, so much power would no doubt be dangerous. I am the only man in the world whom it would be safe to trust with it. Remember, I am a prophet."

There isn't much caution in his declaration, is there? And again he said, "When did I ever teach anything wrong from this stand? When was I ever confounded? I never told you I was perfect, but there is no error in the revelations that I have taught."

The Book of Mormon is a classic example of such definite declarations. I took occasion to extract from the Book of Mormon the word *know* and its derivations, such as *knew, knowledge, known,* etc. Interestingly enough, the phrase "I know" appears in the Book of Mormon no less than 101 times, virtually all of them testimony-oriented, as the prophets declare a knowledge of the gospel of Jesus Christ. Compare that with the ordinary procedure of today. A graduate student in college, for instance, is urged to carefully frame his findings, and probably rightly so, unless some sense of authority has been earned.

Isn't it remarkable that verses of scripture in the Book of Mormon commit God Himself to verify the things that one is reading. They commit God Himself to verify Joseph Smith as a prophet. Here are three examples of this:

> Wherefore, now after I have spoken these words. if ye cannot understand them it will be because ye ask not, neither do ye knock, wherefore

ye are not brought into the light but must perish in the dark, for behold, I say unto you that if ye will enter in by the way and receive the Holy Ghost, it will show you all things that ye must do. (2 Nephi 32:4–5.)

And if they are not the words of Christ, judge ye, for Christ will show unto you with power and great glory that they are His words at the last day. And you and I shall stand face to face before His bar and ye shall know that I have been commanded of Him to write these things, notwithstanding my weakness. (2 Nephi 33:11.)

And when ye shall receive these things, I would exhort you that ye would ask God, the Eternal Father, in the name of Christ, if these things are not true, and if ye shall ask with a sincere heart, with real intent, having faith in Christ, He will manifest the truth of it unto you by the power of the Holy Ghost, and by the power of the Holy Ghost ye may know the truth of all things. (Moroni 10:4.)

The Lord Himself is committed to verify whether the Prophet Joseph Smith was a prophet or an imposter. One has but to accept the challenge and see.

Out of Context

Let me share with you a fundamental lesson I learned a few years ago. Near the end of the course work for my doctorate, I was enrolled in an educational philosophy class with three other students. Two of us were completing our doctorates; the other two were just beginning their graduate work. An issue arose between me and the other doctoral candidate. It had to do with whether or not man is left totally to himself. Is he sufficient to himself, or are there external sources of intelligence to which he can appeal?

The professor of the class was Dr. Henry Aldous Dixon,

who had been the president of Weber State College and of Utah State University and who had retired from the Congress of the United States. He was teaching the course simply because he loved to teach, and he did it superbly well. He deftly moderated — perhaps a better word would be *refereed* — the contest without taking either side.

As the debate became more intense, the other two students took sides, one on each. So there we were, two contestants, each with a "second." The issue grew more important, and each day I left the class feeling more a failure. Why should this concern me? It concerned me because I was right and he was wrong, and I knew it and I thought he knew it; yet he was able to best me in every discussion.

Each day I felt more inadequate, more foolish, and more tempted to capitulate. I spent much time in the library, searched out references, and studied at least as hard as my opponent. Nevertheless, each encounter saw me that much more defeated.

Then one day one of the most important experiences of my entire education occurred. As we were leaving class, his "second" commented, "You're losing, aren't you."

There was no pride left to prevent me from consenting to the obvious. "Yes, I'm losing."

"Do you want to know what's the matter with you?" he asked.

Interested, I answered, "Yes, I would very much like to know."

"The trouble with you," he said, "is that you're fighting out of context." I asked him what he meant. I didn't know, and he didn't explain it. He just said, "You are fighting out of context."

That night I thought continuously about his comment. It wasn't the grade or the credit I would win in the class — it was much bigger than that. I was being beaten and humiliated in my efforts to defend a principle that was true. His statement stayed in my mind, and finally, in my humiliation, I went before the Lord in prayer. Then I knew!

The next day when we returned to class, I stayed in context. When the debate was renewed, instead of mumbling some stilted, sophisticated, educational jargon calculated to show I was conversant with philosophical terminology, I used the words the Lord used on the subject. Instead of saying, "The *a priori* acquisition of intelligence as though from some external source of enlightenment," I said plainly, "Revelation from God!" I talked about the spiritual in the terms that described the spiritual. Suddenly the tables were turned. I was rescued from defeat, and I learned a lesson I shall not soon forget.

The points I had been pressing with so little effect those several weeks suddenly became clear and compelling. I abandoned the foolish process of skirting around spiritual terms in favor of academic jargon.

I stand in debt to that unassuming student from whose remark I learned so much. I will never forget it and would urge everyone who teaches in the Church to teach as the Lord taught, with the tools that He has provided, and not to be drawn out of context. Teach with the Spirit!

CHAPTER THIRTY-NINE

When the Teacher Is Discouraged

Everything is not always rosy for the teacher. There are moments of disappointment; in fact, there are moment of despair. But his mistakes, depressions, disappointments, and problems seem to be a source of growth. A teacher finds that they are not merely tolerable, but they are actually necessary. For "there must needs be opposition in all things," and "after much tribulation cometh the blessings," and "whom the Lord loveth, he chasteneth."

What do you do with discouragement?

A teacher may labor with all the resources at hand and then have a bad day or find that one of his pupils has not responded. One thing that he must never do is give up.

It is comforting to realize that Jesus Himself was not successful in redeeming all with whom He came in contact, that even all those who heard Him speak and teach did not respond — those who were there, who were in the multitudes and listened, who perhaps touched Him. The important thing is that He *wanted* to redeem them all.

"O Jerusalem, Jerusalem . . . how often would I have gathered thy children together, even as a hen gathereth her chickens under her wings, and ye would not!" (Matthew 23:37.)

Good Influence Is Long Lasting

The influence of a teacher may not be in evidence in the classroom or immediately after; there is an interim, a waiting period. If he has taught well, not so much as a good thought is lost. No turn of the mind, however brief or transitory or elusive, if it is good, is ever wasted. No thought of sympathy nor forgiveness nor reflection on generosity or courage or pity, no meditation or humility or gratitude or reverence is ever lost. The frequency with which they are experienced is the measure of the teacher. The more constant they become, the more he is worth, or, in spiritual terms, the more he is worthy. Every clean thought becomes part of him. And when he teaches it, it is somehow recorded and ultimately will redound to his good and the good of those whom he is teaching. So take courage.

We Only Fail If We Give Up

Often when teachers say, "What am I doing wrong?" the answer is, "Nothing. You're doing everything right. You just have to do it longer and more persistently. We have failed only when we have given up." I would say to teachers, take comfort and keep doing what you are doing.

On one occasion Jesus knew He was teaching *at* the people rather than actually instructing them, for He stated: "But whereunto shall I liken this generation? It is like unto children sitting in the markets, and calling unto their fellows,

"And saying, We have piped unto you, and ye have not danced; we have mourned unto you, and ye have not lamented." (Matthew 11:16–17.)

Notice the apperception in His likening of His listeners to children sitting in a marketplace. On another occasion He commented on the hardness of their hearts (Mark 6:52) and reproved them for their lack of faith (Matthew 8:14).

335

Sometimes those closest to Him were a problem to Him. He asked Peter on one occasion, "Are ye also yet without understanding?" (Matthew 15:16.) And there was one time when his students "laughed him to scorn." (Matthew 9:24.)

When a teacher is discouraged and thinks of his failures, he should remember that the accounting is not yet complete. Some students he thinks have heard nothing may have been influenced the most.

Jesus was conscious that some of those He was trying so anxiously to teach did not believe, and He openly stated so: "But there are some of you that believe not. For Jesus knew from the beginning who they were that believed not. . . ." (John 6:64.) And then it was recorded: "From that time many of his disciples went back, and walked no more with him." (John 6:66.)

In this incident is an interesting question to His chosen twelve: "Will ye also go away?" (John 6:67.) It was Peter who responded with an answer that bespeaks his mature judgment and stated that there was nowhere else to obtain the words of eternal life.

I like to read Moroni's pleading to the Lord over his weakness and the Lord's answer to him. Ponder these words:

> And I said unto him: Lord, the Gentiles will mock at these things, because of our weakness in writing; for Lord thou hast made us mighty in word by faith, but thou hast not made us mighty in writing; for thou hast made all this people that they could speak much, because of the Holy Ghost which thou hast given them;
>
> And thou hast made us that we could write but little, because of the awkwardness of our hands. Behold, thou hast not made us mighty in writing like unto the brother of Jared, for thou madest him that the things which he wrote were mighty even as thou art, unto the overpowering of man to read them.

336

Thou hast also made our words powerful and great, even that we cannot write them; wherefore, when we write we behold our weakness, and stumble because of the placing of our words; and I fear lest the Gentiles shall mock at our words.

And when I had said this, the Lord spake unto me, saying: Fools mock, but they shall mourn; and my grace is sufficient for the meek, that they shall take no advantage of your weakness;

And if men come unto me I will show unto them their weakness. I give unto men weakness that they may be humble; and my grace is sufficient for all men that humble themselves before me; for if they humble themselves before me, and have faith in me, then will I make weak things become strong unto them.

Behold, I will show unto the Gentiles their weakness and I will show unto them that faith, hope and charity bringeth unto me—the fountain of all righteousness.

And I, Moroni, having heard these words, was comforted, and said: O Lord, thy righteous will be done, for I know that thou workest unto the children of men according to their faith. (Ether 12:23–29.)

The story is told that someone stopped Elder J. Golden Kimball on the street on one occasion. There had been a little difficulty in Elder Kimball's family that had become publicly known, and whoever it was who stopped him, no doubt with a mind to injure, said, "Brother Kimball, I understand you're having some problems with one of your children." His answer was, "Yes, and the Lord is having some problems with some of his, too."

What Would Pete Think?

Sometimes it is a long time after the instruction that a teacher knows whether or not the lesson has stayed with the student. I knew a teacher who taught seminary in the

Uintah Basin in eastern Utah. In one of his classes was an Indian boy. The teacher endured the boy during that year of school and thought he had done little to help him. He was disturbed at times because the boy appeared disrespectful and referred to him as "Pete." But the teacher tried to remain good-natured and just endured the situation.

Several years later this same student came to see him. He was home on furlough from the military and went to see his former seminary teacher before he talked to anyone else. He gave him the account of this experience.

While he was in military service, he had fallen in with some companions who were not members of the Church and who did not have high moral standards. One weekend when they were on leave in a large city, the other young men decided on a course that was morally disastrous. This young man went along with them, not quite strong enough to resist the group's influence. He told his former seminary teacher that he was on the brink of committing himself to an immoral act when a thought entered his mind: "What would Pete think?" He left his companions and went his way alone.

The seminary teacher learned a great lesson from that interview. He had no idea that anything he was saying in class had found permanent place in the mind of that Indian boy, but several years later, thousands of miles away, his influence asserted itself and saved the young man from a tragic mistake.

A number of years ago I served on a stake high council in Brigham City. On one occasion the stake presidency and members of the high council and their wives attended an evening temple session in the Logan Temple. One of the workers was participating in the instruction for the first time and did very poorly. He had difficulty in remembering his part and was obviously nervous and flustered. He mixed up his presentation in a way that in other places would have been considered humorous. He struggled through, however, and was gently coached and corrected by those who were with him. As much dignity and reverence was maintained as would be possible considering his difficulty.

After the session was over, the brethren from the stake presidency and the high council were standing on the walkway from the temple, waiting for our wives to meet us. One of the brethren commented in some amusement that he surely wouldn't have wanted to be that man, that night. "He really went through an ordeal," he said. "It was like being put on trial before all those people."

President Vernal Willey, characteristically a quiet man, said with some firmness, "Hold on, brethren, let's get one thing straight here. It wasn't that man that was on trial here tonight. We were."

I've never forgotten that and it has made some considerable difference when I have attended a meeting or a performance where those participating did less than ideal.

It is well for a teacher to know, and it is well for students to learn, that many times when we think we are sitting as the judge at a trial, in reality we are one of the defendants.

Don't be too anxious to call yourself a failure or to judge others as failures. When all accounts are settled, you will find that no effort to teach righteousness is ever completely lost. Nothing you do in the way of trying to convey the gospel of Jesus Christ is ever futile.

CHAPTER FORTY

The Teacher

The moment I decided that I wanted to be a teacher is very clear in my mind. It was during World War II, and I was stationed on the little island of Ishima in the Ryukus. This island, a small, lonely one, is just off the northern tip of Okinawa.

One summer evening I went out to sit on the beach to watch the sun go down and ponder on my hopes and dreams in life. I remember looking up at the moon and thinking, "That is the very same moon that shines down on my home in Utah." I was thinking about what I wanted to do with my life after the war, should I be fortunate enough to survive. What did I want to be? It was on that night that I decided I wanted to be a teacher.

Several things helped me make this decision. First, I pondered on the statement of the Prophet Joseph Smith that a man is saved only as fast as he gains knowledge. There would be no better way to gain knowledge than to teach. Since we are here in mortality to learn and to serve, and learning and teaching go so closely together, I determined that I would be a teacher. Then I could learn; then I could be of service to Him.

In the process of meditating there for several hours, I reconciled the fact that if I chose teaching, I could never expect to be a wealthy man. I knew that I could not choose wealth and also choose to teach. Yet I was very content with the decision.

That determination to be a good teacher never left me. I thought from time to time that I would like to be a seminary teacher. It offered a great opportunity to serve, and I held in great admiration President Abel S. Rich, President John P. Lillywhite, and Bishop Harold S. Nelson, who had been my seminary teachers. Each time I thought about that, however, I dismissed it from my mind, realizing that I had not attended college before entering the military service and that no doubt only the best of the finest men available were selected to teach seminary. I just put that thought somewhat above what I should aspire to do.

The opening to teach seminary came, however, in a way that convinced me it was an answer to my prayers, for I truly wanted to be of service. Someday perhaps that story can be told, for it is fundamental to my testimony.

After I had been a teacher for a number of years, one September I wrote the following:

"Last Monday, on one of my rare days at home, I was out in a large grove of trees near our little homestead. My little boys were with me, and we were cutting firewood for the fireplace for winter. It was a beautiful, crisp, September morning. The sun was filtering down through the foliage, and I stood and contemplated the scene before me.

"My little boys began to pick sunflowers to take to their mother. Suddenly I was struck with an impression. It was a spiritual experience. I experienced a reverence for life and a humility that is not always constant with us.

"It was September, and school was about to begin. There came to me once more that excitement that comes every year when school time approaches. I have not been free from it as a teacher any more than I was as a student—

341

the pleasant anticipation of knowing that it is school time once again.

"Soon I would be a teacher again. Perhaps few can understand such a feeling. If you are a teacher by profession and do not understand it, something is missing from your life — something you should seek for and find, even at great cost."

Teaching is a great responsibility. If you are a parent or grandparent, if you are called as an officer or a teacher in the Church, or if you are a missionary, you labor under tremendous responsibility to fulfill your callings faithfully and well.

"Why Hadn't the Instructor Told Us?"

Some years ago I had an experience that taught me this lesson. During the winter of 1943, World War II was raging in full intensity. I had enlisted in the Air Force and was assigned to Thunderbird Field, near Scottsdale, Arizona. We were training in open cockpit Stearman trainers.

One day one of the planes crashed, and one of our classmates lost his life. Flight schedules were immediately intensified. This was war and no time for anyone to become jittery.

The cadets in our class had all soloed, and that afternoon found us practicing landings at an auxiliary field. At the close of the day it was my assignment to take a plane across the valley to the main field.

Out of curiosity I decided to fly over the crash site. It was plainly visible from the air. One could see the spot where the plane had hit, burst into flames, and skidded across the desert floor, burning the chaparral in a long, sooty smear. My curiosity satisfied, I then headed back for the base.

We had been taught the various maneuvers: stalls, loops, spins. In order to lose altitude to enter the landing pattern, I decided to put the plane into a practice spin. That is the quickest way, of course, to lose altitude.

In attempting a recovery from the spin (and perhaps frightened by the thoughts of the accident), I was clumsy and I overcorrected. Instead of a recovery, the plane shuddered violently, stalled, and then flipped over into a secondary spin.

Never have I known such panic. I found myself clawing at the controls. I really don't know what happened—I think I probably let go of the controls. The plane was used extensively as a trainer because it almost had the capacity to fly itself if you'd leave it alone. Finally it pulled out in a long, sweeping skid, just feet above the desert floor.

I quickly recovered my composure and made a normal landing, with the hope that no one had seen my circus performance!

No doubt you too have had a frightening experience where shock set in afterward. Long into that night I experienced almost the same panic as I had had in the plane. My buddy, a member of the Church from southern Utah, who was sleeping in the lower bunk, was awakened by my restlessness. I told him what had happened and asked, "What did I do wrong?"

He told me that his instructor, early in their flight training, had warned against just such an occurrence. He had pointed out the singular danger of a secondary spin and had taken each of his students up and demonstrated how to recover, should it happen. This training, this warning, had insured him against mortal danger.

There arose in me intense resentment for my instructor. Why hadn't he told me? Why hadn't he warned me? Another second or two in that spin, and—well, you would have been spared this story. His negligence as an instructor had come that close to costing me my life.

Great responsibility rests upon those of us who are

leaders and teachers and instructors in the Church. There is the possibility that one for whom we are responsible, if unwarned, may spiritually falter, stall, or spiritually "spin-in."

I resented my instructor because he had failed in his duty to warn me of a mortal danger. The next few days I wasn't very good at flying. I was tense and tied up and frightened.

After a particularly bad flight, my instructor said, "What's the matter with you, Packer? You're no good at this. Why can't you loosen up? You keep this up and we're going to wash you right out of the program!" I was afraid to tell him what was bothering me. And then he said, "I have a special assignment for you this weekend. I want you to go into Phoenix and get right good and drunk. You go get loosened up and relax, and maybe we can make a pilot out of you."

You'd have to know how much I wanted those silver wings to know what a trial that became. I could see the thing that I then wanted more than any other thing on earth slipping away from me. There was a great temptation to follow his advice. To imbibe in spirits would loosen me up, he thought, and restore the confidence I had lost. But those spirits are counterfeit spirits. They lift you and then drop you all the lower.

I did go to Phoenix that weekend, but I sought another kind of Spirit. In association with brethren in the priesthood and with members of the Church in worship service, I found it. There came an inspiration and a restoration of confidence. There came an assurance that has sustained me ever since.

In later years, after I became a teacher, I could see more clearly how my flight instructor, with every intention of doing a worthy job of teaching, may have been distracted, or may have forgotten, or may not really have sensed the importance of that lesson that my buddy's instructor had so thoughtfully given him.

As teachers, we must always be on the alert. From that experience I learned a great lesson about teaching.

Limits Have Been Set

The gift to teach must be earned, and once it is earned, it must be nourished if it is to be kept. If it sleeps too long, it may die. As it works it grows. When a child is born, its little body is created, and, except for the starting process, man has no control over the fact that he is a human being. The Lord in His wisdom has precluded man from tampering with or controlling the development of the human body. The pattern is set. Man cannot make a human into some other animal, or a tree, or an insect. Knowing the ability of man to become wicked, the Lord has set limits on what he may do. Some freedom is given as it relates to plants and animals. Many of the flowers that beautify the world today never existed "naturally." Roses, gladiolas, and camellias as we know them are for the most part the products of the study and efforts of man. He has taken the small, wild variety and through application of natural laws has produced a flower that is more fragrant, more beautiful than any that existed before. The fragrance, the leaf texture, the size, and the color of the flower are controlled by botanists who are familiar with the laws of nature. A botanist can take colors and mix them in flowers almost as an artist would mix paints. But limits are set.

But man cannot cross the species! There are very closely defined limits. A donkey may be crossed with a horse and a mule will be the offspring, but the mule is sterile and cannot reproduce itself. A chicken may be crossed with a pheasant, but the offspring is sterile and cannot reproduce itself. A lion can be crossed with a tiger, but the offspring is sterile and cannot reproduce itself.

Man Controls the Development of Character

These limits keep man, in periods of perversity, from creating monstrosities for his own amusement. Such limitations, however, for some reason do not seem to be in place when it comes to the character and the nature of man. We can tamper with its development and set patterns of creation that can produce a monstrosity. The development lies largely within the control of mankind.

It is the responsibility of the teacher and the parent to mold and build the character and the attitude into something beautiful and enduring. That is a great responsibility. The Lord will not consider lightly how we use the opportunity.

It is good for students when you, as a teacher, will admit on occasion that you love to teach. Such an admission has a good effect upon both the student and you, the teacher. That is true of parents with their children. It gives them great security and makes it possible for them to have trust; it encourages them to bring their questions to be answered. This is important. It is good to let them know on occasion that you love being a parent or a teacher and that it is important. Thereafter you feel an obligation and desire to make your teaching really worthwhile.

A Teacher Should Take Criticism

A teacher should be willing to take constructive criticism. If you can find someone who has the courage to give it to you wisely, it will be among the most valuable contributions to your life.

Shortly after I returned from service in World War II, I was invited to speak in a sacrament meeting in a nearby stake. The patriarch, S. Norman Lee, was a man whom I had known for a number of years. He was on the stand, and after the meeting he complimented me on my talk and said, "I think you mispronounced a word." I was immediately irritated but passed it off by saying, "Oh, is that so? Well, I will have to try to watch that."

I thought seriously about it afterwards, and the next time I saw him I expressed my appreciation to him, for I realized that he was trying to help me.

After sensing that I had come to appreciate his criticism, he was kind enough thereafter to continue. Over the next ten years, I served as an assistant stake clerk, a stake high councilor, a seminary teacher, and a city councilman, and I spoke in many meetings—church and public—where Brother Lee was in attendance. He always had some comment afterwards by way of coaching me, and I was always grateful to him.

On one occasion I was sitting in the audience at the leadership meeting of a stake quarterly conference. A member of the Council of the Twelve was in attendance and the stake president called on me to give the invocation. The request came so unexpectedly that I was greatly frightened. I thought I did not do very well, and as I came back to my seat Brother Lee, who was sitting next to the aisle, took my arm and pulled me down beside him.

"You were frightened, weren't you," he whispered. When I admitted that I was, he whispered a thought or two on how to prepare for such experiences. I will always be grateful for his suggestions and comments.

When I became the president of a mission and had young missionaries, I used the same procedure with them. Some of them I told exactly what I was going to do. I told them that there's one way a person can be relieved from any correction, and that is to show the slightest resentment. One or two of them did, and I never bothered them with correction again. Others were grateful for it, so I did all I could to help them on the way to success. This, of course, is a contribution to the Church, for they will probably develop into substantial leaders.

On one occasion I was interviewing prospective seminary teachers. One of the applicants was not qualified because all of his training had been in elementary education. I was, however, favorably impressed with him.

There was one thing about him that I knew would be a serious limitation to his ability to teach. All during the interview I struggled with the question of whether I should discuss it with him. Since he was not qualified to be a seminary teacher, I thought, "I'm under no obligation. I'll spare myself the discomfort of touching on such a delicate subject." However, the thought entered my mind, "He's your brother." My only motivation was to help, so finally I ventured.

"Has anyone ever talked to you about your teeth?" I asked. Several of them were deformed and so crooked that they protruded though his lips. He told me that earlier in his life he'd had a little dental attention. Some teeth had been pulled, and he was assured that the others would straighten themselves out; however, they did not.

Perhaps unfortunately, his teeth were so healthy that he'd not found it necessary to go to a dentist in the years since.

"Do you know that you can have that problem corrected?" I said.

"Well, not really," he said.

"You have the makings of a very good elementary school teacher, but I think you will not be in the classroom one day without suffering the nickname of Fang, or Sabertooth, or whatever other name the children can invent. You ought not to suffer that when it isn't necessary. Hasn't anyone ever talked to you about this before?"

He told me they had not, and I was appalled that in an otherwise great college of education not one of the professors would counsel him on something so obvious.

348

If We Love Them, Help Them

It is not easy to take criticism. Sometimes it is even harder to give it. But a teacher has that responsibility. If we love our students, we will do all we can to help them, even if at times it has the promise of disturbing the relationship between us. When we are called as a teacher, when we are a parent, we have that authority and that responsibility. We must use it righteously.

> No power or influence can or ought to be maintained by virtue of the priesthood, only by persuasion, by long-suffering, by gentleness and meekness, and by love unfeigned;
>
> By kindness, and pure knowledge, which shall greatly enlarge the soul without hypocrisy, and without guile—
>
> Reproving betimes with sharpness, when moved upon by the Holy Ghost; and then showing forth afterwards an increase of love toward him whom thou hast reproved, lest he esteem thee to be his enemy;
>
> That he may know that thy faithfulness is stronger than the cords of death.
>
> Let thy bowels also be full of charity towards all men, and to the household of faith, and let virtue garnish thy thoughts unceasingly; then shall thy confidence wax strong in the presence of God; and the doctrine of the priesthood shall distil upon thy soul as the dews from heaven.
>
> The Holy Ghost shall be thy constant companion, and thy scepter an unchanging scepter of righteousness and truth; and thy dominion shall be an everlasting dominion, and without compulsory means it shall flow unto thee forever. (D&C 121:41–46.)

That Certain Something

I was called upon almost every day as a seminary supervisor to judge teachers and to judge men—not the ultimate salvation type of judgment, which is correctly reserved for other officers, but a judgment or appraisal of their abilities as teachers and administrators.

There are few characteristics that have been declared essential in this matter of teaching. It has, for instance, nothing to do with how tall a man is or how much he weighs or where he was born or even where he went to school. It has little to do with the color of his hair or his complexion or even his talents. This ability to teach and to lead men is elusively related somehow to the composite of all of them.

In our work, we coined a word for our own use, meaningless to others, but by definition that certain elusive something that makes one a teacher. It is often most obvious by its absence; its presence can be cultivated and improved upon or it can be smothered or neglected.

It is strange to analyze an individual and find that he is not remarkably outstanding in any single characteristic that one might name and yet when all his qualities and characteristics are formed together in a graceful complementary association, he looms head and shoulders above those with whom he associates. He is a teacher!

"I Want You to Learn the Subject"

Among the great teachers I have known was a short, rather unimpressive man, a professor of mathematics at Washington State College in Pullman, Washington. It was during World War II, and there had been established at many of the universities in the country a college-training detachment for the training of air cadets, who were given three months of concentrated academic training before moving to an air base to be trained as pilots.

I was a high school graduate and had done well in the subjects that I enjoyed—and not so well in others. My overall grade was a very average average. In fact, it might be encouraging to some high school students to know that the authorization for me to graduate was held up for a day or two because some work for an English class was not complete. There was a question as to whether I would graduate, for I needed every bit of credit in every course.

Mathematics was not my favorite subject. In fact, years later when I was trying to complete a doctorate degree, that subject posed a great trial for me.

At any rate, World War II erupted when I was a senior in high school, and of course all young men looked forward to military service. I wanted to be a pilot. My older brother, Leon, had already graduated as a pilot. Being a very ordinary student, I felt I probably could not pass the qualifying examinations, but I decided to at least make the effort with one or two other young men from our community.

The test was given at the old Salt Lake Air Base. I will not forget how I agonized over that test because I knew I was an ordinary student. When we were finished the sergeant went over the tests. In order to pass, one needed 125 points. He had a cardboard key that he laid over the test and quickly made the first tabulation. My score was 124. My heart sank. I had failed. But without saying anything, he started going over the paper again and checking something else. Finally he glanced at me, saw my agony, and said, "Some of the questions were in two parts, and we give credit for each part of it if you have it right." I think I prayed up those two-part answers. He found two of them, making a full point, and so I passed the test with the exact minimum score that would qualify me.

I remember to this day that one of the questions was a multiple choice question, "What is ethylene glycol used for?" Since I had worked in my father's garage, I knew it was an ingredient in automobile antifreeze. There were two possible right answers to that question. I had one of them. That little bit of practical knowledge I had gained, without knowing it was worth anything, qualified me to be a pilot and an officer in the Air Force, or at least to make the attempt.

The first assignment was with the college-training detachment at Pullman, Washington. Here there was a great weeding-out of the candidates. We were given an intensive physical and academic training course, and those with deficiencies — physically, emotionally, or academically — were washed out and sent to some other branch of the service, generally to the infantry.

This was sensible, of course, because if we became pilots and were in large planes, we would have the lives of crew members in our hands every moment we were at the controls. Purposely, a lot of pressure was applied in our training, and there was rigid military discipline.

Among the classes was one that loomed as a mighty mountain, impossible for me to climb. That was the course in mathematics. Most of the cadets in our group had attended college for at least a short time and a few were graduates. I went to that class with great apprehension, knowing that surely by comparison I could never pass the course.

But then I met Dr. Schaeffer. He began the course something like this: "During the next three weeks we will spend about two hours a day in the field of mathematics. We will move rather rapidly from basic mathematical computations through an introduction of calculus. What we will do is review all that you have learned in your elementary and high school courses and give you an introduction to the mathematical concepts usually taught the first two years of college."

By that time I was already mentally putting on my infantry boots. But Dr. Schaeffer continued, "I should say at the outset that I am teaching this class for those who do not know the subject, not for those who do. I'm sure

352

many of you have had the college work and that the overview of the basic subject will be boring to you. But I repeat, I am here to teach those who do not know, so we will move at a pace to accommodate them. I will be available to answer any questions, and you may make appointments with me after hours if you wish. And remember, I want you to learn the subject." That's the way he taught.

I did need special help, and he did give it to me. Out of sheer necessity to survive, I asked many questions in class that otherwise might have been embarrassing. I passed that course, the most difficult by every measure that I was subjected to there, with an adequate grade. I learned most of what I know about mathematics from Dr. Schaeffer.

But more than that, I learned from him a great lesson that I later was to use in teaching. It was the source of great satisfaction, years later when I was a supervisor for seminaries in the Church, to be assigned to Washington State College to visit the institute director there. I contacted Dr. Schaeffer, told the above story to him, and fervently thanked him for being the teacher he was.

CHAPTER 41

"Having First Obtained Mine Errand from the Lord"

You have no doubt noted some repetition in these chapters. You may wonder, for instance, why the same scripture is used to illustrate two principles. There is a message in that.

The chapter "Like unto a Glove" demonstrates the use of an object lesson and is placed with the chapters on visual aids. It might quite as well be used as a part of the chapters on apperception.

You will find that basic principles of teaching are closely related. When you practice and use one effectively, you soon find yourself using several of them. It helps to know that you can begin almost anywhere and as you discover and use one principle, you locate the hiding places of many others.

One further word about repetition. Repetition is an important procedure in all teaching. Don't overlook the significance of the fact that Moroni visited Joseph Smith three times during the night and a fourth time the next day, with the same—precisely the same—message. Many teachers and most speakers try to cover too much. They race from one subject to another when they might better be repeating one simple idea. It is good advice to tell your listeners what you are going to tell them, tell them, and then tell them what you have told them. That is a useful technique.

Never apologize for repetition. Someone once asked President Heber J. Grant, "When are you going to stop talking about the Word of Wisdom?" He replied, "As soon as the people begin to live it."

You have been diligent in coming this far in the book and I cannot finish this work without returning to the theme that I hope has been apparent through all of the chapters. The title of the book is found in Doctrine and Covenants 88:77: "Teach ye diligently and my grace shall attend you, that you may be instructed more perfectly in theory, in principle, in doctrine, in the law of the gospel, in all things that pertain unto the kingdom of God, that are expedient for you to understand."

We have talked much about theory and about principle in this book. There is a way in which "you may be instructed more perfectly" in them. I have reserved till the last my comments on this sacred subject.

President J. Reuben Clark, Jr., closed his landmark sermon, "The Charted Course of the Church in Education," with a prayer upon those who teach, which I quote:

> May God bless you always in all your righteous endeavors, may He quicken your understanding, increase your wisdom, enlighten you by experience, bestow upon you patience, charity, and, as among your most precious gifts, endow you with the discernment of spirits that you may certainly know the spirit of righteousness and its opposite as they come to you; may He give you entrance to the hearts of those you teach and then make you know that as you enter there you stand in holy places, that must be neither polluted nor defiled, either by false or corrupting doctrine or by sinful misdeed; may He enrich your knowledge with the skill and power to teach righteousness; may your

faith and your testimonies increase, and your ability to encourage and foster them in others grow greater every day—all that the youth of Zion may be taught, built up, encouraged, heartened, that they may not fall by the wayside, but go on to eternal life, that these blessings coming to them you through them may be blessed also. And I pray all this in the name of Him who died that we might live, the Son of God, the Redeemer of the world, Jesus Christ. Amen.

I have always felt that we stand in holy places when we are given entrance to the hearts of those we teach. There are ways in which we may be sustained spiritually and made equal to the opportunity. One of the most important is found in these lines:

> Wherefore, I Jacob, gave unto them these words as I taught them in the temple, *having first obtained mine errand from the Lord.*
>
> For I, Jacob, and my brother Joseph had been consecrated priests and teachers of this people, by the hand of Nephi.
>
> And we did magnify our office unto the Lord, taking upon us the responsibility, answering the sins of the people upon our own heads if we did not teach them the word of God with all diligence; wherefore, by laboring with our might their blood might not come upon our garments; otherwise their blood would come upon our garments, and we would not be found spotless at the last day. (Jacob 1:17–19. Italics added.)

I emphasize the expression "having first obtained mine errand from the Lord."

There is a great power operative over the Church and kingdom of God. There are sources of intelligence available to all who teach in the Church—if they teach diligently. There is that sacred process by which pure intelligence may be conveyed to the mind in an instant, so that a teacher can know what he needs to know in his moment of need.

We should constantly teach under inspiration. We have the right to teach under inspiration in the home and in the Church. And should we have teaching to do in our other pursuits of life, it is not untoward to call upon the Lord for inspiration in that teaching also.

It is not necessary for a parent or a teacher to know everything. If you are living properly and are prepared to receive inspiration, you may receive it. Consider carefully this verse: "Neither take ye thought beforehand what ye shall say; but treasure up in your minds continually the words of life, and it shall be given you in the very hour that portion that shall be meted unto every man." (D&C 84:85. See also D&C 100:6 and Matthew 10:19.)

On one occasion in a meeting I heard President Marion G. Romney say, "I always know when I am speaking under the inspiration of the Holy Ghost because I always learn something from what I've said."

Parents and teachers in the Church should move forward with confidence and with courage, knowing that they will be sustained if they have in reality "obtained their errand from the Lord." It takes courage. There have been times when I have deserved and I have received chastisement and correction from the Lord because I lacked sufficient courage. I think I shall tell you of one of them.

Shortly after I was called as an Assistant to the Twelve, I had a call in the wee hours of the morning from a very close friend. He and his wife were expecting a new addition to their family, and in the final days before the child was to be born, a critically serious complication had developed. He asked if I would join him in administering to his wife. There was little chance, the doctors thought, that the child would be saved, and the mother's life was in danger as well. At my friend's request, I gave his wife a blessing.

When morning came I went to the office and spent a day in misery and torment. I had been prompted while blessing her to promise that all would be well, but there ran through my mind the prediction of the doctors. Likewise, I had entertained the thought, what happens when exaggerated promises are made in blessings and then not fulfilled? Does that not destroy faith? These thoughts were in my mind at the time we performed the administration. The blessing I pronounced was in general terms; I had not followed the inspiration that came.

That evening when I returned home my friend called to see me again, just to talk. He was beside himself with worry over his wife. We sat down on a bench in the yard and talked. I told him to be at peace, that his wife would be all right and the child would be born without mishap. What is more, I said, "This will be the easiest of her deliveries. That is the blessing that was on my mind this morning, but that I didn't have faith enough to give."

After the conversation, for the first time I felt good. The agony that I had experienced all day had vanished.

The next morning I was called to the hospital in the early hours on another mission, to see someone else. In the hallway I met the family doctor of the woman to whom I had administered. When I inquired about her, he said, "We just brought her from the delivery room. Everything is fine. It was the easiest of her deliveries."

I learned a great lesson from that. We must be sensitive to the Spirit. We must be tuned in, and have the courage and faith to follow the promptings of the Spirit. If we do not listen to the voice of the Spirit, there is not much purpose in the Lord's communicating to us through that channel.

Power comes when a teacher has done all that he can to prepare, not just the individual lesson, but in keeping his life in tune with the Spirit. If he will learn to rely on

358

the Spirit for inspiration, he can go before his class — or, in the case of the parent, he can meet with his children — secure in the knowledge that he can teach with inspiration.

The Master Teacher

And now I should like to close this book where we began — by acknowledging and paying homage to Him who is the Master Teacher. It is He who should be our ideal. No treatise on how to teach compares with a careful study of the four Gospels. Brief though they are, there is enough in these scriptures to open the doors to all the essential principles of teaching necessary to one who would succeed in teaching moral and spiritual values.

The question might be asked, What manner of teacher ought we to be? Even as He is! In the course of my efforts to teach His gospel, I have come to know Him — Jesus Christ, the Son of God, the Only Begotten of the Father.

The account in the New Testament is true. He was born of Mary in the meridian of time. He lived a life that drew Him close, in His early years, to all of the things in the ordinary tangible world about Him. He said and heard and felt all that transpired in the humble village life and the humble family life of His day. Though He was to ascend on high, during His life and during His teaching He was among the people. I have come to know that He lives and have been called to bear special witness of Him.

I stand in reverence before Him with deep regard for *what* He taught and with deep regard for *how* He taught.

Teach ye diligently and His grace shall attend *you,* that *you* may be instructed more perfectly in theory, in principle, in doctrine, in the law of the gospel, in all things pertaining unto the kingdom of God, that are expedient for *you* to understand. Of this I bear witness.

359

The Charted Course of the Church in Education

by President J. Reuben Clark, Jr.

As a school boy I was thrilled with the great debate between those two giants, Webster and Hayne. The beauty of their oratory, the sublimity of Webster's lofty expression of patriotism, the forecast of the civil struggle to come for the mastery of freedom over slavery, all stirred me to the very depths. The debate began over the Foot Resolution concerning the public lands. It developed into consideration of great fundamental problems of constitutional law. I have never forgotten the opening paragraph of Webster's reply, by which he brought back to its place of beginning this debate that had drifted so far from its course. That paragraph reads:

> Mr. President: When the mariner has been tossed for many days in thick weather, and on an unknown sea, he naturally avails himself of the first pause in the storm, the earliest glance of the sun, to take his latitude, and ascertain how far the elements have driven him from his true course. Let us imitate this prudence, and, before we float farther on the waves of this debate, refer to the point from which we departed, that we may at least be able to conjecture where we now are. I ask for the reading of the resolution.

Now I hasten to express the hope that you will not think that I think that this is a Webster-Hayne occasion or that I think I am a Daniel Webster. If you were to think those things — or either of them — you would make a grievous mistake. I admit I am old but I am not that old. But Webster seemed to invoke so sensible a procedure for occasions where, after a wandering on the high seas or in the wilderness, effort is to be made to get back to the place of starting that I thought you would excuse me if I invoked and in a way used this same procedure to restate some of the more outstanding and essential fundamentals underlying our Church school education.

The following are to me those fundamentals:

The Church is the organized Priesthood of God, the Priesthood can exist without the Church, but the Church cannot exist without the Priesthood. The mission of the Church is first, to teach, encourage, assist, and protect the individual member in his striving to live the perfect life, temporally and spiritually, as laid down in the Gospel, "Be ye perfect; even as your Father which is in Heaven is perfect," said the Master; secondly, the Church is to maintain, teach, encourage, and protect, temporally and spiritually, the membership as a group in its living of the Gospel; thirdly, the Church is militantly to proclaim the truth, calling upon all men to repent, and to live in obedience to the Gospel, "for every knee must bow and every tongue confess."

In all this there are for the Church and for each and all of its members, two prime things which may not be overlooked, forgotten, shaded, or discarded:

First: That Jesus Christ is the Son of God, the Only Begotten of the Father in the flesh, the Creator of the world, the Lamb of God, the Sacrifice for the sins of the world, the Atoner for Adam's transgression; that He was crucified; that His spirit left His body; that He died; that He was laid

362

away in the tomb; that on the third day His spirit was reunited with His body, which again became a living being; that He was raised from the tomb a resurrected being, a perfect Being, the First Fruits of the Resurrection; that He later ascended to the Father; and that because of His death and by and through His resurrection every man born into the world since the beginning will be likewise literally resurrected. This doctrine is as old as the world. Job declared: "And though after my skin worms destroy this body, yet in my flesh shall I see God, whom I shall see for myself and mine eyes shall behold, and not another." (Job 19:26,27.)

The resurrected body is a body of flesh and bones and spirit, and Job was uttering a great and everlasting truth. These positive facts, and all other facts necessarily implied therein, must all be honestly believed, in full faith, by every member of the Church.

The second of the two things to which we must all give full faith is: That the Father and the Son actually and in truth and very deed appeared to the Prophet Joseph in a vision in the woods; that other heavenly visions followed to Joseph and to others; that the Gospel and the holy Priesthood after the Order of the Son of God were in truth and fact restored to the earth from which they were lost by the apostasy of the Primitive Church; that the Lord again set up His Church, through the agency of Joseph Smith; that the Book of Mormon is just what it professes to be; that to the Prophet came numerous revelations for the guidance, upbuilding, organization, and encouragement of the Church and its members; that the Prophet's successors, likewise called of God, have received revelations as the needs of the Church have required, and that they will continue to receive revelations as the Church and its members, living the truth they already have, shall stand in need of more; that this is in truth The Church of Jesus

Christ of Latter-day Saints; and that its foundation beliefs are the laws and principles laid down in the Articles of Faith. These facts also, and each of them, together with all things necessarily implied therein or flowing therefrom, must stand, unchanged, unmodified, without dilution, excuse, apology, or avoidance; they may not be explained away or submerged. Without these two great beliefs the Church would cease to be the Church.

Any individual who does not accept the fulness of these doctrines as to Jesus of Nazareth or as to the restoration of the Gospel and Holy Priesthood, is not a Latter-day Saint; the hundreds of thousands of faithful, God-fearing men and women who compose the great body of the Church membership do believe these things fully and completely; and they support the Church and its institutions because of this belief.

I have set out these matters because they are the latitude and longitude of the actual location and position of the Church, both in this world and in eternity. Knowing our true position, we can change our bearings if they need changing; we can lay down anew our true course. And here we may wisely recall that Paul said: "But though we, or an angel from heaven, preach any other Gospel unto you than that which we have preached unto you, let him be accursed." (Galatians 1:8.)

Returning to the Webster-Hayne precedent, I have now finished reading the original resolution.

As I have already said, I am to say something about the religious education of the youth of the Church. I shall bring together what I have to say under two general headings—the students and the teacher. I shall speak very frankly, for we have passed the place where we may wisely talk in ambiguous words and veiled phrases. We must say plainly what we mean, because the future of our youth, both here on earth and in the hereafter, as also the welfare of the whole Church, are at stake.

The youth of the Church, your students, are in great majority sound in thought and in spirit. The problem primarily is to keep them sound, not to convert them.

The youth of the Church are hungry for things of the spirit; they are eager to learn the Gospel, and they want it straight, undiluted.

They want to know about the fundamentals I have just set out—about our beliefs; they want to gain testimonies of their truth; they are not now doubters but inquirers, seekers after truth. Doubt must not be planted in their hearts. Great is the burden and the condemnation of any teacher who sows doubt in a trusting soul.

These students crave the faith their fathers and mothers have; they want it in its simplicity and purity. There are few indeed who have not seen the manifestations of its divine power; they wish to be not only the beneficiaries of this faith, but they want to be themselves able to call it forth to work.

They want to believe in the ordinances of the Gospel; they wish to understand them so far as they may.

They are prepared to understand the truth which is as old as the Gospel and which was expressed thus by Paul (a master of logic and metaphysics unapproached by the modern critics who decry all religion):

> For what man knoweth the things of a man, save the spirit of the man which is in him? even so the things of God knoweth no man but the Spirit of God.
>
> Now we have received, not the spirit of the world, but the spirit which is of God; that we might know the things that are freely given to us of God. (1 Corinthians 2:11, 12.)
>
> For they that are after the flesh do mind the

things of the flesh; but they that are after the Spirit the things of the Spirit. (Romans 8:5.)

This I say then, walk in the Spirit, and ye shall not fulfil the lust of the flesh.

For the flesh lusteth against the Spirit, and the Spirit against the flesh; and these are contrary the one to the other; so that ye cannot do the things that ye would.

But if ye be led of the Spirit, ye are not under the law. (Galatians 5:16–18.)

Our youth understand too the principle declared in modern revelation:

Ye cannot behold with your natural eyes, for the present time, the design of your God concerning those things which shall come hereafter, and the glory which shall follow after much tribulation. (D&C 58:3.)

By the power of the Spirit our eyes were opened and our understandings were enlightened, so as to see and understand the things of God. . . .

And while we meditated upon these things, the Lord touched the eyes of our understandings and they were opened and the glory of the Lord shone round about.

And we beheld the glory of the Son, on the right hand of the Father, and received of his fulness;

And saw the holy angels, and them who are sanctified before his throne, worshiping God, and the Lamb, who worship him for ever and ever. (D&C 76:12, 19–21.)

And now, after the many testimonies which have been given of him, this is the testimony, last of all, which we give of him: That he lives!

For we saw him, even on the right hand of God; and we heard the voice bearing record that he is the Only Begotten of the Father.

That by him, and through him, and of him, the worlds are and were created, and the inhabitants thereof are begotten sons and daughters unto God.

> And while we were yet in the Spirit, the Lord commanded us that we should write the vision. (D&C 76:22–24, 28.)

These students are prepared, too, to understand what Moses meant when he declared:

> But now mine eyes have beheld God; but not my natural, but my spiritual eyes, for my natural eyes could not have beheld; for I should have withered and died in his presence; but his glory was upon me; and I beheld his face, for I was transfigured before him. (Moses 1:11.)

These students are prepared to believe and understand that all these things are matters of faith, not to be explained or understood by any process of human reason, and probably not by any experiment of known physical science.

These students (to put the matter shortly) are prepared to understand and to believe that there is a natural world and there is a spiritual world; that the things of the natural world will not explain the things of the spiritual world; that the things of the spiritual world cannot be understood or comprehended by the things of the natural world; that you cannot rationalize the things of the spirit, because first, the things of the spirit are not sufficiently known and comprehended, and secondly, because finite mind and reason cannot comprehend nor explain infinite wisdom and ultimate truth.

These students already know that they must be honest, true, chaste, benevolent, virtuous, and do good to all men, and that "if there is anything virtuous, lovely, or of good report or praiseworthy, we seek after these things" — these things they have been taught from very birth. They should be encouraged in all proper ways to do these things which they know to be true, but they do not need to have a year's course of instruction to make them believe and know them.

These students fully sense the hollowness of teachings

which would make the Gospel plan a mere system of ethics, they know that Christ's teachings are in the highest degree ethical, but they also know they are more than this. They will see that ethics relate primarily to the doings of this life, and that to make of the Gospel a mere system of ethics is to confess a lack of faith, if not a disbelief, in the hereafter. They know that the Gospel teachings not only touch this life, but the life that is to come, with its salvation and exaltation as the final goal.

These students hunger and thirst, as did their fathers before them, for a testimony of the things of the spirit and of the hereafter, and knowing that you cannot rationalize eternity, they seek faith, and the knowledge which follows faith. They sense by the spirit they have, that the testimony they seek is engendered and nurtured by the testimony of others, and that to gain this testimony which they seek for, one living, burning, honest testimony of a righteous God-fearing man that Jesus is the Christ and that Joseph was God's prophet, is worth a thousand books and lectures aimed at debasing the Gospel to a system of ethics or seeking to rationalize infinity.

Two thousand years ago the Master said: "Or what man is there of you, whom if his son ask bread, will he give him a stone? Or if he ask a fish, will he give him a serpent?" (Matthew 7:10, 11.)

These students, born under the Covenant, can understand that age and maturity and intellectual training are not in any way or to any degree necessary to communion with the Lord and His Spirit. They know the story of the youth Samuel in the temple; of Jesus at twelve years confounding the doctors in the temple; of Joseph at fourteen seeing God the Father and the Son in one of the most glorious visions ever beheld by man. They are not as were the Corinthians, of whom Paul said: "I have fed you with milk and not with meat; for hitherto ye were not able to bear it, neither yet now are ye able." (1 Corinthians 3:2.)

They are rather as was Paul himself when he declared to the same Corinthians: "When I was a child, I spake as a child, understood as a child, I thought as a child: but when I became a man, I put away childish things." (1 Corinthians 13:11.)

These students as they come to you are spiritually working on towards a maturity which they will early reach if you but feed them the right food. They come to you possessing spiritual knowledge and experience the world does not know.

So much for your students and what they are and what they expect and what they are capable of. I am telling you the things that some of you teachers have told me, and that many of your youth have told me.

May I not say now a few words to you teachers?

In the first place, there is neither reason nor is there excuse for our Church religious teaching and training facilities and institutions, unless the youth are to be taught and trained in the principles of the Gospel, embracing therein the two great elements that Jesus is the Christ and that Joseph was God's prophet. The teaching of a system of ethics to the students is not a sufficient reason for running our seminaries and institutes. The great public school system teaches ethics. The students of seminaries and institutes should of course be taught the ordinary canons of good and righteous living, for these are part, and an essential part, of the Gospel. But there are the great principles involved in eternal life, the Priesthood, the resurrection, and many like other things, that go way beyond these canons of good living. These great fundamental principles also must be taught to the youth; they are the things the youth wish first to know about.

The first requisite of a teacher for teaching these principles is a personal testimony of their truth. No amount of learning, no amount of study, and no number of scholastic degrees, can take the place of this testimony, which is the *sine qua non* of the teacher in our Church school system. No teacher who does not have a real testimony of the truth of the Gospel as revealed to and believed by the Latter-day Saints, and a testimony of the Sonship and Messiahship of Jesus, and of the divine mission of Joseph Smith — including in all its reality the First Vision — has any place in the Church school system. If there be any such, and I hope and pray there are none, he should at once resign; if the Commissioner knows of any such and he does not resign, the Commissioner should request his resignation. The First Presidency expects this pruning to be made.

This does not mean that we would cast out such teachers from the Church — not at all. We shall take up with them a labor of love, in all patience and long-suffering, to win them to the knowledge to which as God-fearing men and women they are entitled. But this does mean that our Church schools cannot be manned by unconverted, untestimonied teachers.

But for you teachers the mere possession of a testimony is not enough. You must have besides this, one of the rarest and most precious of all the many elements of human character, — moral courage. For in the absence of moral courage to declare your testimony, it will reach the students only after such dilution as will make it difficult if not impossible for them to detect it; and the spiritual and psychological effect of a weak and vacillating testimony may well be actually harmful instead of helpful.

The successful seminary or institute teacher must also possess another of the rare and valuable elements of character — a twin brother of moral courage and often mistaken for it — I mean intellectual courage — the courage to affirm principles, beliefs, and faith that may not always be considered as harmonizing with such knowledge — scientific or otherwise — as the teacher or his educational colleagues may believe they possess.

Not unknown are cases where men of presumed faith, holding responsible positions, have felt that, since by affirming their full faith they might call down upon themselves the ridicule of their unbelieving colleagues, they must either modify or explain away their faith, or destructively dilute it, or even pretend to cast it away. Such are hypocrites to their colleagues and to their co-religionists.

An object of pity (not of scorn, as some would have it) is that man or woman, who having the truth and knowing it, finds it necessary either to repudiate the truth or to compromise with error in order that he may live with or among unbelievers without subjecting himself to their disfavor or derision as he supposes. Tragic indeed is his place, for the real fact is that all such discardings and shadings in the end bring the very punishments that the weak-willed one sought to avoid. For there is nothing the world so valued and revered as the man, who, having righteous convictions, stands for them in any and all circumstances; there is nothing towards which the world turns more contempt than the man who, having righteous convictions, either slips away from them, abandons them, or repudiates them. For any Latter-day Saint psychologist, chemist, physicist, geologist, archaeologist, or any other scientist, to explain away, or misinterpret, or evade or elude, or most of all, to repudiate or to deny, the great fundamental doctrines of the Church in which he professes to believe, is to give the lie to his intellect, to lose his self-respect, to bring sorrow to his friends, to break the hearts and to bring shame to his parents, to besmirch the Church and its members, and to forfeit the respect and honor of those whom he has sought, by his course, to win as friends and helpers.

371

I prayerfully hope there may not be any such among the teachers of the Church school system, but if there are any such, high or low, they must travel the same route as the teacher without the testimony. Sham and pretext and evasion and hypocrisy have, and can have, no place in the Church school system or in the character building and spiritual growth of our youth.

Another thing which must be watched in our Church institutions is this: It must not be possible for men to keep positions of spiritual trust who, not being converted themselves, being really unbelievers, seek to turn aside the beliefs, education, and activities of our youth, and our aged also, from the ways they should follow, into other paths of education, beliefs, and activities, which (though leading where the unbeliever would go) do not bring us to the places where the Gospel would take us. That this works as a conscience-balm to the unbeliever who directs it is of no importance. This is the grossest betrayal of trust; and there is too much reason to think it has happened.

I wish to mention another thing that has happened in other lines, as a caution against the same thing happening in the Church educational system. On more than one occasion our Church members have gone to other places for special training in particular lines; they have had the training which was supposedly the last word, the most modern view, the ne-plus-ultra of up-to-dateness; then they have brought it back and dosed it upon us without any thought as to whether we needed it or not. I refrain from mentioning well-known and, I believe, well-recognized instances of this sort of thing. I do not wish to wound any feelings.

But before trying on the newest fangled ideas in any line of thought, education, activity, or what not, experts should just stop and consider that however backward they think we are, and however backward we may actually be

372

in some things, in other things we are far out in the lead, and therefore these new methods may be old, if not worn out, with us.

In whatever relates to community life and activity in general, to clean group social amusement and entertainment, to closely knit and carefully directed religious worship and activity, to a positive, clear-cut, faith-promoting spirituality, to a real, every-day, practical religion, to a firm-fixed desire and acutely sensed need for faith in God, we are far in the van of on-marching humanity. Before effort is made to inoculate us with new ideas, experts should kindly consider whether the methods, used to spur community spirit or build religious activities among groups that are decadent and maybe dead to these things, are quite applicable to us, and whether their effort to impose these upon us is not a rather crude, even gross anachronism.

For example, to apply to our spiritually minded and religiously alert youth a plan evolved to teach religion to youth having no interest or concern in matters of the spirit, would not only fail in meeting our actual religious needs, but would tend to destroy the best qualities which our youth now possess.

I have already indicated that our youth are not children spiritually; they are well on towards the normal spiritual maturity of the world. To treat them as children spiritually, as the world might treat the same age group, is therefore and likewise an anachronism. I say once more there is scarcely a youth that comes through your seminary or institute door who has not been the conscious beneficiary of spiritual blessings, or who has not seen the efficacy of prayer, or who has not witnessed the power of faith to heal the sick, or who has not beheld spiritual outpourings, of which the world at large is today ignorant. You do not have to sneak up behind this spiritually experienced youth and whisper religion in his ears; you can come right out, face to face, and talk with him. You do not need to disguise religious truths with a cloak of worldly things; you can bring these truths to him openly, in their natural guise. Youth may prove to be not more fearful of them than you are. There is no need for gradual approaches, for "bedtime" stories, for coddling, for patronizing, or for any of the other childish devices used in efforts to reach those spiritually inexperienced and all but spiritually dead.

You teachers have a great mission. As teachers you stand upon the highest peak in education, for what teaching can compare in priceless value and in far-reaching effect with that which deals with man as he was in the eternity of yesterday, as he is in the mortality of today, and as he will be in the forever of tomorrow. Not only time but eternity is your field. Salvation of yourself not only, but of those who come within the purlieus of your temple, is the blessing you seek, and which, doing your duty, you will gain. How brilliant will be your crown of glory, with each soul saved an encrusted jewel thereon.

But to get this blessing and to be so crowned, you must, I say once more, you must teach the Gospel. You have no other function and no other reason for your presence in a Church school system.

You do have an interest in matters purely cultural and in matters of purely secular knowledge; but, I repeat again for emphasis, your chief interest, your essential and all but sole duty, is to teach the Gospel of the Lord Jesus Christ as that has been revealed in these latter days. You are to teach this Gospel using as your sources and authorities the Standard Works of the Church, and the words of those whom God has called to lead His people in these last days. You are not, whether high or low, to intrude into your work your own peculiar philosophy, no matter what its source or how pleasing or rational it seems to you to be.

To do so would be to have as many different churches as we have seminaries—and that is chaos.

You are not, whether high or low, to change the doctrines of the Church or to modify them, as they are declared by and in the Standard Works of the Church and by those whose authority it is to declare the mind and will of the Lord to the Church. The Lord has declared he is "the same yesterday, today, and forever."

I urge you not to fall into that childish error, so common now, of believing that merely because man has gone so far in harnessing the forces of nature and turning them to his own use, that therefore the truths of the spirit have been changed or transformed. It is a vital and significant fact that man's conquest of the things of the spirit has not marched side by side with his conquest of things material. The opposite sometimes seems to be true. Man's power to reason has not matched his power to figure. Remember always and cherish the great truth of the Intercessory Prayer: "And this is life eternal, that they might know thee the only true God, and Jesus Christ, whom thou hast sent." This is an ultimate truth; so are all spiritual truths. They are not changed by the discovery of a new element, a new ethereal wave, nor by clipping off a few seconds, minutes, or hours of a speed record.

You are not to teach the philosophies of the world, ancient or modern, pagan or Christian, for this is the field of the public schools. Your sole field is the Gospel, and that is boundless in its own sphere.

We pay taxes to support those state institutions whose function and work it is to teach the arts, the sciences, literature, history, the languages, and so on through the whole secular curriculum. These institutions are to do this work. But we use the tithes of the Church to carry on the Church school system, and these are impressed with a holy trust. The Church seminaries and institutes are to teach the Gospel.

In thus stating this function time and time again, and with such continued insistence as I have done, it is fully appreciated that carrying out the function may involve the matter of "released time" for our seminaries and institutes. But our course is clear. If we cannot teach the Gospel, the doctrines of the Church, and the Standard Works of the Church, all of them, on "released time," in our seminaries and institutes, then we must face giving up "released time" and try to work out some other plan of carrying on the Gospel work in those institutions. If to work out some other plan be impossible, we shall face the abandonment of the seminaries and institutes and the return to Church colleges and academies. We are not now sure, in the light of developments, that these should ever have been given up. We are clear upon this point, namely, that we shall not feel justified in appropriating one further tithing dollar to the upkeep of our seminaries and institutes unless they can be used to teach the Gospel in the manner prescribed. The tithing represents too much toil, too much self-denial, too much sacrifice, too much faith, to be used for the colorless instruction of the youth of the Church in elementary ethics. This decision and situation must be faced when the next budget is considered. In saying this, I am speaking for the First Presidency.

All that has been said regarding the character of religious teaching, and the results which in the very nature of things must follow a failure properly know so well the greatness of the problem which faces us and which so vitally and intimately affects the spiritual health and the salvation of our youth, as also the future welfare of the whole Church. We need you, the Church needs you, the Lord needs you. Restrain not yourselves, nor withhold your helping hand.

In closing I wish to pay a humble but sincere tribute to teachers. Having worked my own way through school, high school, college, and professional school, I know something of the hardship and sacrifice this demands; but I know also the growth and satisfaction which come as we reach the end. So I stand here with a knowledge of how many, perhaps most of you, have come to your present place. Furthermore, for a time I tried, without much success, to teach school, so I know also the feelings of those of us teachers who do not make the first grade and must rest in the lower ones. I know the present amount of actual compensation you get and how very sparse it is—far, far too sparse. I wish from the bottom of my heart we could make it greater; but the drain on the Church income is already so great for education that I must in honesty say there is no immediate prospect of betterment. Our budget for this school year is $860,000, or almost seventeen per cent of the estimated total cost of running the whole Church, including general administration, stakes, wards, branches, and mission expenses, for all purposes, including welfare and charities. Indeed, I wish I felt sure that the prosperity of the people would be so ample that they could and would certainly pay tithes enough to keep us going as we are.

So I say I pay my tribute to your industry, your loyalty, your sacrifice, your willing eagerness for service in the cause of truth, your faith in God and in His work, and your earnest desire to do the things that our ordained leader and Prophet would have you do. And I entreat you not to make the mistake of thrusting aside your leader's counsel, or of failing to carry out his wish, or of refusing to follow his direction. David of old, privily cutting off only the skirt of Saul's robe, uttered the cry of a smitten heart; "The Lord forbid that I should do this thing unto my mas-

377

ter, the Lord's anointed, to stretch forth mine hand against him, seeing he is the anointed of the Lord."

May God bless you always in all your righteous endeavors, may He quicken your understanding, increase your wisdom, enlighten you by experience, bestow upon you patience, charity, and, as among your most precious gifts, endow you with the discernment of spirits that you may certainly know the spirit of righteousness and its opposite as they come to you; may He give you entrance to the hearts of those you teach and then make you know that as you enter there you stand in holy places, that must be neither polluted nor defiled, either by false or corrupting doctrine or by sinful misdeed; may He enrich your knowledge with the skill and power to teach righteousness; may your faith and your testimonies increase, and your ability to encourage and foster them in others grow greater every day—all that the youth of Zion may be taught, built up, encouraged, heartened, that they may not fall by the wayside, but go on to eternal life, that these blessings coming to them, you through them may be blessed also. And I pray all this in the name of Him who died that we might live, the Son of God, the Redeemer of the world, Jesus Christ. Amen.

Index

379